privilege

privilege

A Reader

FOURTH EDITION

Michael S. Kimmel and Abby L. Ferber

EDITORS

WESTVIEW
PRESS

Westview Press was founded in 1975 in Boulder, Colorado, by notable publisher and intellectual Fred Praeger. Westview Press continues to publish scholarly titles and high-quality undergraduate- and graduate-level textbooks in core social science disciplines. With books developed, written, and edited with the needs of serious nonfiction readers, professors, and students in mind, Westview Press honors its long history of publishing books that matter.

Published by Westview Press,
An imprint of Perseus Books, a Hachette Book Group company
2465 Central Avenue
Boulder, CO 80301
www.westviewpress.com

Every effort has been made to secure required permissions for all text, images, maps, and other art reprinted in this volume.

Westview Press books are available at special discounts for bulk purchases in the United States by corporations, institutions, and other organizations. For more information, please contact the Special Markets Department at the Perseus Books Group, 2300 Chestnut Street, Suite 200, Philadelphia, PA 19103, or call (800) 810-4145, ext. 5000, or e-mail special .markets@perseusbooks.com.

Library of Congress Cataloging-in-Publication Data

Names: Kimmel, Michael S. | Ferber, Abby L., 1966- | Kimmel, Michael S.,
    editor. | Ferber, Abby L., 1966- editor.
Title: Privilege : a reader / edited by Michael S. Kimmel, Abby L. Ferber.
Description: Fourth Edition. | Boulder, CO : Westview Press, 2016. | Revised
    edition of Privilege, 2014. | Includes bibliographical references and index.
Identifiers: LCCN 2016009658 (print) | LCCN 2016023289 (ebook) | ISBN
    9780813350035 (paperback) | ISBN 9780813350400 (e-book)
Subjects: LCSH: Social classes—United States. | United States—Social
    conditions—1980- | BISAC: SOCIAL SCIENCE / Sociology / General. | SOCIAL
    SCIENCE / Gender Studies. | SOCIAL SCIENCE / Social Classes.
Classification: LCC HN90.S6 P75 2016 (print) | LCC HN90.S6 (ebook) | DDC
    306.0973—dc23
LC record available at https://lccn.loc.gov/2016009658

10 9 8 7 6 5 4 3 2 1

We dedicate this edition to all those
who are learning, daily, to be better allies.

contents

preface

Confronting privilege can be extremely uncomfortable—a productive and healthy discomfort, to be sure, but discomfort just the same. And once the process of confrontation has begun, it's difficult to resist what a colleague once called "premature self-congratulation," the often earnest, if insufferable, proclamations of the newly converted. "Thanks so much for bringing this privilege thing to our attention," we might be tempted to say. "We'll take it from here."

The ability to live with that discomfort and without that preachy self-congratulatory tone is the hallmark of the works we have collected here. It is a struggle, both political and stylistic, and we hope that these essays will prove as unsettling and as discomfiting as they have been for the editors.

After all, we found our way to these essays, and to editing this book together, because we were so unsettled and challenged by confronting our own unearned privilege. The essays in this volume proved both provocative and helpful, not only as we first began to think our way through these issues, but also as we continue the process of confronting privilege today.

A Note to Students

If you are reading this book, odds are your instructors are already themselves engaged in this process. Don't be afraid to talk about it, and to disagree. The way we've organized the book is sort of like peeling back the layers of an onion—the first articles describe the initial shock of realizing that in some way you, too, have experienced both privilege and the absence of privilege. Perhaps you are a working-class student on a scholarship at a private college or university where the students are so wealthy that they often drive nicer cars than the professors. But perhaps you are also white, or straight, or male. But then again, you might be Muslim or Jewish and experience feelings of exclusion around Christmastime. Or an older student, or disabled.

Subsequent sections complicate matters by looking at the ways these different statuses—sexuality, ability, race, class, gender, religion, and the like—each modify and shape the others. Such complication changes the "or" in the preceding paragraph to an "and," or a "but also": What if you are black *and* female? What if you are white *but also* Jewish? As you'll see, these statuses sometimes reinforce each other—as in straight, white, Protestant male—and sometimes collide and undercut each other.

Some years ago, the great sociologist Erving Goffman described the ways these statuses all might coalesce into the "perfect" American male—the one who really has all the privilege:

> In an important sense there is only one complete unblushing male in America: a young, married, white, urban, northern, heterosexual, Protestant, father, of college education, fully employed, of good complexion, weight, and height, and a recent record in sports. . . . Any male who fails to qualify in any one of these ways is likely to view himself—during moments at least—as unworthy, incomplete, and inferior.*

This dynamic is critical. Goffman is saying that every single person will, at some point in life, "fail to qualify" and will feel, at least at moments, "unworthy, incomplete, and inferior." It is those feelings of inadequacy and inferiority that we think often motivate us to resist facing the kinds of privilege we *do* have, because we are so painfully aware of the places and arenas in which we don't measure up. Privilege is far less visible to us than its absence; when we are discriminated against, it is much more painfully obvious than when we belong to the groups that benefit from that discrimination.

One of the editors of this book has a friend, "Jane," who is a black lesbian. Jane says that when she hangs out with a bunch of her black friends, all she can think about is being a lesbian who doesn't fit in. (That is, because virtually all the black people at her school seem to be straight.) But when Jane hangs out with her lesbian friends, all she can think about is how she's black and doesn't fit in (because all the lesbians at her school are white). We see where we *don't* fit in far better than where we *do*.

---

* Erving Goffman, *Stigma* (Englewood Cliffs, NJ: Prentice-Hall, 1963), 128.

One more thing: Sometimes confronting privilege can be painful, but it can also be really funny. When you have a spare 2:40, check out this video of the comedian Louis C.K. describing the moment he realized the privilege he gets for being a white man in America (warning: NSFW—*or school!*): www.youtube.com/watch?v=xqbw4nHrHc0.

Feeling Conscious, Not Guilty

Realizing that you do have privileges—no matter who you are—does not mean feeling miserable and guilty for the rest of your life, just conscious: of both the advantages and the disadvantages that every one of us has because of the statuses we occupy, some by birth and some by choice. Conscious that there simply *are* no level playing fields anywhere—and that every single arena, whether class or race or gender or sexuality or other social identities, is not just a source of identity but also a site of social inequality that is arbitrary and unfair. Knowing how it feels to experience that inequality in one arena should inspire you to help level the playing fields in all arenas.

But feeling conscious is an ongoing process, not a state of being. Consider this: Following the killing of seventeen-year-old Trayvon Martin, three women of color began the Black Lives Matter movement. Hardly a week goes by that discussion of black men and women who end up dead at the hands of law enforcement fills the news. Similarly the number of racist incidents on college campuses across the country is on the rise. We have also seen more and more white allies standing up for racial justice (for example, check out the websites for the group Showing Up for Racial Justice and for the White Privilege Conference).

However, many white folks report experiencing race fatigue, and their involvement decreases. Many black organizers have pointed out, gently but firmly, that they do not have that luxury, that they can't "opt out" of thinking about racism. They live in constant fear for their own lives and for those of their children. This is an example of white privilege.

White allies realizing that they have the privilege of opting out of thinking about racism exemplifies the sort of experiences you will have reading this book. Your task is to be as gentle and as firm when explaining privilege to others, and to be open and accountable to accepting the possibility of a different point of view. To facilitate this process, at the end of each section we have provided issues for discussion and activities for you to engage in. Instead of being "busy work" questions to make sure you're really reading, these are specifically designed to help you engage in the very difficult work of self-examination. Our goal with this volume is not to simply provide you with the latest and most important scholarship on the subject of privilege. Learning about privilege entails examining your own life and experience as well. After all, each one of us has been deeply shaped by the systems and processes examined in these chapters. Understanding privilege is one step in working to dismantle systems of inequality.

This fourth edition of the book incorporates a number of new chapters that provide more recent contributions to the scholarship on privilege, including pieces addressing global, class, transgender, and disability studies perspectives. This was no easy task; the number of publications examining privilege has expanded dramatically since we wrote the first edition of this text and tried to capture the burgeoning new field. Along with this growth has come increased public visibility and debate. We begin the book with a piece attacking the concept of white privilege, written by a Princeton student, that sparked instant and vociferous debate. To capture some of the many responses, we include two here. Our hope is that the remainder of the text will prepare you to contribute to these public discussions with a deeper and more nuanced analysis of the importance of examining privilege if we seek a more socially just and equitable future.

There's an old saying, attributed to Native Americans, that you can't really understand another's experience until you've walked a mile in their moccasins. (Some college campuses help men do just that by "Walking a Mile in Her Shoes"—an organized activity in which men don high heels and attempt to walk across their own campuses.) Truth is, you can't walk a mile in *everyone's* moccasins; you have to trust people when they tell you about their experiences. But only if you really trust them will they be able, in turn, to really listen to your explanation of what it's like to live inside *your* skin.

Acknowledgments

We are so grateful to the authors of the essays in this book for their courage and wisdom. We're grateful to the instructors who feel they can use this book to challenge themselves and their students to think about these issues, all while maintaining a safe space for doing so. And we're grateful to all of the students—past, present, and future—who take the risk of confronting privilege with us.

The process of producing a book like this is as much form as it is content, as much practical concerns as it is political engagement, as much technical as theoretical. We've had a dedicated staff at Westview Press. Over the years and editions, our editors at Westview have been supportive and enthusiastic, none more so than Leanne Silverman, who embraced the project with open arms! Since then, many people at Westview have helped to bring these many editions to life, and we thank them all. A thank-you is also due to Westview's reviewers, who provided valuable advice as we shaped this fourth edition.

Abby thanks: the numerous people of color who have graciously served as patient mentors, especially Eddie Moore Jr., Brenda J. Allen, Rodney Coates, and Donald Cunnigen, who have taught me more about my own privilege and the value and necessity of working in multiracial teams than I could ever learn from any book. I am quite fortunate to have found a home in the Department of Sociology, and the Women's and Ethnic Studies Program (at the University of Colorado, Colorado Springs), where this urgent work is truly valued in an increasingly hostile university culture. I want to thank my mentor, Michael Kimmel, whose work has been truly inspirational for me, and whose friendship, support, and collaboration I value more than he can possibly know.

Most important, I want to thank my family. Joel—I am sustained in everything I do by your love, emotional support, and thoughtful care, which have grown exponentially over the years. And Sydney, my daughter and my friend. I am so proud of you, your maturity, your accomplishments, your values, and the adult you have become. You are *always* more than enough!

Michael thanks: a group of friends (Lillian Rubin, Troy Duster, Martin Sanchez-Jankowski, Angela Harris, Jerry Karabel, and the late and dearly missed Michael Rogin) who began discussing whiteness twenty years ago in a little study group; my longtime friends Harry Brod, Marty Duberman, Michael Kaufman, Mike Messner, and Don Sabo, who have sustained the endless conversation; my European colleagues and friends, notably Chris Beasley, Harry Ferguson, Debra Gimlin, Jeff Hearn, Oystein Holter, Lars Jalmert, and Jorgen Lorentzen; and my friend and co-editor Abby Ferber, for her insightful work and deeply ethical vision; she inspires me constantly. I'm also grateful to my colleagues and students at SUNY Stony Brook, my intellectual home for more than two decades, and to Amy and Zachary, my home forever.

We live in a nation where—despite all ideological assertions about meritocracy, about how individuals are free to rise as high as they can based solely on their individual achievements—race, class, and gender are the best predictors of what we social scientists call "life chances": your level of wealth, occupation, health, even marital happiness. Ours is a nation where characteristics of your birth are the best predictors of where you will end up at your death. On the other hand, we actually do want to live in a nation in which those ideals of individual achievement are actually realized; where talent, motivation, ambition, and hard work actually do pay off; where race, class, sexuality, and gender predict very little about your economic and social life.

Every single day, we are inspired by all the people who have done so much work already to reveal the workings of oppression; all the scholars, writers, and activists who have struggled to make the unseen visible, teaching the privileged about privilege; those who had virtually no choice but to examine race, class, gender, and sexuality as they daily confronted the effects of inequality based on those experiences.

introduction

toward a sociology
of the superordinate

Michael S. Kimmel

This Breeze at My Back

To run or walk into a strong headwind is to understand the power of nature. You set your jaw in a squared grimace, your eyes are slits against the wind, and you breathe with a fierce determination. And still you make so little progress.

To walk or run with that same wind at your back is to float, to sail effortlessly, expending virtually no energy. You do not feel the wind; it feels you. You do not feel how it pushes you along; you feel only the effortlessness of your movements. You feel like you could go on forever. Only when you turn around and face that wind do you realize its strength.

Being white, or male, or heterosexual in this culture is like running with the wind at your back. It feels like just plain running, and we rarely if ever get a chance to see how we are sustained, supported, and even propelled by that wind.

This book tries to make the wind visible.

In recent years, the study of discrimination based on gender, race, class, and sexuality has mushroomed, creating a large literature and increasing courses addressing these issues. Of course, the overwhelming majority of the research has explored the experiences of the victims of racism, sexism, homophobia, and class inequality. These are the "victims," the "others" who have begun to make these issues visible to contemporary scholars and laypeople alike. This is, of course, politically as it should be: the marginalized

1

always understand first the mechanisms of their marginalization; it remains for them to convince the center that the processes of marginalization are in fact both real and remediable.

When presented with evidence of systematic discrimination, majority students are often indifferent, and sometimes even defensive and resistant. "What does this have to do with me?" they ask. The more defensive of them immediately mention several facts that they believe will absolve them of inclusion into the *superordinate* category. "My family never owned slaves," "I have a gay friend," and "I never raped anyone" are fairly typical responses. Virtually none seems able to discuss white people as a group. Some will assert that white people differ dramatically from one another, that ethnicity and religion are more important than race. Others maintain that white people, as a group, are not at all privileged. And virtually all agree that racism is a problem of individual attitudes, of prejudiced people, and not a social problem.

What's more, we seem to be even *more* eager to let ourselves off the collective hook, to refuse to examine these issues from the point of view of the superordinate, than we were even a decade ago. We triumphantly declare America a "postracial" society because we have had an African-American president, and it's not uncommon to hear people "opt out" of understanding racism because they voted for Barack Obama (as if racism were a personal lifestyle option). Indeed, it seems that this self-congratulatory moment has also permitted the return of a more virulent public expression of racism than we've witnessed in decades.

Equally true, try finding a female student who calls herself a feminist. My female students often tell me that feminism was really important back in the day, when, for example, their baby-boomer professor was in college, because things were so unequal then. "But now I can do anything I want; I have completely free choice," the women declare. Gender inequality is a thing of the past; feminism is no longer necessary. "Thank you very much," they seem to be saying to the generations of women who came before them. "We won." (These same students often return to campus a few years later and confess how naive they were, not having entered the labor market or experienced wage discrimination, glass ceilings for promotion, or well-intentioned husbands who can't seem to remember how to wash a dish.)

Such statements are as revealing as they are irrelevant. They tell us far more about the way we tend to individualize and personalize processes that are social and structural. They also tell us that majority students resist discussing inequality because it will require that they feel guilty for crimes someone else committed, as well as to recognize the ways they have benefited from those actions.

Even those students who are willing to engage with these questions tend to personalize and individualize them. They may grudgingly grant the systematic nature of inequality, but to them, racism, sexism, and heterosexism are bad attitudes held by bad people. They are eager to help those bad people see the error of their ways and change their attitudes to good attitudes. This usually will come about through better education.

Those of us who are white, heterosexual, middle class, and/or male need to go further; we need to see how we are stakeholders in understanding structural inequality, how the dynamics that create inequality for some also benefit others. Privilege needs to be made visible.

For the past couple of decades, a spate of exciting new research in a variety of disciplines, including sociology, literature, and cultural studies, has been examining what previously passed as invisible, neutral, and universal. We now can begin to see how the experience of "privilege" also shapes the lives of men, white people, and heterosexuals. Such inquiries, long overdue, are enabling us to more fully understand the social dynamics of race, class, gender, and sexuality, and how they operate in all our lives.

Making Privilege Visible

To be white, or straight, or male, or middle class is to be simultaneously ubiquitous and invisible. You're everywhere you look, you're the standard against which everyone else is measured. You're like water, like air. People will tell you they went to see a "woman doctor," or they will say they saw "the doctor." People will tell you they have a "gay colleague" or they'll tell you about a "colleague." A white person will be happy to tell you about a "black friend," but when that same person simply mentions a "friend," everyone will assume the person is white. Any college course that doesn't have the word "woman" or "gay" or "minority" in the title is, de facto, a course about men, heterosexuals, and white people. But we call those courses "literature," "history," or "political science."

This invisibility is political. I first confronted this invisibility in the early 1980s, when I participated in a small discussion group on feminism. In one meeting, a white woman and a black woman were discussing whether all women were, by definition, "sisters," because they all had essentially the same experiences and because all women faced a common oppression by men. The white woman asserted that the fact that they were both women bonded them, in spite of racial differences. The black woman disagreed.

"When you wake up in the morning and look in the mirror, what do you see?" she asked.

"I see a woman," replied the white woman.

"That's precisely the problem," responded the black woman. "I see a *black* woman. To me, race is visible every day, because race is how I am *not* privileged in our culture. Race is invisible to you, because it's how you are privileged. It's why there will always be differences in our experience."

As I witnessed this exchange, I was startled, and groaned—more audibly, perhaps, than I had intended. Someone asked me, the only man in the room, what my response had meant.

"Well," I said, "when I look in the mirror, I see a human being. I'm universally generalizable. As a middle-class white man, I have no class, no race, and no gender. I'm the generic person!"

Sometimes I like to think that it was on that day that I *became* a middle-class white man. Sure, I had been all those before, but they had not meant much to me. Since then I've begun to understand that race, class, and gender don't refer only to other people, who have been marginalized by race, class, or gender privilege. Those terms also describe me. I enjoy the privilege of invisibility. The very processes that confer privilege to one group and not another group are often invisible to those upon whom that privilege is conferred. What makes us marginal or powerless are the processes we see, partly because others keep reminding us of them. Invisibility is a privilege in a double sense—in describing both the power relations that are kept in place by the very dynamics of invisibility, and in the sense of privilege as a luxury. It is a luxury that only white people have in our society not to think about race every minute of their lives. It is a luxury that only men have in our society to pretend that gender does not matter.

That discussion took place several decades ago, but I was reminded of it when I went to give a guest lecture for a female colleague at my university. We teach the same course on alternate semesters, so she always gives a guest lecture for me, and I do one for her. As I walked into the auditorium, one student looked up at me and said, "Oh, finally, an objective opinion!"

All that semester, whenever my colleague opened her mouth, what this student saw was "a woman." Biased. But when I walked in, I was, in this student's eyes, *unbiased*, an objective opinion. Disembodied western rationality—standing right in front of the class! This notion that middle-class white men are objective and everyone else is biased is the way that inequalities are reproduced.

Let me give you another example of how power is so often invisible to those who have it. You all have e-mail addresses, and you write e-mail messages to people all over the world. You've probably noticed that there is one big difference between e-mail addresses in the United States and e-mail addresses of people in other countries: their addresses have country codes at the end of the address. So, for example, if you were writing to someone in South Africa, you'd put "za" at the end, or "jp" for Japan, or "uk" for England (United Kingdom), or "de" for Germany (Deutschland). Even if you write to someone at a university in another country, you have to use the country code, so, for example, it would be "ac.uk" for an academic institution in Britain, or "edu.au" for an educational institution in Australia. But when you write to people in the United States, the e-mail address ends with "edu" for an educational institution, "org" for an organization, "gov" for a federal government office, or "com" or "net" for commercial Internet providers. Why is it that the United States doesn't have a country code?

It is because when you are the dominant power in the world, everyone else needs to be named. When you are "in power," you needn't draw attention to yourself as a specific entity, but rather you can pretend to be the generic, the universal, the generalizable. From the point of view of the United States, all other countries are "other" and thus need to be named, marked, noted. Once again, privilege is invisible.

There are consequences to this invisibility: privilege, as well as gender, remains invisible. And it is hard to generate a politics of inclusion from invisibility. The invisibility of privilege means that many men, like many white people, become defensive and angry when confronted with the statistical realities or the human consequences of racism or sexism. Since our privilege is invisible, we may become defensive. Hey, we may even feel like victims ourselves.

In *The Envy of the World*, *Newsweek* writer Ellis Cose underscores this issue when he counsels other black people in this way:

> Given such psychologically complex phenomena as racial guilt and racial pain, you are not likely to find much empathy or understanding when you bring racial complaints to whites. The best you can generally hope for is an

awkward silence accompanied by the suspicion that you are crying wolf. (excerpted in *Newsweek*, January 28, 2002, p. 52)

I was reminded of this sort of reaction from the privileged when I appeared on a television talk show opposite three "angry white males"—three men who felt that they had been the victims of workplace discrimination. The show's title, no doubt to entice a large potential audience, was "A Black Woman Took My Job." In my comments to these angry men, I invited them to consider what the word "my" meant in that title, that they felt that the jobs were originally "theirs," that they were entitled to them, and that when some "other" person—black, female—got the job, that person was really taking "their" job. But by what right is that his job? By convention, by a historical legacy of such profound levels of discrimination that we have needed decades of affirmative action to even begin to make slightly more level a playing field that has tilted so decidedly in one direction.

Our task is to begin to make visible the privilege that accompanies and conceals that invisibility.

The Invisible Knapsack

One way to understand how privilege works—and how it is kept invisible—is to look at the way we think about inequality. We always think about inequality from the perspective of the one who is hurt by the inequality, not the one who is helped. Take, for example, wage inequality based on gender. We're used to hearing that women make about 79 cents for every dollar made by a man. In that statistic women's wages are calculated as a function of men's wages; men's wages are the standard (the $1) against which women's wages are calculated. In this way, the discrimination against women is visible—doing the same job, they earn less, just because they are women.

But what if we changed the statistics? What if we expressed men's wages as a function of women's wages? What if we said that for every dollar earned by a woman, men make $1.21? Then it wouldn't be the discrimination that was visible—it would be the privilege. Just for being a male, a male worker received an additional 21 cents. This is what sociologist R. W. Connell calls the "masculinity dividend"—the unearned benefits that accrue to men, just for being men.

One could easily apply this model to race, class, and sexuality. And several of the authors in this volume probe their own experiences as a way to enable others to see what had earlier been invisible. Perhaps no one has done that more successfully than Peggy McIntosh, in her celebrated essay on what she calls the "invisible knapsack." The invisible knapsack contains all the little benefits that come to us simply because we are white, or straight, or middle class, or male. We have to open up that knapsack, dump its contents out, and take a look at all the very different ways that these ascribed characteristics (those we were born with) have become so obscured that we have come to believe that the events of our lives are the results of achieved characteristics.

Making gender, race, class, and sexuality visible—both as the foundations of individual identity and as the social dynamics of inequality—means that we pay some attention to the differences among them as well. Often students argue that gender is different from race, because, as one of my students put it, "you have to live every day with a person of the opposite sex, but you don't have to live so intimately with people of another race." Leaving aside the potential racism or heterosexism of such a statement—one might, after all, live intimately with someone of a different race, or one might not live with someone of the opposite sex—this student does point to an important issue: *just as all forms of inequality are not the same, all forms of privilege are not the same.*

For example, two of the dimensions we discuss in this book—race and gender—appear, at least on the surface, to be based on characteristics present at birth: one's sex or race. That means that they are always visible to an observer. (Well, at least nearly always. There are, of course, people who change their biological sex, or who dress differently from established norms, and those who try to pass as members of another race, and even those, like the late Michael Jackson, who seem to be using draconian surgical techniques to be taken for the other.) Thus the privileges based on gender or race may feel even more invisible because those privileged by race and gender did nothing to earn their privilege.

Privilege based on physical ability is difficult to navigate because the world was made largely by physically able people *for* physically able people. The idea that sidewalks and curbs are not "neutral" would have been a foreign concept indeed to people as recently as the 1970s, when a group in California, at the Center for Independent Living, began the first campaign for ramps. Equal access to public buildings has to, in fact, provide *equal* access to everyone. Equality doesn't mean we all can use the same stairs (e.g., that there is no longer a separate entrance for "white" and for "colored" or for "boys" and "girls"). Equality means we all may have to use *different* means to arrive at the *same* place.

The other dimensions—sexuality, religion, class—however, are not immediately visible to the public. One can more easily pass as a member of a privileged group. But sexual minorities also may feel that their identity is not a social construction but the fulfillment of an inner essence—that is, it is more like race and gender than it is like class. While race and biological sex may seem to be evidently inborn, biologically based, and/or "God-given," sexuality also feels like that to both heterosexuals and homosexuals.

Class, however, does not. In fact, class seems to feel exactly the opposite—a status that one was not born with but that one has earned. Class is less visible than the other dimensions because while our objective position in an economic order depends on empirically measurable criteria (income, occupation, education), class as an everyday experience rests on other people's evaluation of our presentation of self. It is far easier to pass as something we are not—both for people of modest means to effect the lifestyle of the rich and famous and for very wealthy people to effect the styles of the poor. While most of us would like to have everyone think we are wealthier than we actually are, it is often the case that the truly wealthy want everyone to think they are *less* wealthy than they are. We may dress "up" while they dress "down."

Often we will associate ourselves with the trappings of the class to which we aspire as opposed to the class from which we actually come. Take, for example, fashion. I am reasonably certain that most of the readers of this essay have, at some point in their lives, gone bowling. And I am equally certain that very few readers, if any, have ever played polo. And yet I would bet that many of you would be very happy to shell out a lot of money for a garment that identified you as a polo player (for example, a Ralph Lauren Polo shirt with a little polo player on it) than for an equally well-made garment with a little bowler on it. In fact, you would be eager to pay a premium on that Polo shirt precisely because the brand has become associated with a class position to which you can only aspire.

Class can be concealed and class feels like something we have earned all by ourselves. Therefore, class privilege may be the one set of privilege we are least interested in examining because it feels like it is ours by right, not by birth—all the more reason to take a look at class.

Religious privilege can be equally invisible. Imagine that you are Buddhist or Muslim or Taoist or Jewish or Hindu or any one of the thousands of religions in the world, and you live in a country in which people routinely proclaim, "America is a Christian nation!" Just how welcome would you feel? Just how much a part of the nation would you feel? Or imagine you are an atheist, as fully 20 percent of all Americans are, and you have to clench your teeth every single time you say the Pledge of Allegiance and mouth the words "under God" without actually saying them? Religious privilege is when you assume that everyone has a faith, and that everyone's faith is the same generic Christianity as yours. It's called "christonormativity"—the assumption that everyone else is also Christian. And when you wish someone a "Merry Christmas," you might think you are being *inclusive* and genuinely warm and friendly toward them. But the other person may experience this as *exclusionary*, making him or her feel you are cold and unfeeling. If you don't assume someone's religion, or even that they *have* one, you can't offend them.

The Souls of White
(and Straight and Middle-Class and Male) Folk

Taking a look at class is difficult to do, and there is no question that it will make us feel uncomfortable. It's unpleasant to acknowledge that all the good things that have happened to you are not simply the result of your hard work and talent and motivation but the result of something you had no power over. Sometimes it will make us feel guilty, other times defensive. Sometimes we just feel powerless: "What can I possibly do to change this massive system of inequality?"

In a culture such as ours, all problems are thought to be individual problems, based on bad attitudes, wrong choices, or our own frailties and addictions. When confronted with structural or social problems, we think the solutions are either aggregated individual solutions—*everyone* needs to change their attitudes—or that the solutions don't exist. A single, lone individual has no chance, we think, to change the system. You can't fight City Hall.

We feel powerless, impotent. We can become mired in guilt. Some people argue that guilt is a negative emotion and that we shouldn't have to feel guilty for the things that happened generations—even centuries—ago. Occasionally someone is moved by that guilt to attempt to renounce his or her privilege. Books counsel us to become "race traitors," or to "refuse" to be a man.

And sometimes a posture of self-negation feels moral and self-righteous. Guilt isn't always a "bad" emotion, after all. How would you feel about a German student who says that he really didn't want to feel guilty about genocide in World War II? "After all, I never personally sent a Jew to the gas chamber." Or a white South African who proclaimed that she never actually benefited from apartheid, since she got her job and her wealth by virtue of her hard work and determination.

Guilt may be appropriate, even a necessary feeling—for a while. It does not freeze us in abjection, but can motivate us to transform the circumstances that made us feel guilty in the first place, to make connections between our experiences and others' and to become and remain accountable to the struggles for equality and justice around the world. Guilt can politicize us. (Perhaps that's one reason we often resist it.)

While noble in its intention, however, this posture of guilty self-negation cannot be our final destination as we come to understand how we are privileged by race, class, gender, and sexuality. Refusing to be male, white, or straight does neither the privileged nor the unprivileged much good. One can no more renounce privilege than one can stop breathing. It's in the air we breathe.

And it is embedded in the architecture that surrounds us. Renouncing privilege ultimately substitutes an individual solution for a structural and social problem. Inequality is structural and systematic, as well as individual and attitudinal. Eliminating inequalities involves more than changing everyone's attitudes.

Trying to rid oneself of bad attitudes, renouncing one's unearned privilege, also finally brings us no further than the feelings of impotent despair that we often feel in the face of such overwhelming systemic problems. We feel lonely. We feel isolated from our friends, our families, or our classmates. It's the loneliness of the long-distance runner against the wind.

The struggles against inequality are, however, collective struggles, enormous social movements that unite people across geography, race, religion, class, sexuality, and gender. Participating in these struggles to end inequality brings one into a long history of those who have stood alongside the victims of oppression, those who have added their voices to the voices of those who earlier had been silenced. Examining our privilege may be uncomfortable at first, but it can also be energizing, motivating, and engaging.

A Method of Analysis

In this book, we use an "intersectional" approach to explore the ways in which race, class, gender, sexuality, (dis)ability, and religion intersect and interact. This theory was first developed by women of color who argued that in understanding their experiences, the variables of race, class, gender, and sexuality could not be separated. This was a response to the traditional studies of race, which focused on race alone and usually ended up focused narrowly on men of color, and women's studies, which often focused only on the experiences of white women. But some of these theorists asked different questions: Where does the black person stop and the woman begin? How can one analyze the totality of one's experience without examining the ways in which all these categories coincide, collide, contradict?

Intersectionality has now become a buzzword in academia, though it still has virtually no currency outside of colleges and universities. It's clear that the different statuses we occupy—by race, class, gender, sexuality, age, and so forth—all shape and modify one another. Sometimes one of these becomes a master status through which all others are filtered and in which all others become sort of adjectives to its noun. At other times, they shift and sort and collide in ways that can give you a headache. It's complex, and one always runs the risk of a slippery slope into an infinite regress, and by the time you're done enumerating all the different statuses you occupy, you are the only one of that specific combination, and therefore immune to any and all generalizations. Individualism is not the corrective to a social analysis; it's part of it.

What does seem clear, from surveys of young people, is that the places in which we are not privileged are the ones of which we are most aware. In a well-known study, students were asked to list five characteristics about themselves. Not "cool" or "pretty" or "awesome," but five social characteristics. Virtually all the African-American students listed their race; virtually no white students did. (Asians and Latinos were split about 50/50.) About 25 percent of the students listed "Christian" (they were largely evangelicals), but nearly 100 percent of the Jews and Muslims listed their faith. (Virtually no atheists listed that; it's just not that important to them, I guess.) None of the heterosexual students wrote "straight," but virtually all the LGBT students listed something to do with their sexuality. Many students listed their ethnicity—Irish, Italian, Dominican, Russian. Not one student who did not have a disability wrote anything about that; every single physically disabled student noted it. And no one wrote anything to do with class. No one at all.

It's still the case that those parts of our lives in which we feel we stick out, by which we feel marginal, are the most visible to us. We are more aware of where we don't fit in to the dominant groups than where we do. Yet both—our membership in dominant if invisible groups and our membership in visible yet marginalized groups—define us, providing the raw materials from which we fashion an identity. Subordinate and superordinate—these are the statuses that enable us to define who we are.

We need to understand both if we are to understand ourselves, as well as others. We need to see how these different statuses combine and collide, reinforce and contradict one another. This volume uses an intersectional analysis to explore the ways in which race, gender, class, religion, physical ability, and sexuality interact in the lives of those who are privileged by one or more of these identities. We bring together leading thinkers and writers on all of these dimensions, to examine both the parallels and the ruptures among these different but connected relationships. Written both personally and analytically, these essays can bring the reader inside the experiences, and enable us all to begin to theorize our own lives, as well as to explore the ways in which these systems intersect in people's lives.

Ultimately we believe that examining those arenas in which we are privileged as well as those in which we are not privileged will enable us to understand our society more fully, and engage us in the long historical process of change.

part one

seeing—and refusing
to see—privilege

What is privilege? Who has it? Who doesn't?

On virtually every campus in the country, students are debating about privilege. We are being asked to "check our privilege," which often invites a significant amount of self-reflection before speaking—for example, recognizing the specific station from which one speaks.

Privilege is elusive, though, precisely because it is not a thing, not a possession that one "has." For one thing, privilege is not a singular unit: either you have it or you don't. There are so many axes of privilege—by race, class, gender, sexuality, age, religion. The list goes on and on.

For another thing, privilege is neither bad nor good. It's not bad to be privileged. It simply is.

Third, privilege is not like an article of uncomfortable clothing that can simply be discarded once one realizes it's there. Once you are aware of it, though, you don't have to feel guilty. It's like feeling guilty for breathing. But awareness brings responsibility—at least for those who believe, as we, the editors do, that getting an advantage through something other than your own talents and hard work is unfair.

These first readings explore the dimensions of privilege today, making it visible. We start with an effort to deny it, by a white male student at Princeton. In it, he claims that his class background negates all the other ways in which he is privileged: race, gender, able-bodiedness, sexuality, or religion. In this way he reveals something important about how we all navigate the complex world of privilege: that very often what is most visible to us are the

13

ways in which we are not privileged, and what is obscure are those ways in which we are privileged.

It's as if we live in a culture in which no one wants to be privileged; rather, everyone seems to want to be unprivileged. Partly, this is because we want to believe that whatever we have earned has been the result of our own hard work, overcoming obstacles, applying ourselves. We don't want to think that we were handed this all on a silver platter. It's as if we are a medieval society standing on its head: in the medieval era, status was fixed, and members of the hereditary aristocracy knew they were privileged and reveled in it. Peasants could only dream of being lords.

Today, no one wants to claim they are privileged. It's as if owning your privilege is a badge of dishonor.

The essay by Tal Fortgang, denying his privilege, spurred an enormous reaction, as others replied by examining just what sort of privilege he actually might have and explaining why those dimensions of privilege might not be visible to him. (The articles by Charles Clymer and Daniel Gastfriend are examples of this response.)

Following this dialogue, we turn to Peggy McIntosh's brilliant essay in which she discusses the way white privilege and male privilege intersect. McIntosh's pathbreaking discussion of the "invisible knapsack" described and enumerated a wide variety of privileges that white people get, just for being white. White people did nothing to "earn" these; they're just inherited at birth. In this essay, she uses race to talk about gender. In "The Invisible Crutch" Jessica Shea translates this knapsack into a crutch and enumerates a wide array of benefits one gets just for being able-bodied.

In addition, the empirical article by Angelica Guitierrez and Miguel Unzueta examines the effects of affirmative action compared to "legacy admissions" at certain elite colleges and universities. We present them here as a dialogue: the denial of privilege and the beginnings of understanding how some dimensions of privilege might be invisible to us. Next, Juan Cole gives us a satirical yet poignant examination of how whiteness even provides a level of privilege to terrorists. Finally, Bob Pease examines how privilege is not allotted only by social status, but also by geographical position.

In this edition of the book, we've continued to highlight religion as a source of privilege. In 1797, John Adams signed the Treaty of Tripoli, which was ratified unanimously by the Congress. The treaty declared, pretty unequivocally, "The Government of the United States of America is not, in any sense, founded on the Christian religion." And from the signing of the Constitution onward, the separation of church and state has been a foundational principle of American democracy, and no one is to be persecuted for practicing their religion.

Yet is there not a certain privilege given to those who are Christian? Is not Christianity so normative that it is difficult for those who are not Christian to practice their religion? Ironically, in recent years, that has been interpreted to mean that if my religion commands that I discriminate against some people, it should be permitted—because the state can't interfere with the free exercise of religion.

1

checking my privilege

Character as the Basis of Privilege

Tal Fortgang*

There is a phrase that floats around college campuses, Princeton being no exception, that threatens to strike down opinions without regard for their merits, but rather solely on the basis of the person that voiced them. "Check your privilege," the saying goes, and I have been reprimanded by it several times this year. The phrase, handed down by my moral superiors, descends recklessly, like an Obama-sanctioned drone, and aims laser-like at my pinkish-peach complexion, my maleness, and the nerve I displayed in offering an opinion rooted in a personal Weltanschauung. "Check your privilege," they tell me in a command that teeters between an imposition to actually explore how I got where I am, and a reminder that I ought to feel personally apologetic because white males seem to pull most of the strings in the world.

I do not accuse those who "check" me and my perspective of overt racism, although the phrase, which assumes that simply because I belong to a certain ethnic group I should be judged collectively with it, toes that line. But I do condemn them for diminishing everything I have personally accomplished, all the hard work I have done in my life, and for ascribing all the fruit I reap not to the seeds I sow but to some invisible patron saint of white maleness who places it out for me before I even arrive. Furthermore,

* Fortgang, Tal. "Checking My Privilege." *The Princeton Tory*, April 24, 2014. Reprinted by permission of the author.

I condemn them for casting the equal protection clause, indeed the very idea of a meritocracy, as a myth, and for declaring that we are all governed by invisible forces (some would call them "stigmas" or "societal norms"), that our nation runs on racist and sexist conspiracies. Forget "you didn't build that"; check your privilege and realize that nothing you have accomplished is real.

But they can't be telling me that everything I've done with my life can be credited to the racist patriarchy holding my hand throughout my years of education and eventually guiding me into Princeton. Even that is too extreme. So to find out what they are saying, I decided to take their advice. I actually went and checked the origins of my privileged existence, to empathize with those whose underdog stories I can't possibly comprehend. I have unearthed some examples of the privilege with which my family was blessed, and now I think I better understand those who assure me that skin color allowed my family and I to flourish today.

Perhaps it's the privilege my grandfather and his brother had to flee their home as teenagers when the Nazis invaded Poland, leaving their mother and five younger siblings behind, running and running until they reached a Displaced Persons camp in Siberia, where they would do years of hard labor in the bitter cold until World War II ended. Maybe it was the privilege my grandfather had of taking on the local Rabbi's work in that DP camp, telling him that the spiritual leader shouldn't do hard work, but should save his energy to pass Jewish tradition along to those who might survive. Perhaps it was the privilege my great-grandmother and those five great-aunts and uncles I never knew had of being shot into an open grave outside their hometown. Maybe that's my privilege.

Or maybe it's the privilege my grandmother had of spending weeks upon weeks on a death march through Polish forests in subzero temperatures, one of just a handful to survive, only to be put in Bergen-Belsen concentration camp where she would have died but for the Allied forces who liberated her and helped her regain her health when her weight dwindled to barely 80 pounds.

Perhaps my privilege is that those two resilient individuals came to America with no money and no English, obtained citizenship, learned the language and met each other; that my grandfather started a humble wicker basket business with nothing but long hours, an idea, and an iron will—to paraphrase the man I never met: "I escaped Hitler. Some business troubles are going to ruin me?" Maybe my privilege is that they worked hard enough to raise four children, and to send them to Jewish day school and eventually City College.

Perhaps it was my privilege that my own father worked hard enough in City College to earn a spot at a top graduate school, got a good job, and for 25 years got up well before the crack of dawn, sacrificing precious time he wanted to spend with those he valued most—his wife and kids—to earn that living. I can say with certainty there was no legacy involved in any of his accomplishments. The wicker business just isn't that influential. Now would you say that we've been really privileged? That our success has been gift-wrapped?

That's the problem with calling someone out for the "privilege" which you assume has defined their narrative. You don't know what their struggles have been, what they may have gone through to be where they are. Assuming they've benefitted from "power systems" or other conspiratorial imaginary institutions denies them credit for all they've done, things of which you may not even conceive. You don't know whose father died defending your freedom. You don't know whose mother escaped oppression. You don't know who conquered their demons, or may still be conquering them now.

The truth is, though, that I have been exceptionally privileged in my life, albeit not in the way any detractors would have it. It has been my distinct privilege that my grandparents came to America. First, that there was a place at all that would take them from the ruins of Europe. And second, that such a place was one where they could legally enter, learn the language, and acclimate to a society that ultimately allowed them to flourish.

It was their privilege to come to a country that grants equal protection under the law to its citizens, that cares not about religion or race, but the content of your character.

It was my privilege that my grandfather was blessed with resolve and an entrepreneurial spirit, and that he was lucky enough to come to the place where he could realize the dream of giving his children a better life than he had.

But far more important for me than his attributes was the legacy he sought to pass along, which forms the basis of what detractors call my "privilege," but which actually should be praised as one of altruism and self-sacrifice. Those who came before us suffered for the sake of giving us a better life. When we similarly sacrifice for our descendants by caring for the planet, it's called "environmentalism," and is applauded. But when we do it by passing along property and a set of values, it's called "privilege." (And when we do it by raising questions about our crippling national debt, we're called Tea Party radicals.) Such sacrifice of any form shouldn't be scorned, but admired.

My exploration did yield some results. I recognize that it was my parents' privilege and now my own that there is such a thing as an American dream which is attainable even for a penniless Jewish immigrant.

I am privileged that values like faith and education were passed along to me. My grandparents played an active role in my parents' education, and some of my earliest memories included learning the Hebrew alphabet with my Dad. It's been made clear to me that education begins in the home, and the importance of parents' involvement with their kids' education—from mathematics to morality—cannot be overstated. It's not a matter of white or black, male or female or any other division which we seek, but a matter of the values we pass along, the legacy we leave, that perpetuates "privilege." And there's nothing wrong with that.

Behind every success, large or small, there is a story, and it isn't always told by sex or skin color. My appearance certainly doesn't tell the whole story, and to assume that it does and that I should apologize for it is insulting. While I haven't done everything for myself up to this point in my life, someone sacrificed themselves so that I can lead a better life. But that is a legacy I am proud of.

I have checked my privilege. And I apologize for nothing.

Tal Fortgang is a freshman from New Rochelle, NY. He plans to major in either history or politics.

2

this response to that Princeton freshman should be required reading for white males

Charles Clymer*

Tal Fortgang, a freshman at Princeton University, has ignited much of the blogosphere with an op-ed he wrote recently for the *Princeton Tory*, the school's conservative student publication. In it, Fortgang decries being told, "Check your privilege," and denies that he receives a significant benefit from his skin color and gender. He spends much of the piece outlining his Jewish family's tragic history at the hands of Nazi Germany.

Fortgang's column aggressively denies the existence of any "invisible patron saint of white maleness," which he considers an "invisible force" that diminishes the accomplishments of white men. As a fellow straight, white male, however, this argument falls flat. Even with my own personal history of childhood abuse and lack of financial resources, I am acutely aware of the ways I benefit from my skin color and gender every day. To argue anything else is essentially to claim that racism, sexism, homophobia, and transphobia no longer exist.

Fortgang is a white male. He is also straight and ostensibly cisgender (that is, born with the gender with which he identifies). He grew up in New

---

* Clymer, Charles. "This Response to That Princeton Freshman Should Be Required Reading for White Males." *mic.com*, May 6, 2014. Available at http://mic.com/articles/88903 /this-response-to-that-princeton-freshman-should-be-required-reading-for-white -males#.hVpfVTUm8. Reprinted by permission of the author.

Rochelle, N.Y., described by its police department in 2008 as the safest city in New York state and is among the top five safest cities of its size in the country. New Rochelle has an average household income of $108,355, more than twice the household median income in the U.S. Before matriculating in one of the most elite universities in the world, Fortgang attended SAR Academy & High School, a private institution in Riverdale, N.Y., that boasts a theater, a hockey rink, a new "iPad one-to-one curriculum" and a beautiful campus all at an annual tuition cost of only $30,800 ($45,800 for inclusion).

Like Fortgang, I am a white male. I am also straight and cisgender. Unlike him, I have blue eyes and blonde hair, which I've parted to the side since I was a child. I dress conservatively, and I have a generic accent that's difficult to place until I say "y'all" or a similar word or phrase picked up from my upbringing in Texas. As stereotypes go, I am as white as the day is long. I could easily be lost in the crowd at your local country club, which means that I don't "look threatening," that I'm labeled "safe" and a "nice guy" by people who barely know me.

Being a kid wasn't easy for me. I lived at or below the poverty line for most of childhood. My parents divorced when I was 3, and I didn't see my father on a regular basis until I was 12. For several years my mother shuffled my sister and me through a succession of trailer parks, interrupted for a time by a housing project.

My first stepfather was physically abusive, my second stepfather was a manic-depressive alcoholic who pawned or sold the few toys I had for beer money, and throughout all this, my mother sexually abused me over a period of 10 years in an effort to alleviate the longing she had for my father.

I couldn't afford education after high school beyond the first semester my father paid for—scraped together with U.S. savings bonds—at a community college. I was a smart kid. I was talented. I also had nothing, and I was overwhelmed by trying to pursue a dream of success unachievable with my lack of resources.

But this isn't a contest of oppression. I'm not keeping score on who has faced the most shit in life between the two of us. I don't begrudge Fortgang's own upbringing any more than I blame him for my obstacles in life. I outline my life experience here to emphasize the power of white male privilege. No matter how much I've gone through, no matter how many dollars I have in my pocket, I begin every morning with a shower and presentable clothing, and I walk into a world that has been conditioned to accept my appearance and speech as the default. I see white male faces on television and in Congress, white bodies in advertisements and films, white voices on the radio and white males in positions of power on issues that directly affect me.

I have never been harassed by the police or felt nervous around them, for that matter. I have never been followed around in stores, asked where I'm really from or informed that my skin color or gender limit my abilities. I have never been told my heterosexuality is a choice and a sin, never had my life threatened for being a Trayvon Martin in a suburban neighborhood, never specifically planned my route home to avoid being sexually harassed or assaulted or raped, as approximately 238,000 Americans are each year.

Yes, I do struggle with my past trauma and with overcoming that to reach my dreams, but at the end of the day, I can go to sleep without the fear that most of the world believes I was not born to succeed in it.

Fortgang is a child who has lived a privileged existence and has had the misfortune of his sheltered views being validated at every turn until being forced to confront a reality no longer optional for someone of his wealth, gender, race, and sexuality. It's hard to be angry with someone who has been set up for disappointment by being told that everything he's achieved is a result of his hard work, and not partly due to the absence of challenges confronted by people who don't look like him.

I have been active in the feminist community for a few years now, and not once have I been asked to apologize for being a white, straight man, nor have I been asked to apologize for the actions of other white, straight men. On the rare occasion that I have been told to "check my privilege," it's always been in a manner that asks me to examine how my experience clouds my viewpoint on the oppression of others, to acknowledge there are experiences I can't understand because I haven't lived them and to stand beside people who don't look like me, especially when they're not present in white, straight male spaces.

Yet to read Fortgang's piece is to imagine that white, straight males are forced to run across a minefield of inevitable homophobic, transphobic, sexist and racist transgressions in today's society.

He's partially right: Because of our life experience, we will make mistakes. I certainly have. But what's not mentioned is that women and people of color and LGBT folks are the ones running across this minefield while we white, straight men—impervious to social shrapnel—have reached the other side, only to wonder aloud—mockingly, condescendingly—why the rest of these folks can't hurry the hell up because how awful could bigoted shrapnel be, really?

There's a mountain of statistics and studies I can cite, from the wage gap to the way professors respond to student inquiries, that exclusively benefit white men in our society. But this really hammers the point home: *TIME* magazine wound up publishing Fortgang's op-ed, in full, on its website, just a week after unveiling its predominately privileged "*TIME* 100," which excluded Laverne Cox, a transgender woman of color and star of *Orange Is the New Black* who finished among the highest in its website's fan poll.

If Fortgang—unknown but white, straight, and male—were a transgender woman of color, it's doubtful this story would have validated such a life experience or been published in *TIME*.

And you wouldn't know his name. Or mine.

3

reflections on privilege

An Open Letter to Tal Fortgang

Daniel Gastfriend*

Dear Tal,

Like many others, I read your piece this week "Checking My Privilege: Character as the Basis of Privilege"—a retort to the motto "check your privilege," which, you argue, aims to devalue your opinion as a white male and make you feel guilty for your privilege. I was moved to respond because of the similarities we share. Although we do not know each other, we both come from families of Holocaust survivors, grew up in Jewish-American homes, and studied at Princeton. Indeed, our families lived through many of the same horrors and transformations. And I agree—we do not need to apologize for our origins. Nothing about this notion, however, justifies blindness to inequality.

My maternal grandfather grew up in Nuremberg, Germany. After barely escaping a Hitler Youth attempt to drive a nail through his head, he fled with his family in 1938 for the United States. Though he arrived as a poor immigrant who barely spoke English, he managed to receive an education at City College, like your father. He later became chief psychologist at the Northampton State Hospital in Western MA.

* Gastfriend, Daniel. "Reflections on Privilege: An Open Letter to Tal Fortgang." *Huffington Post.com* blog, May 7, 2014. Available at http://www.huffingtonpost.com/daniel-gastfriend /open-letter-tal-fortgang_b_5281169.html. Reprinted by permission of the author.

My paternal grandfather was not so lucky. Born to an orthodox Jewish family in Sosnowiec, Poland, he witnessed at age 13 the annihilation of everything and everyone he held dear under Nazi rule. He describes in his memoir, *My Father's Testament*, the brutality he faced over three years in the concentration camps, the horrors of the death march, the grief of witnessing his dying cousin tossed alive into a mass grave. Through incredible fortitude and luck, he managed to survive. And although the nightmares plague him to this day, he eventually became a successful businessman in the United States, providing a young family with a better life.

Two generations later, I am free from the violence that tormented my grandfathers and have so far enjoyed a life of remarkable opportunity. Like you, I am fiercely proud of how my family came to be where we are today.

One could take a number of different perspectives on how our family histories relate to the notion of privilege. Yours is understandable: Your ancestors fought relentlessly, and against all odds, to build a new life for your family. This is a legacy to be celebrated, and you should not feel guilty for their resilience or success.

But I find another angle more compelling. I grew up with a set of privileges of which my grandfather could only have dreamed. The injustices he faced—and the senseless lottery of birth that condemned him to such suffering—make me inclined to seek out inequality and injustice in whatever forms they take. Included among these are many of the structures that the phrase "check your privilege" means to challenge. While I agree this expression should not be used to silence anyone's opinion, I believe it can make us more cognizant of the privilege that comes with our social position, how that privilege shapes our perspective, and the manifold obstacles that burden so many others which we never need face. Yes, it is possible to achieve prosperity in the face of such inequalities and worse, as our grandparents so remarkably did. This does not mean we should tolerate them.

You vehemently defend the American meritocracy. Indeed, there is something marvelous about a country in which immigrants as extraordinarily disadvantaged as our grandparents could build a new life for themselves and their children. You also write, "It's not a matter of white or black, male or female or any other division which we seek, but a matter of the values we pass along, the legacy we leave, that perpetuates 'privilege.'" I wish this were the entire story.

What your piece misses is a recognition that, despite the successes of families like our own, harmful structural inequalities persist on the basis of class, race, sex, sexual orientation, and gender identity in the U.S. Children growing up in poor areas often attend public schools with significantly less funding than those born in affluent areas (a disparity that does not exist in most developed countries); almost one in five American women are survivors of completed or attempted rape; individuals with non-conforming sexual and gender identities face high rates of workplace discrimination and violent crime; blacks are given harsher prison sentences for the same offenses than whites; resumes with black-sounding names are 50 percent less likely to get called back than equivalent ones with white-sounding names, and emails to university professors [from students] with minority or female names are 25 percent less likely to get responses than those with white male names; the list goes on.

Being aware of these issues—and of the fact that we, by nature of our race and gender, are shielded from many of them—is the first step towards rectifying them. And while I share your enthusiasm for the meritocratic elements of American society that allowed our families to flourish, I find deeply troubling the fact that income mobility is lower in the U.S. than in the vast majority of developed countries; 70 percent of people born into the bottom quintile of the income distribution in America never reach the middle.

Like you, I strive to carry on the spirit of my grandparents' hard work. But I also know I have unfairly benefited from a society that favors affluent, white, heterosexual men. While this privilege is not the entire story of why I am where I am today, it does exist, as do the damaging inequalities that continue to fuel it. My family's painful history does not nullify these injustices; on the contrary, it highlights the imperative to expose and erase them.

Several years ago, my paternal grandfather brought our extended family on a trip to Poland. He took us to the village where he grew up, the ghetto his family was forced into, and finally, to Auschwitz. Shaking with tears, he implored us: "Whenever you see evil in the world, you must cry out, you must act! Never be silent in the face of injustice."

The first step to address injustice is to acknowledge the way it manifests in the world. I am privileged—in part due to the opportunities my grandparents provided me, but also in part due to my social position in American society. And in honor of my grandparents' legacy, I refuse to be content with a society where equality of opportunity is still not extended to all, and where racism, sexism, and prejudice continue to exist—in any form.

Sincerely,
Daniel Gastfriend

4

white privilege and male privilege

Peggy McIntosh*

Through work to bring materials and perspectives from Women's Studies into the rest of the curriculum, I have often noticed men's unwillingness to grant that they are overprivileged in the curriculum, even though they may grant that women are disadvantaged. Denials which amount to taboos surround the subject of advantages which men gain from women's disadvantages. These denials protect male privilege from being fully recognized, acknowledged, lessened, or ended.

Thinking through unacknowledged male privilege as a phenomenon with a life of its own, I realized that since hierarchies in our society are interlocking, there was most likely a phenomenon of white privilege which was similarly denied and protected, but alive and real in its effects. As a white person, I realized I had been taught about racism as something which puts others at a disadvantage, but had been taught not to see one of its corollary aspects, white privilege, which puts me at an advantage.

I think whites are carefully taught not to recognize white privilege, as males are taught not to recognize male privilege. So I have begun in an untutored way to ask what it is like to have white privilege. This paper is a partial record of my personal observations, and not a scholarly analysis. It is based on my daily experiences within my particular circumstances.

I have come to see white privilege as an invisible package of unearned assets which I can count on cashing in each day, but about which I was "meant" to remain oblivious. White privilege is like an invisible weightless knapsack of special provisions, assurances, tools, maps, guides, codebooks, passports, visas, clothes, compass, emergency gear, and blank checks.

Since I have had trouble facing white privilege, and describing its results in my life, I saw parallels here with men's reluctance to acknowledge male privilege. Only rarely will a man go beyond acknowledging that women are (dis)advantaged to acknowledging that men have unearned advantage, or that unearned privilege has not been good for men's development as human beings, or for society's development, or that privilege systems might ever be challenged and *changed*.

I will review here several types or layers of denial which I see at work protecting, and preventing awareness about, entrenched male privilege. Then I will draw parallels, from my own experience, with the denials which veil the facts of white privilege. Finally, I will list 46 ordinary and daily ways in which I experience having white privilege, within my life situation and its particular social and political frameworks.

Writing this paper has been difficult, despite warm receptions for the talks on which it is based.[1] For describing white privilege makes one newly accountable. As we in Women's Studies work to reveal male privilege and ask men to give up some of their power, so one who writes about having white privilege must ask, "Having described it, what will I do to lessen or end it?"

The denial of men's overprivileged state takes many forms in discussions of curriculum change work. Some claim that men must be central in the curriculum because they have done most of what is important or distinctive in life or in civilization. Some recognize sexism in the curriculum but deny that it makes male students seem unduly important in life. Others agree that certain *individual* thinkers are blindly male-oriented but deny that there is any systemic tendency in disciplinary frameworks or epistemology to overempower men as a group. Those men who do grant that male privilege takes institutionalized and embedded forms are still likely to deny that male hegemony has opened doors for them personally. Virtually all men deny that male overreward alone can explain men's centrality in all the inner sanctums of our most powerful institutions. Moreover, those few who will acknowledge that male privilege systems have overempowered them usually end up doubting that we could dismantle these privilege

systems. They may say they will work to improve women's status, in the society or in the university, but they can't or won't support the idea of lessening men's. In curricular terms, this is the point at which they say that they
regret they cannot use any of the interesting new scholarship on women
because the syllabus is full. When the talk turns to giving men less cultural room, even the most thoughtful and fair-minded of the men I know
well tend to reflect, or fall back on, conservative assumptions about the
inevitability of present gender relations and distributions of power, calling
on precedent or sociobiology and psychobiology to demonstrate that male
domination is natural and follows inevitably from evolutionary pressures.
Others resort to arguments from "experience" or religion or social responsibility or wishing and dreaming.

After I realized, through faculty development work in Women's Studies,
the extent to which men work from a base of unacknowledged privilege,
I understood that much of their oppressiveness was unconscious. Then I
remembered the frequent charges from women of color that white women
whom they encounter are oppressive. I began to understand why we are
justly seen as oppressive, even when we don't see ourselves that way. At
the very least, obliviousness of one's privileged state can make a person
or group irritating to be with. I began to count the ways in which I enjoy
unearned skin privilege and have been conditioned into oblivion about its
existence, unable to see that it put me "ahead" in any way, or put my people
ahead, overrewarding us and yet also paradoxically damaging us, or that it
could or should be changed.

My schooling gave me no training in seeing myself as an oppressor, as an
unfairly advantaged person, or as a participant in a damaged culture. I was
taught to see myself as an individual whose moral state depended on her
individual moral will. At school, we were not taught about slavery in any
depth; we were not taught to see slaveholders as damaged people. Slaves
were seen as the only group at risk of being dehumanized. My schooling
followed the pattern which Elizabeth Minnich has pointed out: whites are
taught to think of their lives as morally neutral, normative, and average,
and also ideal, so that when we work to benefit others, this is seen as work
which will allow "them" to be more like "us." I think many of us know how
obnoxious this attitude can be in men.

After frustration with men who would not recognize male privilege, I
decided to try to work on myself at least by identifying some of the daily
effects of white privilege in my life. It is crude work, at this stage, but I will
give here a list of special circumstances and conditions I experience which

I did not earn but which I have been made to feel are mine by birth, by citizenship, and by virtue of being a conscientious law-abiding "normal" person of goodwill. I have chosen those conditions which I think in my case *attach somewhat more to skin-color privilege* than to class, religion, ethnic status, or geographical location, though of course all these other factors are intricately intertwined. As far as I can see, my Afro-American co-workers, friends, and acquaintances with whom I come into daily or frequent contact in this particular time, place, and line of work cannot count on most of these conditions.

1. I can, if I wish, arrange to be in the company of people of my race most of the time.
2. I can avoid spending time with people whom I was trained to mistrust and who have learned to mistrust my kind or me.
3. If I should need to move, I can be pretty sure of renting or purchasing housing in an area which I can afford and in which I would want to live.
4. I can be pretty sure that my neighbors in such a location will be neutral or pleasant to me.
5. I can go shopping alone most of the time, pretty well assured that I will not be followed or harassed.
6. I can turn on the television or open to the front page of the paper and see people of my race widely represented.
7. When I am told about our national heritage or about "civilization," I am shown that people of my color made it what it is.
8. I can be sure that my children will be given curricular materials that testify to the existence of their race.
9. If I want to, I can be pretty sure of finding a publisher for this piece on white privilege.
10. I can be pretty sure of having my voice heard in a group in which I am the only member of my race.
11. I can be casual about whether or not to listen to another woman's voice in a group in which she is the only member of her race.
12. I can go into a music shop and count on finding the music of my race represented, into a supermarket and find the staple foods which fit with my cultural traditions, into a hairdresser's shop and find someone who can cut my hair.
13. Whether I use checks, credit cards, or cash, I can count on my skin color not to work against the appearance of financial reliability.

14. I can arrange to protect my children most of the time from people who might not like them.
15. I do not have to educate my children to be aware of systemic racism for their own daily physical protection.
16. I can be pretty sure that my children's teachers and employers will tolerate them if they fit school and workplace norms; my chief worries about them do not concern others' attitudes toward their race.
17. I can talk with my mouth full and not have people put this down to my color.
18. I can swear, or dress in secondhand clothes, or not answer letters, without having people attribute these choices to the bad morals, the poverty, or the illiteracy of my race.
19. I can speak in public to a powerful male group without putting my race on trial.
20. I can do well in a challenging situation without being called a credit to my race.
21. I am never asked to speak for all the people of my racial group.
22. I can remain oblivious of the language and customs of persons of color who constitute the world's majority without feeling in my culture any penalty for such oblivion.
23. I can criticize our government and talk about how much I fear its policies and behavior without being seen as a cultural outsider.
24. I can be pretty sure that if I ask to talk to "the person in charge," I will be facing a person of my race.
25. If a traffic cop pulls me over or if the IRS audits my tax return, I can be sure I haven't been singled out because of my race.
26. I can easily buy posters, postcards, picture books, greeting cards, dolls, toys, and children's magazines featuring people of my race.
27. I can go home from most meetings of organizations I belong to, feeling somewhat tied in rather than isolated, out-of-place, outnumbered, unheard, held at a distance, or feared.
28. I can be pretty sure that an argument with a colleague of another race is more likely to jeopardize her chances for advancement than to jeopardize mine.
29. I can be pretty sure that if I argue for the promotion of a person of another race, or a program centering on race, this is not likely to cost me heavily within my present setting, even if my colleagues disagree with me.

30. If I declare there is a racial issue at hand, or there isn't a racial issue at hand, my race will lend me more credibility for either position than a person of color will have.
31. I can choose to ignore developments in minority writing and minority activist programs, or disparage them, or learn from them, but in any case, I can find ways to be more or less protected from negative consequences of any of these choices.
32. My culture gives me little fear about ignoring the perspectives and powers of people of other races.
33. I am not made acutely aware that my shape, bearing, or body odor will be taken as a reflection on my race.
34. I can worry about racism without being seen as self-interested or self-seeking.
35. I can take a job with an affirmative action employer without having my co-workers on the job suspect that I got it because of my race.
36. If my day, week, or year is going badly, I need not ask of each negative episode or situation whether it has racial overtones.
37. I can be pretty sure of finding people who would be willing to talk to me and advise me about my next steps, professionally.
38. I can think over many options, social, political, imaginative, or professional, without asking whether a person of my race would be accepted or allowed to do what I want to do.
39. I can be late to a meeting without having the lateness reflect on my race.
40. I can choose public accommodation without fearing that people of my race cannot get in or will be mistreated in the places I have chosen.
41. I can be sure that if I need legal or medical help, my race will not work against me.
42. I can arrange my activities so that I will never have to experience feelings of rejection owing to my race.
43. If I have low credibility as a leader I can be sure that my race is not the problem.
44. I can easily find academic courses and institutions which give attention only to people of my race.
45. I can expect figurative language and imagery in all of the arts to testify to experiences of my race.
46. I can choose blemish cover or bandages in "flesh" color and have them more or less match my skin.

I repeatedly forgot each of the realizations on this list until I wrote it down. For me, white privilege has turned out to be an elusive and fugitive subject. The pressure to avoid it is great, for in facing it I must give up the myth of meritocracy. If these things are true, this is not such a free country; one's life is not what one makes it; many doors open for certain people through no virtues of their own. These perceptions mean also that my moral condition is not what I had been led to believe. The appearance of being a good citizen rather than a troublemaker comes in large part from having all sorts of doors open automatically because of my color.

A further paralysis of nerve comes from literary silence protecting privilege. My clearest memories of finding such analysis are in Lillian Smith's unparalleled *Killers of the Dream* and Margaret Andersen's review of Karen and Mamie Fields' *Lemon Swamp*. Smith, for example, wrote about walking toward black children on the street and knowing they would step into the gutter; Andersen contrasted the pleasure which she, as a white child, took on summer driving trips to the South with Karen Fields' memories of driving in a closed car stocked with all necessities lest, in stopping, her black family should suffer "insult, or worse." Adrienne Rich also recognizes and writes about daily experiences of privilege, but in my observation, white women's writing in this area is far more often on systemic racism than on our daily lives as light-skinned women.[2]

In unpacking this invisible knapsack of white privilege, I have listed conditions of daily experience which I once took for granted, as neutral, normal, and universally available to everybody, just as I once thought of a male-focused curriculum as the neutral or accurate account which can speak for all. Nor did I think of any of these perquisites as bad for the holder. I now think that we need a more finely differentiated taxonomy of privilege, for some of these varieties are only what one would want for everyone in a just society, and others give license to be ignorant, oblivious, arrogant, and destructive. Before proposing some more finely tuned categorization, I will make some observations about the general effects of these conditions on my life and expectations.

In this potpourri of examples, some privileges make me feel at home in the world. Others allow me to escape penalties or dangers which others suffer. Through some, I escape fear, anxiety, or a sense of not being welcome or not being real. Some keep me from having to hide, to be in disguise, to feel sick or crazy, to negotiate each transaction from the position of being an outsider or, within my group, a person who is suspected of having too close links with a dominant culture. Most keep me from having to be angry.

I see a pattern running through the matrix of white privilege, a pattern of assumptions which were passed on to me as a white person. There was one main piece of cultural turf; it was my own turf, and I was among those who could control the turf. I could measure up to the cultural standards and take advantage of the many options I saw around me to make what the culture would call a success of my life. *My skin color was an asset for any move I was educated to want to make,* I could think of myself as "belonging" in major ways, and of making social systems work for me. I could freely disparage, fear, neglect, or be oblivious to anything outside of the dominant cultural forms. Being of the main culture, I could also criticize it fairly freely. My life was reflected back to me frequently enough so that I felt, with regard to my race, if not to my sex, like one of the real people.

Whether through the curriculum or in the newspaper, the television, the economic system, or the general look of people in the streets, we received daily signals and indications that my people counted, and that others *either didn't exist or must be trying, not very successfully, to be like people of my race.* We were given cultural permission not to hear voices of people of other races, or a tepid cultural tolerance for hearing or acting on such voices. I was also raised not to suffer seriously from anything which darker-skinned people might say about my group, "protected," though perhaps I should more accurately say *prohibited,* through the habits of my economic class and social group, from living in racially mixed groups or being reflective about interactions between people of differing races.

In proportion as my racial group was being made confident, comfortable, and oblivious, other groups were likely being made inconfident, uncomfortable, and alienated. Whiteness protected me from many kinds of hostility, distress, and violence, which I was being subtly trained to visit in turn upon people of color.

For this reason, the word "privilege" now seems to me misleading. Its connotations are too positive to fit the conditions and behaviors which "privilege systems" produce. We usually think of privilege as being a favored state, whether earned or conferred by birth or luck. School graduates are reminded they are privileged and urged to use their (enviable) assets well. The word "privilege" carries the connotation of being something everyone must want. Yet some of the conditions I have described here work to systematically overempower certain groups. Such privilege simply *confers dominance,* gives permission to control, because of one's race or sex. The kind of privilege which gives license to some people to be, at best, thoughtless, and at worst, murderous should not continue to be referred to as a desirable attribute. Such "privilege" may be widely desired without being in any way beneficial to the whole society.

Moreover, though "privilege" may confer power, it does not confer moral strength. Those who do not depend on conferred dominance have traits and qualities which may never develop in those who do. Just as Women's Studies courses indicate that women survive their political circumstances to lead lives which hold the human race together, so "underprivileged" people of color who are the world's majority have survived their oppression and lived survivors' lives from which the white global minority can and must learn. In some groups, those dominated have actually become strong through *not* having all of these unearned advantages, and this gives them a great deal to teach the others. Members of so-called privileged groups can seem foolish, ridiculous, infantile, or dangerous by contrast.

I want, then, to distinguish between earned strength and unearned power conferred systemically. Power from unearned privilege can look like strength when it is in fact permission to escape or to dominate. But not all of the privileges on my list are inevitably damaging. Some, like the expectation that neighbors will be decent to you, or that your race will not count against you in court, should be the norm in a just society and should be considered as the entitlement of everyone. Others, like the privilege not to listen to less powerful people, distort the humanity of the holders as well as the ignored groups. Still others, like finding one's staple foods everywhere, may be a function of being a member of a numerical majority in the population. Others have to do with not having to labor under pervasive negative stereotyping and mythology.

We might at least start by distinguishing between positive advantages which we can work to spread, to the point where they are not advantages at all but simply part of the normal civic and social fabric, and negative types of advantage which unless rejected will always reinforce our present hierarchies. For example, the positive "privilege" of belonging, the feeling that one belongs within the human circle, as Native Americans say, fosters development and should not be seen as privilege for a few. It is, let us say, an entitlement which none of us should have to earn; ideally it is an *unearned entitlement.* At present, since only a few have it, it is an *unearned advantage* for them. The negative "privilege" which gave me cultural permission not to take darker-skinned Others seriously can be seen as arbitrarily conferred dominance and should not be desirable for anyone. This paper results from a process of coming to see that some of the power which I originally saw as attendant on being a human being in the United States consisted in *unearned advantage* and *conferred dominance,* as well as other special circumstances not universally taken for granted.

In writing this paper I have also realized that white identity and status (as well as class identity and status) give me considerable power to choose whether to broach this subject and its trouble. I can pretty well decide whether to disappear and avoid and not listen and escape the dislike I may engender in other people through this essay, or interrupt, take over, dominate, preach, direct, criticize, or control to some extent what goes on in reaction to it. Being white, I am given considerable power to escape many kinds of danger or penalty as well as to choose which risks I want to take.

There is an analogy here, once again, with Women's Studies. Our male colleagues do not have a great deal to lose in supporting Women's Studies, but they do not have a great deal to lose if they oppose it either. They simply have the power to decide whether to commit themselves to more equitable distributions of power. They will probably feel few penalties, whatever choice they make; they do not seem, in any obvious short-term sense, the ones at risk, though they and we are all at risk because of the behaviors which have been rewarded in them.

Through Women's Studies work I have met very few men who are truly distressed about systemic, unearned male advantage and conferred dominance. And so one question for me and others like me is whether we will be like them, or whether we will get truly distressed, even outraged, about unearned race advantage and conferred dominance, and if so, what we will do to lessen them. In any case, we need to do more work in identifying how they actually affect our daily lives. We need more down-to-earth writing by people about these taboo subjects. We need more understanding of the ways in which white "privilege" damages white people, for these are not the same ways in which it damages the victimized. Skewed white psyches are an inseparable part of the picture, though I do not want to confuse the kinds of damage done to the holders of special assets and to those who suffer the deficits. Many, perhaps most, of our white students in the United States think that racism doesn't affect them because they are not people of color; they do not see "whiteness" as a racial identity. Many men likewise think that Women's Studies does not bear on their own existences because they are not female; they do not see themselves as having gendered identities. Insisting on the universal *effects* of "privilege" systems, then, becomes one of our chief tasks, and being more explicit about the *particular* effects in particular contexts is another. Men need to join us in this work.

In addition, since race and sex are not the only advantaging systems at work, we need to similarly examine the daily experience of having age advantage, or ethnic advantage, or physical ability or advantage related to nationality, religion, or sexual orientation. Professor Marnie Evans suggested to me that in many ways the list I made also applies directly to heterosexual privilege. This is a still more taboo subject than race privilege: the daily ways in which heterosexual privilege makes married persons comfortable or powerful, providing supports, assets, approvals, and rewards to those who live or expect to live in heterosexual pairs. Unpacking that content is still more difficult, owing to the deeper embeddedness of heterosexual advantage and dominance, and stricter taboos surrounding these.

But to start such an analysis I would put this observation from my own experience: The fact that I live under the same roof with a man triggers all kinds of societal assumptions about my worth, politics, life, and values, and triggers a host of unearned advantages and powers. After recasting many elements from the original list, I would add further observations like these:

1. My children do not have to answer questions about why I live with my partner (my husband).
2. I have no difficulty finding neighborhoods where people approve of our household.
3. My children are given texts and classes which implicitly support our kind of family unit, and do not turn them against my choice of domestic partnership.
4. I can travel alone or with my husband without expecting embarrassment or hostility in those who deal with us.
5. Most people I meet will see my marital arrangements as an asset to my life or as a favorable comment on my likability, my competence, or my mental health.
6. I can talk about the social events of a weekend without fearing most listeners' reactions.
7. I will feel welcomed and "normal" in the usual walks of public life, institutional and social.
8. In many contexts, I am seen as "all right" in daily work on women because I do not live chiefly with women.

Difficulties and dangers surrounding the task of finding parallels are many. Since racism, sexism, and heterosexism are not the same, the advantaging associated with them should not be seen as the same. In addition, it is hard to disentangle aspects of unearned advantage which rest more on social class, economic class, race, religion, sex, and ethnic identity than on other factors. Still, all of the oppressions are interlocking, as the Combahee River Collective statement of 1977 continues to remind us eloquently.[3]

One fact seems clear about all of the interlocking oppressions. They take both active forms which we can see and embedded forms which, as a member of the dominant group, one is taught not to see. In my class and place, I did not see myself as racist because I was taught to recognize racism only in individual acts of meanness by members of my group, never in invisible systems conferring unsought racial dominance on my group from birth. Likewise, we are taught to think that sexism or heterosexism is carried on only through individual acts of discrimination, meanness, or cruelty toward women, gays, and lesbians, rather than in invisible systems conferring unsought dominance on certain groups. Disapproving of the systems won't be enough to change them. I was taught to think that racism could end if white individuals changed their attitudes; many men think sexism can be ended by individual changes in daily behavior toward women. But a man's sex provides advantage for him whether or not he approves of the way in which dominance has been conferred on his group. A "white" skin in the United States opens many doors for whites whether or not we approve of the way dominance has been conferred on us. Individual acts can palliate, but cannot end, these problems. To redesign social systems, we need first to acknowledge their colossal unseen dimensions. The silences and denials surrounding privilege are the key political tool here. They keep the thinking about equality or equity incomplete, protecting unearned advantage and conferred dominance by making these subjects taboo. Most talk by whites about equal opportunity seems to me now to be about equal opportunity to try to get into a position of dominance while denying that *systems* of dominance exist.

It seems to me that obliviousness about white advantage, like obliviousness about male advantage, is kept strongly inculturated in the United States so as to maintain the myth of meritocracy, the myth that democratic choice is equally available to all. Keeping most people unaware that freedom of confident action is there for just a small number of people props up those in power and serves to keep power in the hands of the same groups that have most of it already. Though systemic change takes many decades, there are pressing questions for me and, I imagine, for some others like me, if we raise our daily consciousness on the perquisites of being light-skinned. What will we do with such knowledge? As we know from watching men, it is an open question whether we will choose to use unearned advantage to weaken hidden systems of advantage, and whether we will use any of our arbitrarily awarded power to try to reconstruct power systems on a broader base.

notes

This paper was funded by the Anna Wilder Phelps Fund through the generosity of Anna Emery Hanson. I have appreciated commentary on this paper from the Working Papers Committee of the Wellesley College Center for Research on Women, from members of the Dodge seminar, and from many individuals, including Margaret Andersen, Sorel Berman, Joanne Braxton, Johnnella Butler, Sandra Dickerson, Marnie Evans, Beverly Guy-Sheftall, Sandra Harding, Eleanor Hinton Hoytt, Pauline Houston, Paul Lauter, Joyce Miller, Mary Norris, Gloria Oden, Beverly Smith, and John Walter.

1. This paper was presented at the Virginia Women's Studies Association conference in Richmond in April 1986 and the American Educational Research Association conference in Boston in October 1986 and discussed with two groups of participants in the Dodge Seminars for Secondary School Teachers in New York and Boston in the spring of 1987.

2. Andersen, Margaret, "Race and the Social Science Curriculum: A Teaching and Learning Discussion," *Radical Teacher*, November 1984, pp. 17–20. Smith, Lillian, *Killers of the Dream*, New York, 1949.

3. "A Black Feminist Statement," The Combahee River Collective, pp. 13–22 in Hull, Scott, Smith, eds., *All the Women Are White, All the Blacks Are Men but Some of Us Are Brave: Black Women's Studies*, New York: Feminist Press, 1982.

5

the invisible crutch

Jessica Shea*

The Invisible Knapsack of White Privilege, conceived by Peggy McIntosh, discusses the many things a white person takes for granted, in list form. As a white person, I was uncomfortable reading many of these things, but I also saw reflected in them what men, wealthy people, and non-disabled people take for granted.

I've decided to build an invisible crutch from things that constitute abled privilege, without repeating too much of what is in McIntosh's list (so read her list, and substitute "disability" for "color" for many of those items).

1. I can, if I wish, arrange to attend social events without worrying if they are accessible to me.
2. If I am in the company of people who make me uncomfortable, I can easily choose to move elsewhere.
3. I can easily find housing that is accessible to me, with no barriers to my mobility.
4. I can go shopping alone most of the time and be able to reach and obtain all of the items without assistance, know that cashiers will notice I am there, and can easily see and use the credit card machines.
5. I can turn on the television and see people of my ability level widely and accurately represented.

---

* Shea, Jessica. "The Invisible Crutch," *She Dances on the Sand* blog, April 23, 2009. Available at rioiriri.blogspot.com/2009/04/invisible-crutch.html. Reprinted by permission of the author.

6. I can be pretty sure of my voice being heard in a group where I am the only person of my ability level represented—and they will make eye contact with me.

7. I can advocate for my children in their schools without my ability level being blamed for my children's performance or behavior.

8. I can do well in a challenging situation without being told what an inspiration I am.

9. If I ask to speak to someone "in charge," I can be relatively assured that the person will make eye contact with me and not treat me like I am stupid.

10. I can belong to an organization and not feel that others resent my membership because of my ability level.

11. I do not have to fear being preyed upon because of my ability level.

12. I can be reasonably assured that I won't be late for meetings due to mobility barriers.

13. I can use most cosmetics and personal care products without worrying that they will cause a painful or dangerous reaction.

14. I can usually go about in public without other people's personal care products causing me painful or dangerous reactions.

15. My neighborhood allows me to move about on sidewalks, into stores, and into friends' homes without difficulty.

16. People do not tell me that my ability level means I should not have children.

17. I can be reasonably sure that I will be able to make it to a regular job every day.

18. I know that my income can increase based on my performance, and I can seek new and better employment if I choose; I do not have to face a court battle to get an increase in my income.

19. My daily routine does not have to be carefully planned to accommodate medication or therapy schedules.

20. I can share my life with an animal companion without my ability to care for it being called into question due to my financial and ability situations.

21. If I am not feeling well and decide to stay in bed, I will likely be believed and not told that I am lazy and worthless.

I am sure there are more I haven't thought of. Do keep in mind that I've tried *not* to copy Ms. McIntosh's work, because there's no need—most of what she says applies to this list as well.

6

are admissions decisions based on family ties fairer than those that consider race?

Social dominance orientation and attitudes toward legacy vs. affirmative action policies

Angélica S. Gutiérrez and Miguel M. Unzueta*

Introduction

A large body of literature has examined people's attitudes toward affirmative action policies (Bobo, 2000; Dovidio & Gartner, 1996; Sears, Hetts, Sidanius, & Bobo, 2000; Lowery, Unzueta, Knowles, & Goff, 2006). Intended to increase the representation of underrepresented groups in higher education and in the workplace, affirmative action is a collection of policies that takes into consideration racial group membership in hiring and admissions decisions (Gurin, Dey, Hurtado, & Gurin, 2002). Although examining individuals' reactions to affirmative action is important, examining reactions to other selection policies like legacy admissions policies may provide insight into people's underlying motivations for supporting or opposing such policies.

*Gutiérrez, Angélica S., and Miguel M. Unzueta. "Are admissions decisions based on family ties fairer than those that consider race? Social dominance orientation and attitudes toward legacy vs. affirmative action policies." *Journal of Experimental Social Psychology* 49 (2013) 554–558. DOI:10.1016/j.jesp.2012.10.011. Copyright © 2012 Published by Elsevier Inc. Adapted with permission from Elsevier.

Previous research suggests that opposition to affirmative action policies is motivated by principled motives (Sniderman & Piazza, 1993). Scholars contend that although racism once influenced attitudes toward affirmative action, opposition is now driven by race-neutral values such as fairness and merit (Carmines & Merriman, 1993; Sniderman, Crosby, & Howell, 2000). In the present paper we challenge the view that meritocratic principles are the only source of opposition to policies that provide opportunities on the basis of beneficiaries' group membership. Although some opponents of affirmative action may legitimately oppose these policies on the premise that they violate meritocracy—i.e., the ideal that people should be rewarded based only on competence and effort rather than group membership (Bobocel, Son Hing, Davey, Stanley, & Zanna, 1998; Heilman, Battle, Keller, & Lee, 1998)—we argue that there may be others who, consistent with their desire to maintain social inequality, differentially support policies that deviate from meritocracy. To test this hypothesis we examine reactions to two policies that grant selection preferences to individuals based on group membership: legacy policies and affirmative action.

What are legacy policies?

Legacy policies give an admissions boost to children and grandchildren of university alumni (Ladewski, 2010). Given that legacy admissions are based on past patterns of university enrollment, legacy preferences disproportionately benefit White applicants, whose parents are more likely than parents of racial minority applicants to have attended universities (Lamb, 1993). Studies suggest that applicants whose parents graduated from a university are 45% more likely to gain admission over applicants with no familial connection to the university in question; applicants who have a sibling, aunt, uncle, or grandparent who graduated from a university are 14% more likely to be admitted relative to someone with no legacy status (Hurwitz, 2011).

How legacy policies may differ from affirmative action policies

One reason why people may react differently to legacy vs. affirmative action policies is that these policies have opposing consequences for racial equality. Whereas affirmative action policies promote equality by attempting to reduce racial gaps in access to jobs and educational opportunities (Blumer, 1958; Bobo, 1998; Sidanius & Pratto, 1999), legacy policies could be thought of as promoting inequality by primarily benefitting members of the dominant racial group (i.e., Whites; Ladewski, 2010). Given that affirmative action and legacy policies may have distinct consequences for the racial hierarchy, people's social dominance orientation (SDO)—i.e., the degree to which individuals desire inequality between social groups (Pratto, Sidanius, Stallworth, & Malle, 1994)—may differentially predict support for these policies. Specifically, if such policies are, in fact, thought to have opposing effects on racial equality, then SDO should predict opposition to hierarchy-*attenuating* affirmative action policies and support for hierarchy-*enhancing* legacy policies.

The present research

In the present research we examine whether the differential effect of legacy and affirmative action policies on the racial hierarchy affects people's support for such policies. In Study 1, we assess people's support for legacy vs. affirmative action as a function of SDO. Consistent with social dominance theory (Sidanius, Liu, Pratto, & Shaw, 1994; van Laar, Sidanius, Rabinowitz, & Sinclair, 1999), we argue that support for these policies reflects individuals' desire to preserve or minimize racial inequality regardless of whether such policies actually benefit the ingroup. To this end, in Study 2 we directly assess whether SDO reflects a general desire to maintain inequality (Pratto, Sidanius, & Levin, 2006; Sidanius & Pratto, 1999) or a specific desire to protect ingroup interests (Lehmiller & Schmitt, 2007; Schmitt, Branscombe, & Kappen, 2003) by manipulating the purported beneficiaries of legacy admission policies.

Study 1

Study 1 tested the hypothesis that a desire to preserve the racial hierarchy differentially influences people's attitudes towards legacy vs. affirmative action policies. Consistent with past research, we expect to find that affirmative action is opposed as a function of SDO (Pratto et al., 1994). Conversely, given that legacy policies are likely to reinforce the racial hierarchy by overwhelmingly benefitting Whites (Ladewski, 2010), we expect to find a positive relationship between legacy policy support and SDO.

Participants

Eighty participants (51 women, 29 men) were recruited from an online participant database maintained at UCLA (38 Asians, 36 Whites, 4 Latinos, 2 participants indicated more than one racial identity). The age ranged from 18 to 36 ($M = 20.76$, $SD = 2.87$).

Procedure

Participants were told that they would be completing two unrelated surveys. Participants first completed an SDO measure, which was described as a survey of individuals' views of groups in society. The second survey was described as a survey of individuals' policy views. Participants were randomly assigned to evaluate either a legacy or an affirmative action policy. In the legacy condition, participants read a vignette indicating that Ivy League schools and other major universities, including UCLA,* currently use a legacy admissions policy; this policy was described as giving children and grandchildren of alumni a "nudge" in the admissions process. In the affirmative action condition, participants read a similar vignette but the term "legacy" was substituted with "affirmative action" and the beneficiaries of this policy were described as "university applicants who are underrepresented at a particular institution." Participants were then asked to indicate their support for the policy.

Measures

Social dominance orientation. SDO was measured using an eight-item scale (Sidanius & Pratto, 1999). Participants were asked to indicate how negatively or positively they felt about various items. Sample items include: "If certain groups stayed in their place, we would have fewer problems" and "It's probably a good thing that certain groups are at the top and other groups are at the bottom" (1 = very negative, 7 = very positive; $\alpha = .93$; $M = 2.43$, $SD = .94$).

Policy support

To assess participants' policy support, they were asked to respond to the following items: "How fair do you think is this policy?" (1 = not fair at all,

---

*Participants were debriefed with UCLA's admissions policy and told that UCLA does not grant preferential treatment on the basis of an applicant's family ties (i.e., legacy) or race (i.e., affirmative action).

7 = very fair), "To what extent do you agree or disagree that this policy is legitimate and should be continued?" (1 = strongly disagree, 7 = strongly agree), "How much do you oppose or support the policy that you read in the previous screen?" (1 = strongly oppose, 7 = strongly support), "This admissions policy will help admit highly qualified individuals," "UCLA will be a much better place if this policy continues to be used in the admissions process," "Given that university rankings are based on the caliber of students that attend an institution, UCLA will continue to increase in rankings with this admissions policy," "As a future alumnus of UCLA, I am more likely to be engaged in university activities if UCLA continues to use this admissions policy than if it were to discontinue its use," "If money is no obstacle in the future, I will donate money to UCLA if it continues to use this admissions policy" (1 = strongly disagree, 7 strongly agree; $\alpha = .92$; $M = 3.05$, $SD = 1.16$).

Discussion

Study 1 uncovered a positive relationship between SDO and policy support in the legacy condition, a finding consistent with the idea that people motivated to preserve status hierarchies support policies that reinforce racial inequality by benefitting the dominant racial group. Conversely, and consistent with past research, SDO was negatively associated with support for hierarchy-attenuating affirmative action policies—i.e., policies that benefit minority group members.

Although the present findings are consistent with the idea that dominance motives predict support for legacy admissions preferences and opposition to affirmative action preferences, it is possible that these findings reflect a desire to protect the ingroup and not status hierarchies per se. Specifically, the positive relationship between SDO and legacy policy support in Study 1 may reflect participants' support for a policy from which they think their group will benefit. Recent research suggests that social dominance orientation may not capture a general desire to maintain status hierarchies but rather a specific desire to maintain hierarchies in which one's ingroup stands to benefit. This research posits that the position of one's ingroup in the social structure is an important influence on attitudes towards inequality (Oakes, Haslam, & Turner, 1994; Schmitt et al., 2003; Turner & Reynolds, 2003). According to the group-interest perspective, groups that benefit from inequality are more likely to support it relative to groups that are disadvantaged by it because inequality protects the status and power of the privileged group. As such, a desire to protect ingroup interests and not a general desire to protect the status hierarchy may explain why SDO was positively related to support for legacy policies in Study 1. Consistent with this alternative explanation is the fact that the sample used in Study 1 is primarily White and Asian, two groups that are well represented at UCLA and therefore likely to benefit from legacy admission preferences in the future.*

Study 2

Study 2 was designed to examine whether a general desire to maintain the status hierarchy or a specific desire to protect ingroup interests explains differential attitudes towards legacy policies. Recall that Study 1 did not explicitly state who would likely benefit from legacy preferences. As such, it is possible that both Asian and White participants, who composed the majority of our sample and are currently the most well-represented groups in the university where these studies were conducted, believed that their own group would benefit from legacy policies. If both groups believed that their own group would benefit, then policy support may reflect a desire to protect the ingroup's interests and not a desire to maintain status hierarchies.

---

*UCLA does not employ legacy or affirmative action policies in the university admissions review process. The following is UCLA's admissions policy: Each year, UCLA considers many more excellent applicants for freshmen admission than it can possibly admit. The goal of the campus' admissions review process is to single out from a large and growing pool of academically strong applicants those unique individuals who have demonstrated the intellectual curiosity, tenacity, and commitment to community service expected of the UCLA graduate. These select applicants are the ones who would contribute the most to UCLA's dynamic learning environment: they are also the applicants who would make the most of being immersed in it. Although high school grade point average and standardized test scores are important indicators of academic achievement used in UCLA's admissions review, they only tell part of the story. As a public, land grant institution of higher learning, UCLA has a mandate to serve the State of California by educating its future leaders in research, industry, and the arts. California's future depends heavily on this important charge. While California law prohibits the consideration of an applicant's race and/or gender in individual admission decisions, the University also has a mandate to reflect the diversity of the state's population in its student body. Student diversity is a compelling interest at UCLA. It contributes to a rich and stimulating learning environment, one that best prepares leaders-in-the-making for the challenges and opportunities of California, the nation, and beyond (http://www.admissions.ucla.edu/policies.htm).

Examining the attitudes of Asian participants when they are told that either the ingroup (i.e., Asians) or an outgroup (i.e., Whites) would benefit from legacy admissions policies would enable us to determine whether a desire to protect ingroup interests or a desire to protect the status hierarchy accounts for differences in policy support. To this end, in Study 2 we explicitly stated that either the ingroup or the dominant outgroup (i.e., Whites) benefits from these policies. If SDO is capturing a general desire for hierarchy maintenance (Sibley, Robertson. & Wilson, 2006; Sidanius & Pratto, 1999), then as a function of SDO, Asian perceivers should support a legacy policy that benefits Whites but oppose one that benefits fellow Asians. However, if SDO is capturing ingroup interests (Lehmiller & Schmitt, 2007; Schmitt et al., 2003), then we should find that SDO predicts support for a policy that benefits Asians and opposition for a legacy policy that benefits Whites.

Participants
Fifty-four self-identified Asian participants (16 men, 37 women, 1 unreported) were recruited from an online participant database maintained at UCLA. The age ranged from 18 to 35 ($M = 20.31$, $SD = 2.53$).

Procedure
The same procedure from Study 1 was used, but the scenarios also explicitly stated that either Asians or Whites would benefit from the legacy admissions policy. Since our main predictions concern differences in these two key conditions, we omitted the affirmative action condition in Study 2.

Measures
Social dominance orientation. SDO was assessed using the same scale in Study 1 (Sidanius & Pratto, 1999; $\alpha = .93$; $M = 2.77$, $SD = .97$).

Policy support. Policy support was assessed using the same eight-item measure as Study 1 ($\alpha = .93$; $M = 3.41$, $SD = 1.07$).

Discussion

Study 2 found a positive relationship between SDO and policy support among Asian participants in the condition in which Whites were the perceived beneficiaries of the legacy policy. Conversely, there was a non-significant negative relationship between SDO and policy support among Asians in the condition where Asians were the perceived beneficiaries of the legacy policy. These findings suggest that legacy policy support depends, in part, on its effect on the status hierarchy and not on its effect on the ingroup.

In sum, Study 2 suggests that as a function of SDO, Asian participants support legacy policies thought to benefit Whites. The positive relationship in the condition in which Whites were the perceived beneficiaries is consistent with the group dominance perspective, which suggests that groups will support policies that are hierarchy enhancing even when these policies disadvantage their own ingroup (Pratto et al., 2006; Sidanius & Pratto, 1999). Additionally, the non-significant relationship in the condition where Asians were the perceived beneficiaries suggests that group-interest may not explain differential reactions to legacy preferences (Lehmiller & Schmitt, 2007; Schmitt et al., 2003). Instead, the present study suggests that a desire to preserve status hierarchies in general explains why legacy policies are supported by individuals relatively high in SDO.

General discussion

The present findings provide a direct test of the competing hypotheses that attitudes towards inequality reflect group interests (Schmitt et al., 2003) vs. a generalized orientation towards status hierarchies (Sidanius & Pratto, 1999). The results from two studies provide evidence that general dominance motives seem to account for differential reactions to policies that disproportionately privilege some groups and disadvantage others. Even when the ingroup (Asians; Study 2) is privileged by legacy policies, there is a predisposition to support such policies consistent with one's level of SDO only when such policies benefit the dominant group (i.e., Whites).

Moreover, our studies suggest that meritocratic principles are not the core reason why people high in SDO oppose affirmative action. If this were the case, then we should have found that SDO predicts opposition to both affirmative action and legacy policies. However, in Study 1 we found that SDO actually predicts legacy policy support. This finding is consistent with past work suggesting that " . . . seemingly mainstream values . . . simply mask desires for group dominance . . . " (Frederico & Sidanius, 2002, p. 489; see also Sidanius & Pratto, 2001). In all, these findings suggest that attitudes toward selection policies (i.e., legacy, affirmative action) will depend not on their specific content or objectives, but rather on their assumed effect on status hierarchies.

Conclusion

The reported studies, to our knowledge, are the first to explore attitudes toward legacy admission policies. These studies suggest that individuals motivated to maintain social inequality support legacy policies because these policies are thought to benefit the dominant racial group and, by extension, maintain racial inequality. As such, the reported studies cast further doubt on the idea that attacks on affirmative action are purely based on the desire to uphold the principle of meritocracy (see also Frederico & Sidanius, 2002). Rather, it appears that some "unmeritocratic" policies are acceptable so long as these policies contribute to the enhancement, rather than the attenuation, of race-based inequality.

references

Blumer, H. (1958). Race prejudice as a sense of group position. *The Pacific Sociological Review, 1,* 3–7.

Bobo, L. (1998). Race, interests, and beliefs about affirmative action. *American Behavioral-Scientist, 41,* 985–1003.

Bobo, L. (2000). Race and beliefs about affirmative action. In D. O. Sears, J. Sidanius, & L. Bobo (Eds.), *Racialized politics: The debate about racism in America* (pp. 137–164). Chicago: University of Chicago Press.

Bobocel, D. R., Son Hing, L. S., Davey, L. M., Stanley, D. J., & Zanna, M. P. (1998). Justice-based opposition to social policies: Is it genuine? *Journal of Personality and Social Psychology, 75,* 653–669.

Carmines, E. G., & Merriman, R. W., Jr. (1993). The changing American dilemma: Liberal values and racial policies. In P. M. Sniderman, P. E. Tetlock, & E. G. Carmines (Eds.), *Prejudice, politics, and the American dilemma* (pp. 237–255). Stanford, CA: Stanford University Press.

Dovidio. J. F., & Gartner, S. L. (1996). Affirmative action, unintentional racial biases, and intergroup relations. *Journal of Social Issues, 52,* 51–75.

Frederico, C. M., & Sidanius, J. (2002). Sophistication and the antecedents of Whites' racial policy attitudes: Racism, ideology, and affirmative action in America. *Public Opinion Quarterly, 66,* 145–176.

Gurin, P., Dey, E. L., Hurtado. S., & Gurin, G. (2002). Diversity and higher education: Theory and impact on educational outcomes. *Harvard Educational Review, 72,* 330–366.

Heilman, M. E., Battle, W. S., Keller, C. E., & Lee, R. A. (1998). Type of affirmative action policy: A determinant of reactions to sex-based preferential selection. *The Journal of Applied Psychology, 83,* 190–205.

Hurwitz, M. (2011). The impact of legacy status on undergraduate admissions at elite colleges and universities. *Economics of Education Review, 30,* 480–492.

Ladewski (2010). Preserving a racial hierarchy: A legal analysis of the disparate racial impact of legacy preferences in university admissions. *Michigan Law Review, 10*, 577–601.

Lamb, J. D. (1993). The real affirmative action babies: Legacy preferences at Harvard and Yale. *Columbia Journal of Law and Social Problems, 26*, 491–521.

Lehmiller, J. J., & Schmitt, M. T. (2007). Group domination and inequality in context: Evidence for the unstable meanings of social dominance and authoritarianism. *European Journal of Social Psychology, 37*, 704–724.

Lowery, B. S., Unzueta, M. M., Knowles, E. D., & Goff, P. A. (2006). Concern for the ingroup and opposition to affirmative action. *Journal of Personality and Social Psychology, 90*, 961–974.

Oakes, P. J., Haslam, S. A., & Turner, J. C. (1994). *Stereotyping and social reality*. Oxford: Blackwell.

Pratto, F., Sidanius, J., & Levin, S. (2006). Social dominance theory and the dynamics of intergroup relations: Taking stock and looking forward. *European Review of Social Psychology, 17*(1), 271–320.

Pratto, F., Sidanius, J., Stallworth, L. M., & Malle, B. F. (1994). Social dominance orientation: A personality variable predicting social and political attitudes. *Journal of Personality and Social Psychology, 67*, 741–763.

Schmitt, M. T., Branscombe, N. R., & Kappen, D. M. (2003). Attitudes toward group-based inequality: Social dominance or social identity? *The British Journal of Social Psychology, 42*,161–186.

Sears, D. O., Hetts, J. J., Sidanius, J., & Bobo, L. (2000). Race in American politics. In D. O. Sears, J. Sidanius, & L. Bobo (Eds.), *Racialized politics: The debate about racism in America* (pp. 1–43). Chicago: University of Chicago Press.

Sibley, C. G., Robertson, A., & Wilson, M. S. (2006). Social dominance orientation and right wing authoritarianism: Additive and interactive effects. *Political Psychology, 27*, 755–768.

Sidanius, J., Liu, J., Pratto, F., & Shaw, J. (1994). Social dominance orientation, hierarchy-attenuators and hierarchy-enhancers: Social dominance theory and the criminal justice system. *Journal of Applied Social Psychology, 24*, 338–366.

Sidanius, J., & Pratto, F. (1999). *Social dominance: An intergroup theory of social hierarchy and oppression*. New York: Cambridge University Press.

Sidanius, J., & Pratto, F. (2001). *Social dominance: An intergroup theory of social hierarchy and oppression*. New York: Cambridge University Press.

Sniderman, P. M., Crosby, G. C., & Howell, W. G. (2000). The politics of race. In D. O. Sears, J. Sidanius. & L. Bobo (Eds.), *Racialized politics: Values, ideology, and prejudice in American public opinion* (pp. 236–279). Chicago: University of Chicago Press.

Sniderman, P. M., & Piazza, T. (1993). *The scar of race*. Cambridge, MA: Harvard University Press.

Turner, J., & Reynolds, K. (2003). Why social dominance theory has been falsified. *The British Journal of Social Psychology, 42*(2), 199–206.

van Laar, C., Sidanius, J., Rabinowitz, J., & Sinclair, S. (1999). The three Rs of academic achievement: Reading, riting, and racism. *Personality and Social Psychology Bulletin, 25*, 139–151.

7

top ten differences between white terrorists and others

Juan Cole*

1. White terrorists are called "gunmen."[†] What does that even mean? A person with a gun? Wouldn't that be, like, everyone in the US? Other terrorists are called, like, "terrorists."
2. White terrorists are "troubled loners." Other terrorists are always suspected of being part of a global plot, even when they are obviously troubled loners.
3. Doing a study on the danger of white terrorists at the Department of Homeland Security will get you sidelined by angry white congressmen.[‡] Doing studies on other kinds of terrorists is a guaranteed promotion.
4. The family of a white terrorist is interviewed, weeping as they wonder where he went wrong. The families of other terrorists are almost never interviewed.
5. White terrorists are part of a "fringe." Other terrorists are apparently mainstream.

---

*Cole, Juan. "Top Ten Differences between White Terrorists and Others," *Informed Consent* blog, August 9, 2012, www.juancole.com/2012/08/top-ten-differences-between-white -terrorists-and-others.html. Copyright 2012, *Informed Consent*. Reprinted by permission of the author.

† www.latimes.com/news/nation/nationnow/la-na-nn-sikh-temple-gunman-201208 08,0,6572009.story.

‡ www.wired.com/dangerroom/2012/08/dhs/all.

6. White terrorists are random events, like tornadoes. Other terrorists are long-running conspiracies.

7. White terrorists are never called "white." But other terrorists are given ethnic affiliations.

8. Nobody thinks white terrorists are typical of white people. But other terrorists are considered paragons of their societies.

9. White terrorists are alcoholics, addicts, or mentally ill. Other terrorists are apparently clean-living and perfectly sane.

10. There is nothing you can do about white terrorists. Gun control won't stop them. No policy you could make, no government program, could possibly have an impact on them. But hundreds of billions of dollars must be spent on police and on the Department of Defense, and on TSA, which must virtually strip-search 60 million people a year, to deal with other terrorists.

8

globalizing privilege

Bob Pease*

Much of the recognition of privilege and oppression is framed within a taken-for-granted, geographically bordered sovereign state (Fraser 2008). Working for social justice, all too often, addresses only citizens within national borders, with little consideration given to the way in which privilege within those geographical boundaries is likely to impact on those outside of them. Just as there is growing recognition among some progressive social movements that injustice must be targeted across national borders, so, too, the recognition of privilege must be understood within an international or global frame.

Schwalbe (2002) notes that non-Western, foreign university students in North America tend to know more about the United States than most North American students. This is because non-Western students' lives are shaped by the policies of the United States government and the diffusion of North American cultural hegemony, whereas North American students do not have the same need to understand the policies of their own government or those of non-Western countries. The reality is that most Westerners are simply unaware of the impact of the West on non-Western countries (Bonnett 2004; Gray and Coates 2008). Like most of my contemporaries, I grew up in ignorance of the privileges associated with my geo-political position.

---

* Pease, Bob. "Globalizing Privilege," pp. 41–49 in *Undoing Privilege: Unearned Advantage in a Divided World*, by Bob Pease. Copyright 2010 by Zed Books. Reprinted by permission of the publisher.

In my lifestyle, my professional practice and my political work, unwittingly I perpetuated a Eurocentric vision of the world.

The Idea of the West*

To understand global privilege, it is necessary to interrogate the concept of 'the West', which has been presented as an ideal model of progress for all countries in the world. Developments in the West are seen as flowing down to inspire traditional societies along similar routes of progress (Slater 2004).

Modernisation is a concept used to describe the growing gap between the industrialised countries of the West and the impoverishment of the non-West (R. Marks 2002). The premise is that all countries of the world should adopt the values that informed the rise of the West. This belief in the superiority of Western values and rationality is what constitutes the myth of Eurocentrism, which Marks argues is no more than an ideology that distorts the truth and masks Western global dominance. In fact, the greatest power that the West has is not its economic and technological supremacy, but its power to define what is progress and ultimately what it means to be human (Sardar 1999a).

While Western culture portrays itself as the only culture that is capable of engaging in a reflexive critique of its own accomplishments (Slater 2004), there is very little indication of reflections about the premises of Western superiority. On the contrary, Western dominance is sustained by what Slater refers to as 'imperial knowledge'. By this, he means a belief in the need to intervene in other 'less-advanced' societies, a belief in the legitimacy of imposing Western values on non-Western societies and a belief that non-Western cultures are inferior and consequently that their rights can be legitimately denied. Thus Western supremacy requires the silencing of non-Western cultures and demonstrates no interest in learning from these cultures.

---

* Mohanty (2004) notes that terms like West and East and North and global South focus on countries in the northern and southern hemispheres; they do not totally capture the divisions between affluence and deprivation. Jolly (2008) further argues that these geographical terms tend to dehistoricise and naturalise inequalities between nations. Kothari (in Harcourt 2007) believes that these terms have become meaningless because there is growing affluence in some parts of the South and extensive deprivation and disadvantage in parts of the North. Notwithstanding these inequalities within countries, it is still meaningful to use these terms to analyse institutionalised inequalities in wealth and power between nations.

Of course, it is understandable that the West will view history from a European perspective. This ethnocentrism would not be such a problem if the West accepted that it was simply **one** of many ethnocentric views of the world. However, it is the claim of the West's universal applicability of its culture to the rest of the world that constitutes it as Eurocentrism. Western countries refuse to acknowledge that their claimed superiority is based on their values and their biased perceptions of the past. Rather, they claim to base their superiority on scholarship and scientific evidence (R. Marks 2002).

A number of writers have challenged the view that the West pioneered the modern world, arguing that the West and East have been historically interconnected. In this view, the East has played an important role in the development of Western civilisation (Blaut 1993; Gran 1996; Hobson 2004). R. Marks (2002) provides an alternative historical account of the origins of the Western world and demonstrates how the West was able to present itself as progressive, while constructing Asia, Africa and Latin America as backward. Hobson (2004) also illustrates how many so-called Western concepts have Eastern origins. Similarly, Narayan (2000) challenges the view that concepts such as human rights, democracy and equality are Western. Hence, it is not simply a matter of imposing Western values on to non-Western cultures, but rather the propagation of the myth that these concepts have solely Western origins that reinforces Western supremacy.

If Western supremacy is to be challenged, it is necessary to question the rational and scientific premises of modernisation and technological development. Sardar (1999a) believes that such challenges must come from the non-West, as they formulate and advocate new concepts. This does not imply uncritical acceptance of all that comes out of the non-West. However, there will need to be a capacity on the part of the West to engage with and respect determinations that are different from their own.

If the gap between the wealthy and poorest nations of the world is to be eliminated, a move beyond Eurocentric understanding of the modern world is needed. This means endeavouring to get outside Western ways of knowing and acknowledging that such ways of knowing are Eurocentric.

Moving Beyond Eurocentrism

Essentially, Eurocentrism involves the belief that Europeans are superior to non-Europeans. Blaut (1993) refers to it as 'the colonizer's model of the world' because it is premised on the view that European civilisation has superior qualities associated with race and culture compared with non-Western cultures. Western culture is also predominantly white culture. While the dimensions of white privilege are explored in Chapter 6, it is necessary to establish here that there is a direct link between Western expansion in the world and the concept of whiteness. Thus there is a close connection between Western global dominance and white cultural influences (Shorne 1999).

While all countries that constitute the West are capitalist, there is a need to mask this historical and culturally specific formation to avoid any suggestion of alternatives. Thus the West is presented as the best of all possible worlds. The economic development of the West must then be portrayed as a transhistorical social formation based upon eternal truths and instrumental rationality (Amin 1989). Dominant ideologies in the West legitimate capitalist societies as the only possible form of economic and political relations. Eurocentrism then grows out of colonial domination and provides a legitimation of inequalities between nations (Gheverghese et al. 1990).

Amin (1989) refers to Eurocentrism as a form of prejudice that distorts theoretical understanding. However, Western social sciences are so embedded within Eurocentric assumptions that most social scientists are unaware of their European bias. Eurocentrism underlies all social science disciplines, including history (Gran 1996); sociology (Connell 2007); psychology (Naidoo 1996); social work (Midgley 1983); urban theory (McGee 1995) and geography (Blaut 1993). To challenge Eurocentrism is to question the taken-for-granted assumptions that underpin all Western social science disciplines.

Blaut (1993) raises questions about the term 'Eurocentrism' because it implies a form of prejudiced attitudes. If that is so, then it can be eliminated through enlightened thought. However, Eurocentrism functions not just as a matter of attitudes, but rather is founded on beliefs informed by scholarship and science and it purports to be based on scientific and empirical evidence. If this is so, then it is validated as a form of truth about the world. Highly educated and supposedly unprejudiced Europeans are consequently not likely to critically interrogate the assumptions underpinning it.

Non-Western intellectuals have also been influenced by Eurocentrism. They are encouraged to borrow theoretical constructs and categories that have value in Western societies and relate them to their own context where their value may be questionable (Gheverghese et al. 1990). This raises difficult and complex issues when progressive Westerners encounter these developments. In 1998, I was a member of a small Australian delegation to an Asia and Pacific Social Work Conference in Beijing that was to launch the first social work course in China. As someone who was committed to local knowledge and culturally grounded social work practice, I supported efforts by Chinese academics to develop their own conceptual frameworks for social work theory and practice. However, a number of leading Chinese academics who founded the course had undertaken their PhDs in North America and adapted North American models of social work and psychology to the Chinese situation. I found myself in the uncomfortable position of promoting local knowledge that went against the views of some Chinese delegates who had cognitively adopted North American models of theory and practice.

A more inclusive form of world history requires recognition that Eurocentric world views are only appropriate to understanding the West as a historical and cultural construct. A non-Eurocentric history involves developing a more holistic understanding of global issues. Western social science understandings of the non-West requires decolonising practices and locally based scholarship (Gray and Coates 2008).

Orientalism: Constructing the Non-West

One of the most significant early challenges to Eurocentrism was Edward Said's *Orientalism,* first published in 1978. Orientalism is 'a body of ideas, beliefs, cliches or learning about the East' (Said 2003:205). It forms the basis of representations of the Orient in Western consciousness. However, it is not simply a body of knowledge about non-Western societies. Rather, it involves an ideological construction of the Orient that is mythical and transhistorical. It further presents characteristics of the East as immutable and in opposition to the West (Amin 1989) and proclaims the inherent superiority of the West over the East (Hobson 2004).

Thus Orientalism goes beyond the disciplines and practices associated with the study of oriental societies. It involves an epistemological and ontological approach, which sets up a polarised division between the Orient and the West (Turner 1994). The West is portrayed as productive, hard-working, mature, honest and progressive and the East is constructed as the opposite of these values. Said (2003) demonstrates how this process of 'othering' maintains unequal power relations throughout the world and provides the legitimation for Europe to 'manage' the Orient.

Through Orientalism, the West perpetuates its dominance over the non-West by attributing essences to both the Orient and the Occident. Orientalism becomes a colonialist method of subjugation because it legitimates colonialist interventions (Sardar 1999b). Twenty-five years after the first edition of his book, Said (2003) argued that his analysis still holds true. Orientalism fuelled the anti-Islam views that were propagated under the presidential administration of George Bush in North America. While the West continues to be appropriated by neo-liberal capitalism that supports military interventions into non-Western countries, anti-Western sentiment will continue to influence the rise of radical Islamism (Bonnett 2004).

Although Said's work has been criticised by some as an anti-Western polemic, it does not set out to portray the West as evil. However, some have argued that in response to the debates about Orientalism, a form of Occidentalism arose where everything to do with the West was subjected to critique. Turner (1994) says, for example, that it is inappropriate to regard all Western analyses of the Orient as negative. Otherwise, all Indigenous and non-Western frameworks would have to be accepted as legitimate. This may, in some cases, promote political conservatism and equally distorted and prejudiced views of the West.

Said is also accused of portraying the West as monolithic and unchanging (Sardar 1999b). If all Western intellectuals are Orientalist, then does that mean that there is no progressive thought in the West? There were and are counter-hegemonic intellectuals in the West who were opposed to colonialism and who resisted imperialism and ethnocentrism (McLeod 2000). Paranjape (1993) makes the point that it is important to acknowledge that the West is a divided entity and not a monolith. It is ideologically and ethically divided in relation to the global South. Hence, it is possible to forge alliances with progressive groups within the West to promote more socially just relations.

The Poverty of Development

A number of development writers have noted that after more than thirty years of development programmes and foreign aid, the poorest countries of the world are worse off than they were before Western interventions (Verhelst 1990; Escobar 1995; Tucker 1999; Munck 1999). Esteva (in Harcourt

2007) has noted that in 1960, the rich countries had twenty times the wealth of the poor countries. Twenty years later, following development interventions, they were forty-six times richer. Today the gap is even wider. Given these outcomes, one must ask whether the dominant model of Western development is part of the problem. This is especially so in the context of espoused individualistic and capitalist accumulative principles rather than redistributive and justice-based principles.

White European men wrote the history of development and established the foundations of truth that are universalised for all (Munck 1999). As early as the 1970s, critics of development were identifying the Eurocentric assumptions underpinning modernisation and Westernisation and how these interventions had increased the dependency of non-Western nations on the West. Not only had they failed to improve the living conditions of those in the non-West, they had actually intensified the poverty and hardship faced by the masses in these nations.

Peet and Hartwick (1999: 1) posit that development 'is a founding belief of the modern world'. While Western affluence was propagated as a dream for all, the reality was that it was only achievable for a few. Tucker (1999: 1) defines development as 'a process whereby other peoples are dominated and their destinies are shaped according to an essentially Western way of conceiving and perceiving the world'. Thus in this view development is connected to imperialism where developed countries impose their control over non-Western countries. This control operates not just in terms of economic processes, but also in relation to cultural meanings about the nature of the world. Tucker challenges the view of development as a natural and transcultural process, arguing that it is premised upon Western myths. Modernisation theories of development invalidate the cultures of traditional societies and impose a Western model of progress upon them whereby the imitation of the Western model of development is presented as the only solution to the growing gap between the wealthy and poorest countries of the world. Tucker points out that slavery, genocide and colonialism have all been legitimated under the guise of progress.

The challenge to those in the West to become aware of their Eurocentrism and their monocultural prejudice is not new (Verhelst 1990). However, it would appear that many NGOS that claim to be in solidarity with the people of the non-West have failed to heed this challenge. This may be due in part to the fact that development has become an industry. People are educated and credentialed at universities to work in the development sector. Thus development practitioners establish comfortable and well-paid careers. Horn (in Harcourt 2007) says that there is a tension between unpaid, mass-based social movements for social justice and the salaried end of the development sector.

In the last few years, a number of publications have documented the experiences of Western development workers who went to non-Western countries to 'help', only to discover that what they had to offer was not what was needed. Subsequently, as they developed awareness of their own assumptions and the assumptions of the programmes they were embedded within, they wrote about the failures of dominant models of development (Danaher 2001; Bouler 2003; Goudge 2003; Bolten 2008). Danaher (2001) reflects on how he was once told by a grassroots activist in Africa that, while it was appreciated that he came there because he wanted to help, if he really wanted to help, he could do more by going back to his own country and working to change government and corporate policies which supported undemocratic leaders in non-Western countries.

There is an ongoing debate about the effectiveness of foreign aid and whether it is allocated fairly. For many years, anti-development writers have been arguing that foreign aid entrenches the privilege of wealthy groups. However, at the time of writing, Peter Singer had just published a book arguing why people in affluent countries should donate money to aid agencies to fight world poverty (Singer 2009). He provides a compelling moral argument to persuade affluent people that they should not purchase luxury goods once their basic living costs have been met, but should instead donate excess money to save lives in non-Western countries. In contrast, Moyo (2009) argues that foreign aid to Africa has increased corruption and despotism and done nothing to address poverty.

Easterly (2007) has challenged the utopian agenda of trying to use aid to eliminate poverty and change political systems. He argues that the best aid can do is to improve the lives of the poor in practical and material ways. Like many development economists, Easterly seems to regard the problem of aid as having more to do with problems in social engineering rather than with corporate globalisation. Chang (2007), in contrast, argues that the rich countries, in alliance with the IMF and the World Bank, use aid to force developing countries to develop neo-liberal policies in their own countries.

Goudge (2003) argues that foreign aid not only fails to help the non-West, but also that it falsely creates the impression that the West is doing something when it is not. An alternative to aid is to change the international trading system to benefit poorer countries. Held and Kaya (2007), for example, point out that agricultural subsidies provided in rich countries are ten nines the total amount of aid given to Africa. Thus a number of writers have argued that changing the agricultural subsidies given to farmers in rich countries to supplement their income would provide more concrete benefits to poor countries (Milanovic 2007).

Furthermore, Gronemeyer (1995) asks people to reflect upon their responses if they knew someone was coming to their home with the expressed purpose of doing them some good. Citing Thoreau, she suggests that one would run for their life in case some of the good was done to them. Gronemeyer demonstrates how the concept of 'helping' the non-West has become an instrument of power with its own self-justification. Goudge (2003) distinguishes between specific forms of help that are requested and help that is imposed on others using Western theories and methodologies.

Shiva (1993) observes that whenever countries in the North intervene in the lives of people in the South, their interventions are premised upon a notion of superiority, usually legitimated on the notion of the 'white man's burden'. If the crisis in the South were to be overcome, it would require a decolonisation of the North whereby its Eurocentric assumptions and internalised dominance were critically interrogated.

The argument here is that as important as it is to be aware of the exploitative role of the IMF and the World Bank and the interventionist policies of Western governments, people must also engage in the more painful step of acknowledging their own personal Western privilege (Goudge 2003). How do the individual actions of Westerners reproduce global inequalities? Goudge argues that the more individuals in the West gain benefits from the exploitation of poorer nations, the greater their responsibility for doing something about it. The ecological argument is 'live simply so that others can simply live.'

discussion questions and activities

Discussion or Journal Questions

1. What was most surprising/challenging/compelling for you in reading this section? Why?
2. When we study topics like race, gender, and sexuality, we often think first about the oppressed (people of color; women; LGBTQ people; etc.). Why is that?
3. Identify the various systems of privilege introduced in this section. Is it possible for someone to experience both oppression and privilege in their life? What factors make it difficult to recognize that?
4. McIntosh distinguishes between unearned advantage and conferred dominance. Does this distinction work when applied to other systems of privilege besides race and gender?
5. While research on privilege has been a growing field in the social sciences and humanities, its introduction to the public has largely come from the media. The first three chapters provide insight into the debates that occasionally flare up in the media. What do you think are some of the factors that make this a controversial public topic? After completing the Social Identity Development Activity below, try to place each of the three authors into a specific stage, and explain why.

Personal Connections

The following questions and activities are designed to be completed either on your own or in class, and then discussed as a group. As you share your insights with others, think about the patterns and similarities that emerge, as well as the differences among your answers.

A. Identifying Yourself

Considering some of the most significant social identity categories examined in this text (race, gender, sexual orientation, class, religion, and ability), which have you thought about most in terms of their importance in *your* own life? Why? Which system of privilege have you thought about least? Why? Has the relative importance of these identities in your life changed over time at all? Or in different contexts?

B. Examining Your Privilege

Part One provided a number of chapters that list or identify privileges associated with specific social identities. Select another category of privilege (class, religion, age, or cisgender), and create a list of the often invisible privileges afforded to this group.

C. Locating Yourself

Social Identity Development Theory describes the identity development process for members of privileged and oppressed identity groups. Identity is more complex than this overview suggests. People may not move neatly from one stage to the next and may experience several stages simultaneously; some may even backslide. Nevertheless, reflecting upon these stages can be a useful tool for self-reflection. As you read about the developmental process, select two of your own social identities to examine, with at least one being a privileged social group identity (white, heterosexual, able-bodied, etc.). Write a two- to three-page discussion of where you see yourself in terms of these two identities and why.

Social Identity Development Stages

Social identities to consider: race, gender, class, sexual identity, ability/disability, nationality

Stage I: Naive

At this stage people are just becoming aware of differences between self and members of other social groups, are unaware of the complex codes of appropriate behavior, and are learning what it means to be a member of their social group. Numerous events transform and socialize children to accept their group's privileged or oppressed position. Significant socializers include family, education, media, religion, etc.

Stage II: Acceptance

This stage represents some degree of internalization (not necessarily conscious) of the dominant culture's ideology. At this stage, hierarchical systems of privilege appear natural, "the way things are." Codes of appropriate behavior are mostly internalized. Individuals engage in blaming the victim, and may dismiss experiences that contradict what they have internalized.

Stage III: Resistance

This stage represents a paradigm shift. People are likely to enter this stage by questioning previously accepted "truths" about the way things are, and gain increased awareness of the existence of privilege/oppression. As a result of new knowledge that challenges their previously accepted ideology and self-definition, people entering resistance begin formulating new views and challenging social factors that have shaped their identity. People become more skilled at identifying oppression and privilege, may begin experiencing conflict with others, and experience strong emotions including anger, pain, shame, and more.

Stage IV: Redefinition

In this stage, people begin developing an identity liberated from the hierarchy of oppression and privilege. They might isolate themselves as they begin developing a positive social identity and locate aspects of their culture and social group that are affirming. Members of oppressed social identity groups may seek the company of others in their group and at the same stage of identity development.

Stage V: Internalization

This stage represents an ongoing process of internalizing and integrating the new sense of social identity into various facets of one's life until it becomes natural. It may involve renegotiating relationships and interactions with significant people in their lives, as well as cultivating greater empathy for oppressed groups. There is no end to this stage; rather, people continue to grow stronger and more secure with their new consciousness, even if it is not valued by others.

Numerous authors have developed social identity models. This version is adapted from Diane Goodman, *Promoting Diversity and Social Justice: Educating People from Privileged Groups*, 2nd ed. (New York: Routledge, 2011).

part two

understanding privilege

What does privilege feel like? How do we know we have it?

The essays in this section take us deeper inside the actual experience of privilege and try to excavate the experience of the privileged coming to terms with their privilege. For example, Allan Johnson and Michael Messner each begin to unravel the processes in which they "became" straight or white or male—and the consequences for those upon whom their identities were built.

Sonny Nordmarken makes it clear that whether you are male or female, there is a certain privilege that comes from actually being—and feeling yourself to be—one or the other. Sure, it's true that gender is an axis of privilege, but being within the confines of the binary of male and female is, itself, a comfort to those who feel themselves to fall outside of it.

Woody Doane begins to complicate these axes of privilege by exploring the gradual aging of one who was born privileged (middle class, white, male, heterosexual) through the growing realization that privilege by age is no longer his. This moment of realization can be both the source of Tal Fortgang's refusal to acknowledge his privilege and a source of empathic understanding of others' experiences. Both Diana Kendall and Paul Kivel explore the continuing realities of class and religious privilege.

Finally, Cara Liebowitz addresses that question that many of us constantly ask when we first learn about privilege: Are we "wrong" or "bad" just because we're privileged? Are we supposed to feel guilty? Liebowitz offers an emphatic no—with a caveat that acknowledging that you have received something that is not rightfully yours obligates you to fight for a system in which everyone can, and does, play on an even playing field. Otherwise, it would be like being told the deck was stacked and deciding to play anyway, as if it weren't.

9

privilege, power, difference, and us

Allan Johnson*

To do something about the trouble around difference, we have to talk about it, but most of the time we don't, because it feels too risky. This is true for just about everyone, but especially for members of privileged categories, for whites, for men, and for heterosexuals. As Paul Kivel writes, for example, "Rarely do we whites sit back and listen to people of color without interrupting, without being defensive, without trying to regain attention to ourselves, without criticizing or judging."

The discomfort, defensiveness, and fear come in part from not knowing how to talk about privilege without feeling vulnerable to anger and blame. They will continue until we find a way to reduce the risk of talking about privilege. The key to reducing the risk is to understand what makes talking about privilege *seem* risky. I don't mean that risk is an illusion. There is no way to do this work without the possibility that people will feel uncomfortable or frightened or threatened. But the risk isn't nearly as big as it seems, for like the proverbial (and mythical) human fear of the strange and unfamiliar, the problem begins with how people *think* about things and who they are in relation to them.

Individualism, or the Myth That Everything Is Somebody's Fault

We live in a society that encourages us to think that the social world begins and ends with individuals. It's as if an organization or a society is just a collection of people, and everything that happens in it begins with what each one thinks, feels, and intends. If you understand people, the reasoning goes, then you also understand social life. It's an appealing way to think because it's grounded in our experience as individuals, which is what we know best. But it's also misleading, because it boxes us into a narrow and distorted view of reality. In other words, it isn't true.

If we use individualism to explain sexism, for example, it's hard to avoid the idea that sexism exists simply because men *are* sexist—men have sexist feelings, beliefs, needs, and motivations that lead them to behave in sexist ways. If sexism produces evil consequences, it's because men *are* evil, hostile, and malevolent toward women. In short, everything bad in the world is seen as somebody's fault, which is why talk about privilege so often turns into a game of hot potato.

Individualistic thinking keeps us stuck in the trouble by making it almost impossible to talk seriously about it. It encourages women, for example, to blame and distrust men. It sets men up to feel personally attacked if anyone mentions gender issues, and to define those issues as a "women's problem." It also encourages men who don't think or behave in overtly sexist ways—the ones most likely to become part of the solution—to conclude that sexism has nothing to do with them, that it's just a problem for "bad" men. The result is a kind of paralysis: people either talk about sexism in the most superficial, unthreatening, trivializing, and even stupid way ("The Battle of the Sexes," *Men Are from Mars, Women Are from Venus*) or they don't talk about it at all.

Breaking the paralysis begins with realizing that the social world consists of a lot more than individuals. We are always participating in something larger than ourselves—what sociologists call social systems—and systems are more than collections of people. A university, for example, is a social system, and people participate in it. But the people aren't the university and the university isn't the people. This means that to understand what happens in it, we have to look at both the university and how individual people participate in it. If patterns of racism exist in a society, for example, the reason is never just a matter of white people's personalities, feelings, or intentions. We also have to understand how they participate in particular kinds of behavior, and what consequences it produces.

Individuals, Systems, and Paths of Least Resistance

To see the difference between a system and the people who participate in it, consider a game like Monopoly. I used to play Monopoly, but I don't anymore because I don't like the way I behave when I do. Like everyone else, as a Monopoly player I try to take everything from the other players—all their money, all their property—which then forces them out of the game. The point of the game is to ruin everyone else and be the only one left in the end. When you win, you feel good, because you're *supposed* to feel good. Except that one day I realized that I felt good about winning—about taking everything from everyone else—even when I played with my children, who were pretty young at the time. But there didn't seem to be much point to playing without trying to win, because winning is what the game is *about*. Why land on a property and not buy it, or own a property and not improve it, or have other players land on your property and not collect the rent? So I stopped playing.

And it worked, because the fact is that I don't behave in such greedy ways when I'm not playing Monopoly, even though it's still me, Allan, in either case. So what's all this greedy behavior about? Do we behave in greedy ways simply because we *are* greedy? In a sense, the answer is yes, in that greed is part of the human repertoire of possible motivations, just like compassion, altruism, or fear. But how, then, do I explain the absence of such behavior when I'm not playing Monopoly? Clearly, the answer has to include both me as an individual human being who's capable of making all kinds of choices *and* something about the social situation in which I make those choices. It's not one or the other; it's both in relation to each other.

If we think of Monopoly as a social system—as "something larger than ourselves that we participate in"—then we can see how people and systems come together in a dynamic relationship that produces the patterns of social life, including problems around difference and privilege. People are indisputably the ones who make social systems happen. If no one plays Monopoly, it's just a box full of stuff with writing inside the cover. When people open it up and identify themselves as players, however, Monopoly starts to *happen*. This makes people very important, but we shouldn't confuse that with Monopoly itself. We aren't Monopoly and Monopoly isn't us.

I can describe the game and how it works without saying anything about the personal characteristics of all the people who play it or might play it.

People make Monopoly happen, but *how*? How do we know what to do? How do we choose from the millions of things that, as human beings, we *could* do at any given moment? The answer is the other half of the dynamic relation between individuals and systems. As we sit around the table, we make Monopoly happen from one minute to the next. But our participation in the game also shapes how *we* happen as people—what we think and feel and do. This doesn't mean that systems control us in a rigid and predictable way. Instead, systems load the odds in certain directions by offering what I call "paths of least resistance" for us to follow.

In every social situation, we have an almost limitless number of choices we might make. Sitting in a movie theater, for example, we could go to sleep, sing, eat dinner, undress, dance, take out a flashlight and read the newspaper, carry on loud conversations, dribble a basketball up and down the aisles—these are just a handful of the millions of behaviors people are capable of. All of these possible paths vary in how much resistance we run into if we try to follow them. We discover this as soon as we choose paths we're not supposed to. Jump up and start singing, for example, and you'll quickly feel how much resistance the management and the rest of the audience offer up to discourage you from going any further. By comparison, the path of least resistance is far more appealing, which is why it's the one we're most likely to choose.

The odds are loaded toward a path of least resistance in several ways. We often choose a path because it's the only one we see. When I get on an elevator, for example, I turn and face front along with everyone else. It rarely occurs to me to do it another way, such as facing the rear. If I did, I'd soon feel how some paths have more resistance than others.

I once tested this idea by walking to the rear of an elevator and standing with my back toward the door. As the seconds ticked by, I could feel people looking at me, wondering what I was up to, and actually wanting me to turn around. I wasn't saying anything or doing anything to anyone. I was only standing there minding my own business. But that wasn't all that I was doing, for I was also violating a social norm that makes facing the door a path of least resistance. The path is there all the time—it's built in to riding the elevator as a social situation—but the path wasn't clear until I stepped onto a different one and felt the greater resistance rise up around it.

Similar dynamics operate around issues of difference and privilege. In many corporations, for example, the only way to get promoted is to have a mentor or sponsor pick you out as a promising person and bring you along by teaching you what you need to know and acting as an advocate who opens doors and creates opportunities. In a society that separates and privileges people by gender and race, there aren't many opportunities to get comfortable with people across difference. This means that senior managers will feel drawn to employees who resemble them, which usually means those who are white, straight, and male.

Managers who are white and/or male probably won't realize they're following a path of least resistance that shapes their choice until they're asked to mentor an African American woman or someone else they don't resemble. The greater resistance toward the path of mentoring across difference may result from something as subtle as feeling "uncomfortable" in the other person's presence. But that's all it takes to make the relationship ineffective or to ensure that it never happens in the first place. And as each manager follows the system's path to mentor and support those who most resemble them, the patterns of white dominance and male dominance in the system as a whole are perpetuated, regardless of what people consciously feel or intend.

In other cases, people know alternative paths exist but they stick to the path of least resistance anyway, because they're afraid of what will happen if they don't. Resistance can take many forms, ranging from mild disapproval to being fired from a job, beaten up, run out of town, imprisoned, tortured, or killed. When managers are told to lay off large numbers of workers, for example, they may hate the assignment and feel a huge amount of distress. But the path of *least* resistance is to do what they're told, because the alternative may be for them to lose their own jobs. To make it less unpleasant, they may use euphemisms like "downsizing" and "outplacement" to soften the painful reality of people losing their jobs. (Note in this example how the path of least resistance isn't necessarily an easy path to follow.)

In similar ways, a man may feel uncomfortable when he hears a friend tell a sexist joke, and feel compelled to object in some way. But the path of least resistance in that situation is to go along and avoid the risk of being ostracized or ridiculed for challenging his friend and making *him* feel uncomfortable. The path of least resistance is to smile or laugh or just remain silent.

What we experience as social life happens through a complex dynamic between all kinds of systems—families, schools, workplaces, communities, entire societies—and the choices people make as they participate in them and help make them happen. How we experience the world and ourselves, our sense of other people, and the ongoing reality of the systems themselves all arise, take shape, and happen through this dynamic. In this way, social life produces a variety of consequences, including privilege and oppression. To understand that and what we can do to change it, we have to see how systems are organized in ways that encourage people to follow paths of least resistance. The existence of those paths and the choice we make to follow them are keys to what creates and perpetuates all the forms that privilege and oppression can take in people's lives.

What It Means to Be Involved in Privilege and Oppression

Individuals and systems are connected to each other through a dynamic relationship. If we use this relationship as a model for thinking about the world and ourselves, it's easier to bring problems like racism, sexism, and heterosexism out into the open and talk about them. In particular, it's easier to see the problems in relation to us, and to see ourselves in relation to them.

If we think the world is just made up of individuals, then a white woman who's told she's "involved" in racism is going to think you're telling her she's a racist person who harbors ill will toward people of color. She's using an individualistic model of the world that limits her to interpreting words like *racist* as personal characteristics, personality flaws. Individualism divides the world up into different kinds of people—good people and bad, racists and nonracists, "good guys" and sexist pigs. It encourages us to think of racism, sexism, and heterosexism as diseases that infect people and make them sick. And so we look for a "cure" that will turn diseased, flawed individuals into healthy, "good" ones, or at least isolate them so that they can't infect others. And if we can't cure them, then we can at least try to control their behavior.

But what about everyone else? How do we see *them* in relation to the trouble around difference? What about the vast majority of whites, for example, who tell survey interviewers that they aren't racist and don't hate or even dislike people of color? Or what about the majority of men who say they favor an Equal Rights Amendment to the US Constitution? From an individualistic perspective, if you aren't consciously or openly prejudiced or hurtful, then you aren't part of the problem. You might show disapproval of "bad" people and even try to help out the people who are hurt by them. Beyond that, however, the trouble doesn't have anything to do with you so far as you can see. If your feelings and thoughts and outward behavior are good, then *you* are good, and that's all that matters.

Unfortunately, that isn't all that matters. There's more, because patterns of oppression and privilege are rooted in systems that we all participate in and make happen. Those patterns are built into paths of least resistance that people feel drawn to follow every day, regardless of whether they think about where they lead or the consequences they produce. When male professors take more seriously students who look like themselves, for example, they don't have to be self-consciously sexist in order to help perpetuate patterns of gender privilege. They don't have to be bad people in order to play a "game" that produces oppressive consequences. It's the same as when people play Monopoly—it always ends with someone winning and everyone else losing, *because that's how the game is set up to work as a system.* The only way to change the outcome is to change how we see and play the game and, eventually, the *system itself* and its paths of least resistance. If we have a vision of what we want social life to look like, we have to create paths that lead in that direction.

Of course there are people in the world who have hatred in their hearts—such as neo-Nazi skinheads who make a sport of harassing and killing blacks or homosexuals—and it's important not to minimize the damage they do. Paradoxically, however, even though they cause a lot of trouble, they aren't the key to understanding privilege or to doing something about it. They are participating in something larger than themselves that, among other things, steers them toward certain targets for their rage. It's no accident that their hatred is rarely directed at privileged groups, but instead those who are culturally devalued and excluded. Hate-crime perpetrators may have personality disorders that bend them toward victimizing *someone,* but their choice of whom to victimize isn't part of a mental illness. That's something they have to learn, and culture is everyone's most powerful teacher. In choosing their targets, they follow paths of least resistance built into a society that everyone participates in, that everyone makes happen, regardless of how they feel or what they intend.

So if I notice that someone plays Monopoly in a ruthless way, it's a mistake to explain that simply in terms of their personality. I also have to ask how a system like Monopoly rewards ruthless behavior more than other games we might play. I have to ask how it creates conditions that make such behavior appear to be the path of least resistance, normal and unremarkable. And since I'm playing the game, too, I'm one of the people who make it happen as a system, and its paths must affect me, too.

My first reaction might be to deny that I follow that path. I'm not a ruthless person or anything close to it. But this misses the key difference between systems and the people who participate in them: We don't have to be ruthless *people* in order to support or follow paths of least resistance that lead to behavior with ruthless *consequences*. After all, we're all trying to win, because that's the point of the game. However gentle and kind I am as I take your money when you land on my Boardwalk with its four houses, take it I will, and gladly, too. "Thank you," I say in my most sincerely un-ruthless tone, or even "Sorry," as I drive you out of the game by taking your last dollar and your mortgaged properties. Me, ruthless? Not at all. I'm just playing the game the way it's supposed to be played. And even if I don't try hard to win, the mere fact that I play the game supports its existence and makes it possible, especially if I remain silent about the consequences it produces. Just my going along makes the game appear normal and accept-able, which reinforces the paths of least resistance for everyone else.

This is how most systems work and how most people participate in them. It's also how systems of privilege work. Good people with good intentions make systems happen that produce all kinds of injustice and suffering for people in culturally devalued and excluded groups. Most of the time, people don't even know the paths are there in the first place, and this is why it's important to raise awareness that everyone is always following them in one way or another. If you weren't following a path of least resistance, you'd certainly know it, because you'd be on an alternative path with greater resistance that would make itself felt. In other words, if you're not going along with the system, it won't be long before people notice and let you know it. All you have to do is show up for work wearing "inappropriate" clothes to see how quickly resistance can form around alternative paths.

The trouble around difference is so pervasive, so long-standing, so huge in its consequences for so many millions of people that it can't be written off as the misguided doings of a small minority of people with personality problems. The people who get labeled as bigots, misogynists, or homo-phobes are all following racist, sexist, heterosexist paths of least resistance that are built into the entire society.

In a way, "bad people" are like ruthless Monopoly players who are doing just what the game calls for even if their "style" is a bit extreme. Such extremists may be the ones who grab the headlines, but they don't have enough power to create and sustain trouble of this magnitude. The trouble appears in the daily workings of every workplace, every school and university, every government agency, every community. It involves every major kind of social system, and since systems don't exist without the involvement of people, there's no way to escape being involved in the trouble that comes out of them. If we participate in systems the trouble comes out of, and if those systems exist only through our participation, then this is enough to involve us in the trouble itself.

Reminders of this reality are everywhere. I see it, for example, every time I look at the label in a piece of clothing. I just went upstairs to my closet and noted where each of my shirts was made. Although each carries a US brand name, only three were made here; the rest were made in the Philippines, Thailand, Mexico, Taiwan, Macao, Singapore, or Hong Kong. And although each cost me twenty to forty dollars, it's a good bet that the people who actually made them—primarily women—were paid pennies for their labor performed under terrible conditions that can sometimes be so extreme as to resemble slavery.

The only reason people exploit workers in such horrible ways is to make money in a capitalist system. To judge from the contents of my closet, that clearly includes *my* money. By itself, that fact doesn't make me a bad person, because I certainly don't intend that people suffer for the sake of my wardrobe. But it does mean that I'm involved in their suffering because I participate in a system that produces that suffering. As someone who helps make the system happen, however, I can also be a part of the solution.

But isn't the difference I could make a tiny one? The question makes me think of the devastating floods of 1993 along the Mississippi and Missouri Rivers. The news was full of powerful images of people from all walks of life working feverishly side by side to build dikes to hold back the raging waters that threatened their communities. Together, they filled and placed thousands of sandbags. When the waters receded, much had been lost, but a great deal had been saved as well. I wonder how it felt to be one of those people. I imagine they were proud of their effort and experienced a satisfying sense of solidarity with the people they'd worked with. The sandbags each individual personally contributed were the tiniest fraction of the total, but each felt part of the group effort and was proud to identify with the consequences it produced. They didn't have to make a big or even measurable difference to feel involved.

It works that way with the good things that come out of people pulling together in all the systems that make up social life. It also works that way with the bad things, with each sandbag adding to the problem instead of the solution. To perpetuate privilege and oppression, we don't even have to do anything consciously to support it. Just our silence is crucial for ensuring its future, for the simple fact is that no system of social oppression can continue to exist without most people choosing to remain silent about it. If most whites spoke out about racism; if most men talked about sexism; if most heterosexuals came out of their closet of silence and stood openly against heterosexism, it would be a critical first step toward revolutionary change. But the vast majority of "good" people are silent on these issues, and it's easy for others to read their silence as support.

As long as we participate in social systems, we don't get to choose whether to be involved in the consequences they produce. We're involved simply through the fact that we're here. As such, we can only choose *how* to be involved, whether to be just part of the problem or also to be part of the solution. That's where our power lies, and also our responsibility.

10

becoming 100 percent straight

Michael A. Messner*

Many years ago I read some psychological studies that argued that even for self-identified heterosexuals it is a natural part of their development to have gone through "bisexual" or even "homosexual" stages of life. When I read this, it seemed theoretically reasonable, but did not ring true in my experience. I have always been, I told myself, 100 percent heterosexual! The group process of analyzing my own autobiographical stories challenged the concept I had developed of myself, and also shed light on the way in which the institutional context of sport provided a context for the development of my definition of myself as "100 percent straight." Here is one of the stories.

When I was in the ninth grade I played on a "D" basketball team, set up especially for the smallest of high school boys. Indeed, though I was pudgy with baby fat, I was a short 5'2", still prepubescent with no facial hair and a high voice that I artificially tried to lower. The first day of practice I was immediately attracted to a boy I'll call Timmy, because he looked like the boy who played in the *Lassie* TV show. Timmy was short, with a high voice, like me. And like me, he had no facial hair yet. Unlike me, he was very skinny. I liked Timmy right away, and soon we were together a lot. I noticed things about him that I didn't notice about other boys: he said some words a certain way, and it gave me pleasure to try to talk like him. I remember liking the way the light hit his boyish, nearly hairless body. I thought about him when we weren't together. He was in the school band, and at the football games I'd squint to see where he was in the mass of uniforms. In short, though I wasn't conscious of it at the time, I was infatuated with Timmy—I had a crush on him. Later that basketball season, I decided—for no reason that I could really articulate then—that I hated Timmy. I aggressively rejected him, began to make fun of him around other boys. He was, we all agreed, a geek. He was a faggot.

Three years later Timmy and I were both on the varsity basketball team, but had hardly spoken a word to each other since we were freshmen. Both of us now had lower voices, had grown to around 6 feet tall, and we both shaved, at least a bit. But Timmy was a skinny, somewhat stigmatized reserve on the team, while I was the team captain and starting point guard. But I wasn't so happy or secure about this. I'd always dreamed of dominating games, of being the hero. Halfway through my senior season, however, it became clear that I was not a star, and I figured I knew why. I was not aggressive enough.

I had always liked the beauty of the fast break, the perfectly executed pick and roll play between two players, and especially the long 20-foot shot that touched nothing but the bottom of the net. But I hated and feared the sometimes brutal contact under the basket. In fact, I stayed away from the rough fights for rebounds and was mostly a perimeter player, relying on my long shots or my passes to more aggressive teammates under the basket. But now it became apparent to me that time was running out in my quest for greatness: I needed to change my game, and fast. I decided one day before practice that I was gonna get aggressive. While practicing one of our standard plays, I passed the ball to a teammate, and then ran to the spot at which I was to set a pick on a defender. I knew that one could sometimes get away with setting a face-up screen on a player, and then as he makes contact with you, roll your back to him and plant your elbow hard in his stomach. The beauty of this move is that your own body "roll" makes the elbow look like an accident. So I decided to try this move. I approached the defensive player, Timmy, rolled, and planted my elbow deeply into his solar plexus. Air exploded audibly from Timmy's mouth, and he crumbled to the floor momentarily.

Play went on as though nothing had happened, but I felt bad about it. Rather than making me feel better, it made me feel guilty and weak. I had to admit to myself why I'd chosen Timmy as the target against whom to test out my new aggression. He was the skinniest and weakest player on the team.

At the time, I hardly thought about these incidents, other than to try to brush them off as incidents that made me feel extremely uncomfortable.

Years later I can now interrogate this as a sexual story, and as a gender story unfolding within the context of the heterosexualized and masculinized institution of sport. Examining my story in light of research conducted by Alfred Kinsey a half century ago, I can recognize in myself what Kinsey saw as a very common fluidity and changeability of sexual desire over the lifecourse. Put simply, Kinsey found that large numbers of adult "heterosexual" men had previously, as adolescents and young adults, experienced sexual desire for males. A surprisingly large number of these men had experienced sexual contact to the point of orgasm with other males during adolescence or early adulthood. Similarly, my story invited me to consider what is commonly called the "Freudian theory of bisexuality." Sigmund Freud shocked the post-Victorian world by suggesting that all people go through a stage, early in life, when they are attracted to people of the same sex.[1] Adult experiences, Freud argued, eventually led most people to shift their sexual desire to what he called an appropriate "love object"—a person of the opposite sex. I also considered my experience in light of what lesbian feminist author Adrienne Rich called the institution of compulsory heterosexuality. Perhaps the extremely high levels of homophobia that are often endemic in boys' and men's organized sports led me to deny and repress my own homoerotic desire through a direct and overt rejection of Timmy, through homophobic banter with male peers, and the resultant stigmatization of the feminized Timmy. Eventually I considered my experience in the light of what radical theorist Herbert Marcuse called the sublimation of homoerotic desire into an aggressive, violent act as serving to construct a clear line of demarcation between self and other. Sublimation, according to Marcuse, involves the driving underground, into the unconscious, of sexual desires that might appear dangerous due to their socially stigmatized status. But sublimation involves more than simple repression into the unconscious. It involves a transformation of sexual desire into something else—often into aggressive and violent acting out toward others. These acts clarify the boundaries between oneself and others and therefore lessen any anxieties that might be attached to the repressed homoerotic desire.

Importantly, in our analysis of my story, the memory group went beyond simply discussing the events in psychological terms. The story did perhaps suggest some deep psychological processes at work, but it also revealed the importance of social context—in this case, the context of the athletic team. In short, my rejection of Timmy and the joining with teammates to stigmatize him in ninth grade stands as an example of what sociologist

R. W. Connell calls a moment of engagement with hegemonic masculinity, where I actively took up the male group's task of constructing heterosexual/ masculine identities in the context of sport. The elbow in Timmy's gut three years later can be seen as a punctuation mark that occurred precisely because of my fears that I might be failing in this goal.

It is helpful, I think, to compare my story with gay and lesbian "coming out" stories in sport. Though we have a few lesbian and bisexual coming out stories among women athletes, there are very few from gay males. Tom Waddell, who as a closeted gay man finished sixth in the decathlon in the 1968 Olympics, later came out and started the Gay Games, an athletic and cultural festival that draws tens of thousands of people every four years. When I interviewed Tom Waddell over a decade ago about his sexual identity and athletic career, he made it quite clear that for many years sports was his closet:

> When I was a kid, I was tall for my age, and was very thin and very strong. And I was usually faster than most other people. But I discovered rather early that I liked gymnastics and I liked dance. I was very interested in being a ballet dancer . . . [but] something became obvious to me right away—that male ballet dancers were effeminate, that they were what most people would call faggots. And I thought I just couldn't handle that. . . . I was totally closeted and very concerned about being male. This was the fifties, a terrible time to live, and everything was stacked against me. Anyway, I realized that I had to do something to protect my image of myself as a male—because at that time homosexuals were thought of primarily as men who wanted to be women. And so I threw myself into athletics—I played football, gymnastics, track and field. . . . I was a jock—that's how I was viewed, and I was comfortable with that.

Tom Waddell was fully conscious of entering sports and constructing a masculine/heterosexual athletic identity precisely because he feared being revealed as gay. It was clear to him, in the context of the 1950s, that being known as gay would undercut his claims to the status of manhood. Thus, though he described the athletic closet as "hot and stifling," he remained there until several years after his athletic retirement. He even knowingly played along with locker room discussions about sex and women as part of his "cover."

I wanted to be viewed as male, otherwise I would be a dancer today. I wanted
the male, macho image of an athlete. So I was protected by a very hard shell.
I was clearly aware of what I was doing. . . . I often felt compelled to go along
with a lot of locker room garbage because I wanted that image—and I know
a lot of others who did too.

Like my story, Waddell's points to the importance of the athletic institution as a context in which peers mutually construct and reconstruct
narrow definitions of masculinity. Heterosexuality is considered to be a
rock-solid foundation of this concept of masculinity. But unlike my story,
Waddell's may invoke a dramaturgical analysis.[2] He seemed to be consciously "acting" to control and regulate others' perceptions of him by
constructing a public "front stage" persona that differed radically from
what he believed to be his "true" inner self. My story, in contrast, suggests
a deeper, less consciously strategic repression of my homoerotic attraction. Most likely, I was aware on some level of the dangers of such feelings,
and was escaping the risks, disgrace, and rejection that would likely result
from being different. For Waddell, the decision to construct his identity
largely within sport was to step into a fiercely heterosexual/masculine
closet that would hide what he saw as his "true" identity. In contrast, I
was not so much stepping into a "closet" that would hide my identity;
rather, I was stepping out into an entire world of heterosexual privilege.
My story also suggests how a threat to the promised privileges of hegemonic masculinity—my failure as an athlete—might trigger a momentary
sexual panic that can lay bare the constructedness, indeed, the instability
of the heterosexual/masculine identity.

In either case, Waddell's or mine, we can see how, as young male athletes, heterosexuality and masculinity were not something we "were," but
something we were doing. It is significant, I think, that although each of
us was "doing heterosexuality," neither of us was actually "having sex" with
women (though one of us desperately wanted to). This underscores a point
made by some recent theorists that heterosexuality should not be thought
of simply as sexual acts between women and men. Rather, heterosexuality
is a constructed identity, a performance, and an institution that is not necessarily linked to sexual acts. Though for one of us it was more conscious
than for the other, we were both "doing heterosexuality" as an ongoing
practice through which we sought to do two things:

- avoid stigma, embarrassment, ostracism, or perhaps worse if we were even suspected of being gay;
- link ourselves into systems of power, status, and privilege that appear to be the birthright of "real men" (i.e., males who are able to compete successfully with other males in sport, work, and sexual relations with women).

In other words, each of us actively scripted our own sexual and gender performances, but these scripts were constructed within the constraints of a socially organized (institutionalized) system of power and pleasure.

Questions for Future Research

As I prepared to tell this sexual story publicly to my colleagues at the sport studies conference, I felt extremely nervous. Part of the nervousness was due to the fact that I knew some of them would object to my claim that telling personal stories can be a source of sociological insights. But a larger part of the reason for my nervousness was due to the fact that I was revealing something very personal about my sexuality in such a public way. Most of us are not accustomed to doing this, especially in the context of a professional conference. But I had learned long ago, especially from feminist women scholars, and from gay and lesbian scholars, that biography is linked to history. Part of "normal" academic discourse has been to hide "the personal" (including the fact that the researchers are themselves people with values, feelings, and, yes, biases) behind a carefully constructed facade of "objectivity." Rather than trying to hide or be ashamed of one's subjective experience of the world, I was challenging myself to draw on my experience of the world as a resource. Not that I should trust my experience as the final word on "reality." White, heterosexual males like me have made the mistake for centuries of calling their own experience "objectivity," and then punishing anyone who does not share their worldview by casting them as "deviant." Instead, I hope to use my experience as an example of how those of us who are in dominant sexual/racial/gender/class categories can get a new perspective on the "constructedness" of our identities by juxtaposing our subjective experiences against the emerging worldviews of gay men and lesbians, women, and people of color.

Finally, I want to stress that in juxtaposition neither my own nor Tom Waddell's story sheds much light on the question of why some individuals "become gay" while others "become" heterosexual or bisexual. Instead, I should like to suggest that this is a dead-end question, and that there are far more important and interesting questions to be asked:

- How has heterosexuality, as an institution and as an enforced group practice, constrained and limited all of us—gay, straight, and bi?
- How has the institution of sport been an especially salient institution for the social construction of heterosexual masculinity?
- Why is it that when men play sports they are almost always automatically granted masculine status, and thus assumed to be heterosexual, while when women play sports, questions are raised about their "femininity" and sexual orientation?

These kinds of questions aim us toward an analysis of the workings of power within institutions—including the ways that these workings of power shape and constrain our identities and relationships—and point us toward imagining alternative social arrangements that are less constraining for everyone.

notes

1. The fluidity and changeability of sexual desire over the life-course is now more obvious in evidence from prison and military populations and single-sex boarding schools. The theory of bisexuality is evident, for example, in childhood crushes on same-sex primary schoolteachers.

2. Dramaturgical analysis, associated with Erving Goffman, uses the theater and performance to develop an analogy with everyday life.

references

Haug, Frigga. 1987. *Female Sexualization: A Collective Work of Memory.* London: Verso.

Lenskyj, Helen. 1986. *Out of Bounds: Women, Sport and Sexuality.* Toronto: Women's Press.

———. 1997. "No Fear? Lesbians in Sport and Physical Education," *Women in Sport and Physical Activity Journal* 6 (2): 7–22.

Messner, Michael A. 1992. *Power at Play: Sports and the Problem of Masculinity.* Boston: Beacon Press.

———. 1994. "Gay Athletes and the Gay Games: An Interview with Tom Waddell," in M. A. Messner and D. F. Sabo (eds.), *Sex, Violence and Power in Sports: Rethinking Masculinity.* Freedom, CA: Crossing Press, pp. 113–119.

Pronger, Brian. 1990. *The Arena of Masculinity: Sports, Homosexuality, and the Meaning of Sex.* New York: St. Martin's Press.

11

becoming ever more monstrous
Feeling Gender In-Betweenness

Sonny Nordmarken*

Introduction: Being Transgender, Performing Instructor

It is an unusually warm Tuesday morning in March. This is the first semester I am teaching my own class. I am 31 years old, but I appear to be 20. As I am young-looking, I wear a costume to make my class believe I am the instructor: professional khaki pants, dress shoes, a button-up shirt, an argyle sweater, and a tie. For the first 2 weeks of the semester, I am so nervous to perform "instructor" that I do not sleep the night before I teach.

For today's class, we have read an article on trans people's experiences in workplaces. I have some personal experience I could share regarding this topic, as the classroom is my workplace and I am trans. I explain the differences between "MTF" ("male to female") and "FTM" ("female to male") and several other common transgender identities. My 35 students sit, intrigued expressions on their faces. I explain: "Someone who transitions from male to female is a trans woman, and trans women usually use the pronoun 'she.'" Out of my earshot, a student retorts, "How can you call that a woman?" Oblivious to this comment, I continue. I face the board, and write the words "stealth" and "out." I turn to face the students.

---

* Nordmarken, Sonny. "Becoming Ever More Monstrous: Feeling Gender In-Betweenness," *Qualitative Inquiry* 20, no. 1 (2014): 37–50. DOI: 10.1177/1077800413508531. Reprinted by permission of SAGE Publications, Inc.

"What does this term, 'stealth,' mean?" I ask, pointing to the word. A student raises her hand. "When a trans person does not tell people they are trans," she states. "Good," I say. Standing there, I am performing "stealth." My students are not aware of my transness. I have not come out to them. I hesitate, considering telling them I am performing stealth as we speak, to demonstrate the concept. I would "out" myself in that speech act, and I would no longer be stealth. I feel lucid. It seems a perfect time to come out, since we are discussing the terms, but I do not feel at ease with the idea of them knowing this about me. It has been only months since my gender ambiguity has become less visible, and it has been a relief to receive fewer otherizing looks and comments in that time. But I am still hypervigilant about how I am being read. I decide to just go on with the lesson without mentioning my personal connection to the material.

I write the word "passing" on the board. I say: "'Passing' is when a person 'passes' as 'not trans,' intentionally does not come out as 'trans.' The term 'passing' is problematic though. Can you imagine why?" A student offers, "It assumes that a person is not 'really' who they are." I reply, "Exactly. This concept can invalidate trans people. The term 'stealth' also suggests deception, which supports negative stereotypes about trans people."

A student wonders, "Doesn't a trans man benefit from male privilege when he 'passes'?" "Yes," I say, "he does, in many cases like any other man." I have noticed how students treat me with more respect now than they ever did before I began hormonal transition. Before, I presumed that they read me as a gender-nonconforming female, and that they were confused about my gender. I want to share this but I don't. And it is good that I don't.

Because in the next moment, I notice a student gazing at my crotch. I feel a shooting of deep discomfort through my body. I presume that he wonders if I am trans and is looking for "evidence." I can't let on that I see his expression, because I need to remain in "instructor mode." My job is to teach the class. I have to contain my anxiety, and I have to contain the 35 students who are looking at me expectantly, as well as the one who is looking at me intently, concentrating on the last part of my body I want attention on.

I feel mixed feelings, writing about this nascent teaching experience. I wonder whether it is ethical to write about you, my students. I wonder what you would think or how you would feel if you read this. I wonder whether it would surprise you to know that your subtle actions impact me, or whether it would shock you to know that I am trans.

As a transmasculine person, I encounter particular indignities in everyday life. Interpersonal interactions are often uncomfortable, sometimes painful. Analyzing the case of my transgender life, its melding with others', and the parallels with the monster's life in Shelley's *Frankenstein*, I explore sensations of selves and others, separations within and between selves and others, and possibilities for reconnection and freedom. Claiming humanity in my monstrosity as a transsexual,* I make my monstrosity human. Charting my socioemotional gendered transitions on my gender journey, I expose others' marginalizing actions, I question the locatedness of positionalities, and I make my many selves legible. I aim to build connections across difference, with you, reader, for cisgender[†] people and for shape-shifters alike, so that we might see ourselves in each other, and that, together, we might work against injustice and distance, and toward a deeper kind of intimacy and freedom for us all.

Complicating Locations: Transgender In-Betweenness

It is April of 2012, a year since I began testosterone treatment. I am 32 years old. You might wonder who I am now. I am not a different self, but my social locations are shifting. I prefer to consider, not who, but how am I, now? Under what circumstance am I, now (Minh-ha, 1989)? What contexts shape me, what movements make me? I want to share with you about the last year and the few years before. In my journey, I have felt many feelings. I have experienced the world experiencing me in drastically different ways. People respond to me very differently when they read me as female from how they do when they read me as male, and when they cannot read my gender. Yet, I am the same person, even as I transition.

As we all are, I am a betweener (Diversi & Moreira, 2009). Marcelo Diversi and Claudio Moreira define betweener as an "(un)conscious body experiencing life in and between two cultures" (Diversi & Moreira, 2009, p. 19). Betweeners who cross between two cultures are understood in terms of race and class differently depending on the cultural context. I am a slightly different kind of betweener. Though I do not move between

---

* Transsexuals are targets of trans-specific hate violence in addition to discrimination. For more information, see Kidd and Witten (2008).

† "Cisgender": nontransgender. "Cis," a prefix used in chemistry to refer to molecular structure, means "on the same side"; "cisgender" refers to people whose gender identity and expression match their assigned gender.

cultures as often as they do, at different times, I am read differently within the same cultural context. My betweener-ness is complex. It is an in-betweenness. I live in the in-betweenness of genders and in the border-lands of oppressions. I live as different kinds of "oppressor" and as different kinds of "oppressed." I move in the world as White and able-bodied, with socioeconomic and educational privilege, and as queer.

As a transgender being, my gendered shifting moves me into more be-tweennesses. I am *queerly between*: I occupy multiple positions at once, and different positions at different times, depending on how people read me—in regard to age and ability as well as gender. I am socially subjugated as transgender, even as I am beginning to experience in a new way what White male privilege is. And the subjugations of femaleness still shape my life. In social interactions, I still behave, perform, and position myself in the ways I have habitually done so, as someone who has been socialized fe-male. I feel the feelings I have habitually felt as a result of being positioned as female and treated as inferior. Yet, now people often position me as male in social interactions. In many of these moments, I experience a feeling of inclusion that I have not ever felt, and in others, I feel excluded in ways I have never felt. Yet, at times, the femininity I continue to embody as a transmasculine* being leads people to look at me funny. I feel new feelings particular to transness: anxiety, fear, hypervigilance. It can be dangerous to be a transsexual. It can be a lot of emotional work to navigate the cisgender world. I experience sexism, homophobia, transphobia, and White, male, able-bodied privilege. These positions and states feel very different from each other. These borderlands of oppression are places of astonishment, pain, humility, and deep understanding.

My age is queer: I look much younger than I am. Similarly, I am si-multaneously enabled, constrained, and defined by disability. According to Rosemarie Garland-Thomson (2005),

> People with chronic or acute illnesses, appearance impairments such as birthmarks or fatness, traumatic injuries, congenital impairments or anom-alies, sensory impairments, latent conditions such as HIV or hereditary

---

*I use the term "transmasculine" to denote the general gender grouping I place my-self within. Some in this group might also describe themselves as "female-to-male (FTM) spectrum" or "masculine-of-center." The adjective "trans" can describe people whose gender and/or sex identities, expressions, bodies, and/or histories depart from normative conceptions.

conditions, learning disabilities, and mental, developmental, or emotional illnesses are grouped together under the medical-scientific rubric of abnormality and its accompanying cultural sentence of inferiority. (p. 1558)

Mine is a complicated (dis)ability status. I take testosterone. The high levels of androgens in my body enhance some of my muscular abilities. I am also medically diagnosed with "Gender Identity Disorder," which classifies me legally as mentally disordered. This diagnosis is what allows me to obtain testosterone "treatment." My androgyny might be understood as an "appearance impairment." I am also simultaneously privileged and subjugated through the institution of gender. As I continue to change shape, I am becoming more transsexed. My body is becoming more monstrous, but my monstrousness is becoming less outwardly obvious than it was before. I am becoming new betweenings.

I am self and Other, self-as-Other, and Other-as-self: In various ways, I am becoming another social way of being. A multiple kind of outsider within (Collins, 1986)—as a queer female coming into a male body in a male-dominated society dominated by heteropatriarchal epistemologies, and as a trans person in a cisgender-dominated society dominated by cisgender epistemologies. This is a story about becoming different kinds of genderednesses and betweennesses. A story about being liminal, moving between bodies and between locations, and being in many bodies at once. And a story about being decidedly queer. "Being half in and half out of identities, subject positions, and discourses, and being fluid in a world relentlessly searching for stability and certainty" (Adams & Jones, 2011, p. 114). This story is a body of many stories and many bodies. An ongoing space-time-body of transit. A queer time and place (Halberstam, 2005).

Becoming More Monstrous: Working Toward Freedom and Connection

As we all are, I am becoming—never actually occurring, but "always forthcoming and already past" (Deleuze, 1990, p. 80). My movement is not a journeying from one static state to another. It is a state of constant movement. An articulating of *movements* rather than a sequence of *moments*. I am moving in multiple directions at once. My body is becoming what we call more "masculine" than it was before, even as I am becoming what we call more "feminine" than I am now. I am becoming more masculine in shape and yet, more feminine in movement. I find myself embodying a certain femininity that I did not feel comfortable in, in movements before, when my body looked more female. Though my voice now is in male-octaves, I am speaking more softly than I did. This is a masculine-bodied femininity. It is how my new movement is expressing itself in this new shaping I am taking. And, as I am "always forthcoming and already past," this gendered expression is both new movement and remnant of itself, which has and will continue to change.

I am becoming more and less recognizable, in different ways, simultaneously. My body ruptures categories and threatens ideas of body normativity, renouncing "beauty" to be "beast," while breaking the binary meaning of beauty and beast by being monstrously beautiful. This is a corporeal resistance. It is both intentional and unintentional. This "monstering" brings me freedom and joy, yet also danger and fear. Being "monstered"—being made into a monster through others' eyes—can hurt. Like Susan Stryker, I relate to Frankenstein's monster. Stryker (1994) says,

> I find a deep affinity between myself as a transsexual woman and the monster in Mary Shelley's *Frankenstein*. Like the monster, I am too often perceived as less than fully human due to the means of my embodiment; like the monster's as well, my exclusion from human community fuels a deep and abiding rage in me that I, like the monster, direct against the conditions in which I must struggle to exist. (p. 238)

Though I am not a transsexual woman, but a transsexual male-ish being, I see myself reflected in this experience. As the descriptor "monstrosity" sticks differently to different monstered bodies, I wonder whether it is right to liken my particular, White transmasculine experiences—which afford me certain privileges—to transfeminine experiences, to experiences of trans people of color, or to those of any other Others, for that matter. While privilege is important to account for, it is also true that I too feel excluded from human community—the human community that grows between what we imagine as "Western," White, able-bodied, cisgender, male, heteronormative, economically advantaged bodies. I too feel indignity and rage at my exclusion, and the effects of social trauma.

As I conduct research interviews, I find connection and resonance listening to other trans people's stories. Sam tells me about how in his Japanese American family, there is a culture of silence. They do not talk about the internment of World War II. He tells me about the loud silence, the guilt, and obligation. Trauma gets regenerated in the next generation, but those in the next generation do not know where it is coming from or why they are traumatized. His family's silence feels isolating. Their distancing and misrecognition of his gender almost feels normal to Sam, who is used to silence and isolation. I listen, relating to his stories. The knowledge of Judaism has been lost over generations in my family. I have not learned much about my Jewishness or about the trauma I have inherited. But the silence is there. The guilt is there. The anxiety is there. War traumatized me too. My grandfather fought as a soldier in World War II. My ancestors lived with fear in the midst of genocide, and the next generations inherited their guilt about surviving. This trauma is ever present. I do not know the story. But I can feel it. I feel it in my isolation from my family. In my isolation from myself, and in the persistent fear that I've done something wrong or that I do not deserve intimacy. This makes my isolation as a transsexual more vivid. Hearing Sam's story, I better understand and reclaim my lost past. Connecting with him helps me connect to myself. And put my fragmented self back together.

How can this isolation, this pain, this rage engender productive possibilities for resistance? How can we find freedom in and through the monsters in ourselves? What freedom can this be? Frankenstein's monster resists dehumanization by learning to speak, enacting subjectivity and claiming himself as a subject. He makes himself legible by speaking about his experience of exclusion. "Like that creature," Stryker (1994) says, "I assert my worth as a monster in spite of the conditions my monstrosity requires me to face, and redefine a life worth living" (p. 250). We shape-shifters are making ourselves legible by speaking our truths. We are rejecting subjugation. We are invoking and claiming abject positions—femininities and queer genderednesses—as a form of resistance. We resist dehumanization by making ourselves, our pain, and our complex lives legible. We talk back.

But, I wonder about the limits of language. I wonder about the limits of recognition as a strategy for liberation. And I wonder: Is it right to put the onus on us? We are not the only ones injured by our oppression. People suffer from their separation from us, from coercing each other into enacting harm, and in feeling remorse from that harm. We all suffer from this separation from each other. Oppression is a form of collective trauma. It is inside all of us. We are not singular entities separate from each other— we all have multiple selves, and we all form a collective body. Oppression separates us all from parts of ourselves as well as from each other. And we need to work together with ourselves and each other to transform it.

What is monstrous? Who is a monster, and to whom? "Monstrous" seems to mean terrifying otherness—"Other" by definition, a definitional inferiorization. However, the capacity to evoke terror is a certain kind of power. I seek to claim that power through claiming monstrousness in myself. The word "monster" derives from verbs: "the Latin 'monere,' to warn, and 'demonstrare,' to show or make visible" (Botting, 1991, p. 142). "'Daemon'"—a term Shelley uses to describe the monster—"is the Latinate transliteration of the Greek *daimon*, [meaning] *eros*, or love" (Wittman, 1998, p. 89). And as Deleuze and Guattari (1987) observe, "It is not the slumber of reason that engenders monsters, but a vigilant and insomniac rationality" (cited in Botting, 1991, p. 161). I thus use this term in an oppositional way, by returning it to its roots, and returning myself to mine in the process. I "monster," or make visible the dehumanization I have faced, which is a result of dominant, rational ways of thinking—what individuals deploy to render me "monstrous." I take power in exhibiting others' terrorizing behavior. Perhaps surprisingly, love has a part in shaping our stories of monstering and of being made into monsters.

Monstering with Glee: Creating Confusion as Resistance

It is 5 years ago, a time before I began testosterone treatment. My age is 27. My queer gender appears indiscernible to many people.* It is a "'discreditable identity' that must be confirmed, repeatedly through discourse and action" (Foucault, 1978; Goffman, 1963; Yoshino, 2006; as cited in Adams, 2011, p. 88). This is true of many identities. In particular, indigenous identities, like trans identities, are imagined in many contexts as mythological or as not "really" existing. However, being disavowed fundamentally defines trans experience. The hegemony of biological essentialism means that, for example, the existence of cisgender individuals is taken for granted. Their identities are not questioned—they are assumed to exist. Trans people, in contrast, are assumed to not exist; they are assumed to

---

* How do I know how I am being read when I state that others cannot categorize me? Can I really claim to know what these others know or aim to know? This is an important epistemological question. I do not know in every case, but the repetitive evidence that accompanies many baffled expressions—such as stares at my chest—lead me to gather that this apparent confusion is about my gender.

"actually" be something else—something that can be known by viewing their bodies. Biological essentialism thus discredits trans identity. Trans people must therefore continually re-assert their identities.

As a trans person, I occupy a particularly between kind of betweenness. Among my other legible positionalities, I am read as sexually deviant because I appear gender-deviant. In this historical movement, I enjoy pushing people to think about gender in a nonbinary way.

On the bus, I sit, on my way to work. I look out the window, thinking about the children I will see soon. In the next moment, I feel energy reaching out to me. I sense eyes following me. I am being watched—realization dawns in an instant.

Glancing up, I confront eyes querying me. Eyes wondering. Boy or girl? Man or woman? This is beyond curiosity. It is desire. It is the wanting to possess, the intention to extract, it is the mission to obtain for oneself information—no: Truth.

I feel a sense of amusement watching the eyes' confusion, their concentration. I enjoy the chaos my body prompts. These eyes feel and imagine themselves to be legitimate knowers. How dare I, as Other, challenge their abilities to "know"? My very ambiguity challenges their understanding of themselves as omniscient. My ambiguity moves into their space, cornering their minds. They do not know which way to turn. My androgyny fucks with their imagined able-bodiedness: I impair their ability to categorize me. I challenge their conceptions of gender; I shake the foundations of their narrative. I upheave their ideas of Truth and their trusty methods to know it. I am successfully undoing gender (Butler, 2004) by being illegible. I am living the unlivable. Their failure to attribute a gender category to me makes my ambiguous gender performance a form of resistance. I take power in their confusion. I feel a rush of heat and euphoria in this moment of freedom—as I monster gender-fuck and gender-terrorize.

Political Economies of Looking: Claiming Power with Movements of Rage

It is 2 years ago, a time before I began testosterone treatment. I am 30 years old. My gender appears indiscernible to many people. In this moment, I wish my gender queerness were not so visible. I have been moving over the years toward a more male identity, and I no longer enjoy others' confusion about my body. Now, their energetic intrusions irritate me.

On the bus, I sit, reading. On my way to work. The fascinating, densely written book requires my full attention. My eyes trace lines of a paragraph. The words enter and exit my head, leaving no remnants. I am distracted, thinking about the deadlines I have to meet soon. In the next moment, I become aware of some other kind of discomfort. I feel energy reaching out to me. Eyes boring into me. The unease of being watched.

In the menu of gazes, there are many types. There are the double-takes, the trying-to-be-discreet-corner-of-the-eye extended glimpses, the persistent looks of confusion, and the more obvious, blatant stares. I encounter them all. Glancing up, I confront eyes reaching into me. Eyes opposite me, staring openly, shamelessly. Gawking. Eyes sitting to my right, trying to resist the draw to me, pretending to be uninterested. I feel their pull into me, the bodies facing forward, the eyes straining as far to the left as they can. Trying to appear like they are not looking. I feel their strain, the dull ache of over-extending the limit of the organ. These eyes know well their own rudeness.

I feel the pull of their need to see, to discern for themselves. Eyes demanding—needing to know. Boy or girl? Man or woman? This is beyond curiosity. It is desire. It is the wanting to possess, the intention to extract, it is the mission to obtain for oneself "Truth." This pull is based on their imagining themselves to be legitimate knowers. Within the act of staring is the entitlement to stare, to know, to determine, to proclaim (Serano, 2007). The internalized belief in oneself as omniscient being: "If I don't know, it does not exist." The logic of reality through self-determination, through self-proclamation. And of course, I, as Other, am not "able" to speak, to know, to determine, to proclaim (Spivak, 1988). How dare I, as Other, challenge their abilities to "know"? My very ambiguity is an assault to their understanding of themselves as omniscient. My androgyny fucks with their imagined able-bodiedness.

The gender-normate to my left tightens her body movements. Unease with my body. This same experience as staree—the receiver of stares—5 years ago brought me a feeling of excitement. I had felt a triumphant rush of joy, knowing that I had successfully confused the people on the bus. I took power in their discombobulated state. I was a successful gender terrorist. Monstering successfully.

Now, the cumulative experience of strangers' attention to my gender ambiguity feels like stigma. Eyes exercise power through interacting. Eyes express feeling, and they elicit feeling. The exercise of looking and being looked at creates a structure of feeling—a feeling of surveillance.

The eyes are still staring. The energy is smothering. Suffocating. I feel cornered. Suddenly, I feel hot with rage. Can't they see it? Their gazing is a continuous attack. Their confusion, which used to feel exciting to me, now feels like relentless probing. Their faces say: "You are a freak. You are less than human, a monster." Like Frankenstein's monster, I wonder, is "there no injustice in this? Am I to be thought the only criminal, when all human-kind sinned against me?" (Shelley, 2003, p. 211).

How dare they? Have I lost the power of monstrosity? How have I allowed them to make me a monster? How can I find my gender terrorist joy again? How can I return my monstrous power to myself?

According to Diversi and Moreira (2009), "We cannot erase the oppression in the marked body. But we can allow the wounds to speak up in their own bodies." So, I can speak. I can speak "from the wound in my mouth" (Weems, 2003). I can speak in many ways, with words and with actions. Perhaps speaking through my wounds can create a new way of seeing.

The starers see me seeing them. I feel the corners of my mouth curling, a growl rising in my throat. My jaw opens to strike out, to bite them. I look at them, staring back. My face speaks my anger. Like many starees do, I dare them to keep looking when they can see me seeing them gawking at me (Garland-Thomson, 2009).

The eyes to my right look away, then. But their energy has not moved; it remains in my space. I still feel their attunement to my movements, their awareness of me. After a moment or two, they try to sneak back in. These looks are "microaggressions," or often unconscious, often indirect, other-ing actions (Solorzano, Ceja, & Yosso, 2000).

Microaggressions

The blatant starers keep on looking. What do I do?
 I revolt.
 I glare back.
 My indignant anger
 Moves out of my body.
 My eyes rip the anger out from inside me.
 "Rage
 gives me back my body
 as its own fluid medium" (Stryker, 1994, p. 247).
 I embrace the monster

That I am continuing to become.
"Rage
throws me back at last
into this mundane reality
in this transfigured flesh
that aligns me with the power of my Being" (Stryker, 1994, p. 248).

I return the me that I lost to myself; I sit on my own side, alongside myself, and in so doing, take back my power.

"Through the operation of rage, the stigma itself becomes the source of transformative power" (Stryker, 1994, p. 249).

We, as shape-shifters, resist abjection by making our own selves. In so doing, we question and deconstruct dominant epistemologies, which assume the existence of an essential "self." We acknowledge that ideas of what constitutes the human and how we know this are just ideas. We create trans epistemologies, which locate authority to know in the *feeling* about our gendered selves (Anzaldua, 2007, p. 22). I make "freedom to carve and chisel my own face, to staunch the bleeding with ashes, to fashion my own gods out of my entrails" (Anzaldua, 2007, p. 22). I am not only challenging the ability of the person on the bus to know my truths. I am challenging the structures of knowledge and power in this society—the idea of a knowable, objective "Truth." I am challenging this academy that claims itself as legitimate knower and knowledge producer and its methods that claim to be legitimate ways of knowing and producing knowledge. As a scholar and as a member of society, I produce knowledge. I am inside the politics of representation. And I participate in the politics of the material world. I challenge the structures of knowledge production even as I maintain them. And I question my own abilities to know, as I question others'. In so doing, I reclaim my monstrous self and power in my monstrosity. Yet, this self is not ahistorical or decontextual. As I remake myself, I see and feel the histories, contexts and movements that shape me and the meaning I make of myself and the world.

My body is a site of a war over mis/recognition and mis/representation. I am an emoting, living revolt against the hegemony of gender, though this is not my point anymore. I am a continuous resistance, whether I mean to be or not. My corporeality is a weapon that threatens the system of body normativity. This weapon, my unruly body, demands to be disciplined, to be stared at. My gender that refuses assimilation is my home, a border, a wound that runs down the length of my body. My gendered body is a wound that runs down the length of society, embodying the trauma that body normativity creates.

My embodied, affective resistance is human, more human than violent eyes. They are inhuman in their inhumaneness, their unhuman performativity and performance.

Becoming More Monstrous:
Being in Movements of Joy, Considering Power

I am 31; it is May 2011. Life feels fast in this moment, in these movements. It has been 6 weeks and a day since I began testosterone. I have been feeling overwhelming joy in this time. I have heard emotional narratives of other transsexual men and natal females of many genders who start testosterone. Some feel calmer than before. Some feel irritable or angsty. Some lose the facility to cry, and with it, the release crying brings.

In these first weeks, I feel an amazing joy. I am euphoric. I am overjoyed about the changes taking place in my body. The first day of testosterone treatment, I smell different. My face is oily. I have so much energy. This exhilarating auto-poiesis, this self-creation.

On the fifth day of testosterone, standing in line to order dinner in a restaurant, I cannot help but jump up and down. Frenziness in my chest moves into and through my legs and arms. My mouth is smiling of its own accord. Muscles are growing, moving parts of me into a more "male" form. As parts of my body are looking more "male," yet other parts still appear more "female," I am becoming more monstrous. And my monstrous joy is a powerfully queer feeling.

A week into my treatment, I run faster and further, and—extraordinarily— am not fatigued. I am in multiple bodies at once. My waifiness as sinewy and wiry is a faggoty masculinity, a boyish femininity. A leaping lizard type of body. What once was Tyrannosaurus Rex-like in masculine female form is returning to become a queerer monster. Hormones moving flesh in my body, shifting like tectonic plates, pushing fat deposits and muscle densities into new formations. A slight monster, evolving quickly into a denser monster. Becoming new names, so rarely realized. Voicing sounds never before heard, only almost imagined. Being and becoming many monstrous beasts in amphibious forms. Every week, a new body, a new beast. Living in two realms, moving to the next, learning to breathe and locomote in new ways. We are gaying the drab landscape with our many queer bodies. Isn't that so joyful?

I am going through puberty for the second time. But this time, I am loving every minute of it. I am ecstatic. What is this joy about? What does it mean in the context of power structures of Whiteness, patriarchy, and able-bodiedness? Am I becoming more of an "oppressor"?

A distinct discomfort at this thought. A position I want to move out of more than any other. What does it mean, to be an "oppressor"? Must an "oppressor" exist, for oppression to exist? Even as I am becoming, I am the same person I was, I am the same person I was, so there is no inherent power in any body—it is all created in the movement of people perceiving me, and I them; this creates the position. I will now be, in moments, in movements, a recipient of privilege in ways I was not before. In many ways, it feels to me that the world around me is changing, more than I am. How is it to be "oppressor" and yet "oppressed" in the same body, in the same life? What about the distinct trans oppression that this binary conception of gender oppression leaves out? It is a distinct experience to feel many sides of the same oppression, in the same body. Am I becoming oppressor in moments when I am read as oppressor, though nothing I am doing is changing? What, then, is oppression? Is it oppression if a "new" "oppressor" is not oppressing, and has suffered the very same oppression? As betweeners, we all are in some ways oppressor, and in other ways oppressed.

Oppression is not bodies themselves, it is the institutionalized movement of some bodies against others. Complex structural forces, not individuals, reproduce oppression. In my experience, there is more to power than the appearance of a body. Though I will read more as male, my gender will still be complex. I am a feminine sort of masculine being. I still have my life history of living in the world as female, I still have my feminist perspective, and I still identify with women. As I am aware of male privilege, I still make efforts to challenge sexism and misogyny, just as I always have. So, using the term "oppressor" for me is inaccurate. I resist oppression in how I occupy an embodied site of what we would call "oppressor." My monstrous movement, my life histories, and the histories I inherit queer oppression even in moments I benefit from it.

However, my Whiteness is still White. I may queer the concept of oppression by embodying many parts of it at once, but my Whiteness is compounded by the parts of me becoming more masculine. I am becoming ever more monstrous, and yet, I am also moving into a position of ever more privilege. I have a new kind of responsibility to hold myself accountable to: the responsibility to be vigilant about how I move power in the world as someone who is perceived to be an able-bodied White man, and to move this power strategically against all forms of oppression and in the service of allyship to and resistance alongside people of color, disabled people, women, and other Others.

After 6 weeks and a day, I am again and still, a betweener. I am always a betweener who is becoming. We are all always becoming, but I am becoming now in a rapid, visible way. People still stare at me. I am still illegible to them. But I am in love somehow with my body that is becoming more monstrous and my new relationalities in the world. A feeling of euphoria I have never felt.

Will people still stare at me when I am absorbed back into a sea of normative-appearing masculinity? When my gender ambiguity becomes less than it appears? How will I be in the world, if people become able to see me? I am becoming at once more legible as human, more invisible as monstrous, and yet I am becoming even more monstrous than before. How bizarre. How absurd. Though, it is true. My monstrosity is becoming more visible in the parts of my body that are hidden from view, and less visible in the more exposed parts. I am becoming more monstrous, and I can't remember when I have felt this happy.

As I embrace my monstrous body, my rage births joy. "In this act of magical transformation, I recognize myself again. I am groundless and boundless movement. I am a furious flow" (Stryker, 1994, p. 247). I return to myself and reclaim my power in the monster that I am being and becoming. "Here at last is the chaos I held at bay. Here at last is my strength. I am not the water—I am the wave, and rage is the force that moves me" (Stryker, 1994, p. 247). Enraged joy fills my monstrous chest. My beating heart reaches out beyond my body, spilling out through the wound in my mouth (Weems, 2003). I am being and becoming a being—both human and inhuman. Am I not? I have come from a turning inward of pain, to a joyful rage of autonatality, a contentedly calming storm.*

---

*Incidentally, there is no reason for my transition. This seems to be a question that many people are curious about, and I have no answer for them. What I can share is that how I felt about myself just started shifting until it was a different shape than before. I did technically decide to start hormone therapy; that felt like a natural step for me, like how I presume puberty is for most people. I started T because it became more and more painful for me to be invisible and misread—perhaps some of that comes through in my story here. If you are asking this question—why did you transition?—I encourage you to question yourself: Why do I not transition? Then, you might see the absurdity of the question. Obviously, you do not transition because it is not you. I transition because to transition is to be me.

New Legibilities, New Illegibilities, New Inclusions, New Exclusions

It is 3.5 months since I began testosterone. I am still 31. I am conducting research—interviewing trans people about their everyday interactions. How is my betweenness shifting? What is this new betweenness, which makes me? It is multiple betweennesses. The shift depends on the interpretive eye of the beholder. As my legibility as male (rather than female or "indiscernible") becomes clearer to others, my legibility as a person, as human, becomes clearer to others. I experience people in a new way.

As I walk through the airport, people engage with me, their eyes reaching out to welcome me: greeting me, inviting me, including me. I stand in line waiting to order a sandwich. From behind me, a middle-aged, White woman speaks. Her words smile out from her mouth like hands to touch me. "What are you going to order?" Her eyes and face are twinkling, open, soft, engaged. She is smiling at me. Her entire being is winking at me.

I am astonished. Confused. I wonder why she is talking to me. What does she want? Why is she acting so friendly? She does not think I am a monster. Then, a dawning thought: She sees me as a White, able-bodied, cisgendered, straight, male youth. This is the register in which I am legible to her. The first time in 6 years that I have felt this privilege of mirroring; she sees me as one of her kind: normatively gendered. For the first time in my life, I feel how it feels to be seen as a "normal" male body. This is the shape, the articulation of gender normative, White male privilege. Belonging is what this configuration of privilege feels like. The energy moving through the eyes: a way of looking that communicates inclusion, camaraderie, comfort. An ease in the taking of me as one of them.

For this moment, my gender queernesses are unseen. Moving as a gender outcast in the world for 6 years, I became accustomed to people distancing themselves from me: staring at me or avoiding eye contact. Belonging: the privilege of legibility.

Legibility does not always mean friendliness, though. Recognition as male and queer brings another complicated betweenness to navigate. I walk to the park, holding hands with my then-lover, another FTM shapeshifter. A truck barrels past us. A passenger yells, "Faggots!" at us as they pass. I feel a strange mix of excitement and fear. This is the first time I have felt recognized by a stranger for who I am: a queer, socially male being. It is exciting to be validated. It is also the first time I have received this particular form of hate speech. I feel an acute vulnerability and terror. What an interesting welcome into this world of masculinities. I am again, a monster, in a new form.

Tensions of power live in between the different positionalities I inhabit. Though it is precarious, there is a power in "passing" as male—and as a White male in particular. This iterative accomplishment of masculinity is a movement that grants me cisgender male privilege—benefits of the gender power structure. Alternatively, being seen as a gender-defying male threatens the ideology of masculinity and this same gender power structure. Masculinity is inherently fragile because its ideal instantiation is not achievable and therefore, it is always in need of being accomplished (Kaufman, 2001). Gender-fucking while being legible as male is a form of resistance against oppressive gender systems—patriarchy and cisgender normativity—as it makes the fragility of both masculinity and gender as we know it visible. Being gender-illegible in this way can claim a particular power because it disrupts the ideas of gender stability and masculinity. However, gender-fucking and "passing" as male are both precarious; in moments of trans visibility or "discovery," I am vulnerable to violent gender regulations. Thus, I receive particular forms of power in movements when I incite or escape confusion in others. I also always face risks. What creates vulnerability also threatens the gender power structure.

My betweenness is moving. I am a multiple betweener. Receiving belongingness privilege when I am seen as a straight male, the me I have been my whole life up until now is angry at the me I am today. This old me is still fully me, though others could not and cannot see. I occupy new illegibilities: the erasure of gender complexity and of my history, the erasure of my humanness in my new, more masculine, queer monstrosity, the erasure of me as myself. I do not know what to make of these new illegibilities. They come about because of cisnormativity, the assumption that people are all cisgender. Few imagine possibilities for multigendered identities and histories. Few imagine we might be trans. Being seen as a straight male frustrates me even as it protects me; being seen as a gay male frightens me even as it validates me. I am not transitioning as much as the world is transitioning around me.

Becoming More Monstrous, Becoming More Separated

Six months on testosterone. In boxing class at the gym, I'm helping Bill rig the punching bags. He addresses me, looking me in the eye: "So, you're in graduate school?" I say: "Yes, I'm in sociology." As I speak, he attends to my chest, as if it is speaking. I feel distinctly uncomfortable. My head feels dull and thick. I slow down. I feel like I am not who I am.

Alienation
   n. Being isolated from a group; loss of identity in which the self seems unreal, thought to be caused by difficulties in relating to society.

Dissociation is a familiar sensation. An odd feeling of being displaced out of my body—that my chest is not mine. It is an uneasy feeling of de-territorialization: feeling forced to psychically vacate myself, because I am being taken for something I am not. Losing myself a little bit for a moment each time I encounter interactions like this one, when I am scrutinized.

Since starting testosterone, my chest is the most conspicuous remaining feminine marker on my body. The thing that most easily reveals my monstrosity now. Receiving stares into the chest made me squirm before I came into my transness, when I was female-identified. A life of familiarity with everyday sexual objectification. In this moment, I experience a mix of feelings. Indignity. Disbelief. Anger. For me, gender dysphoria is a result of interactive experiences like these.

This intrusion is a normal way of interacting with me. People are not hateful, or even overtly transphobic. They just look at my body in a way that disregards the fact that I might feel uncomfortable with them looking at me that way. They look at my face, then my chest, then my face. It is a kind of double take specific to transmasculine experience. A transmasculine-specific microaggression. I am still squirming inside, but it would create more discomfort for me, were I to say anything about his action. It would draw more attention to the issue that I want to be a nonissue.

The class comes in. I feel the energy of the teacher looking at me with wonderment. He's not looking at anyone else this way. As the class starts, we begin calisthenics, and minutes pass, the students silently following me with their eyes as they exercise. I have everyone's attention, and I do not want it. I try to move my body in a "masculine" way, punching the bag, weaving. Trying to convince them that I am not interesting enough to be worth looking at.

They feel entitled to look at me, still. After 6 months on testosterone, my voice is deeper, my face and body are more masculinized, I am growing more facial hair. And yet, after 6 months, I am still a spectacle. I'm looking more like a guy but something about me is still feminine enough, makes me monstrous enough, to make them wonder. No one in these attentive audiences says anything, but their silence does. The silent stare is a statement. Looking and not speaking is also speaking.

After 6 months on testosterone, how am I now? I am again and still, a betweener. I feel like a different creature from "women" or "men." My gender and sexed transience move my betweennesses around into new configurations. My sex-gender journeying shifts the shape of my social being in other ways, too. I feel this shifting through the energy of how other people interact with me. I resist the inhumanity of their eyes. I am fully human in my gender-fucking, transsexualizing monstrosity.

Humiliation, Humility, Humanity

It is 9 months since I began testosterone. I am still 31, almost 32. It is my first time designing and teaching my own course on the sociology of gender. I shave my beard when I return from break. I do not like how food gets stuck in it, and it grows in patchy, so I want to try for a clean start with the semester. I soon realize how important facial hair is for male gender attribution.

I go out to eat with a friend. We sit in the cozy, dimly lit restaurant. The server, an apparent young, White, pony-tailed woman with a spritely smile bounces toward our table: "Hello, Ladies!" Startled, I exchange a look with my friend. *Ouch.* This hasn't happened for a while. My jaw is tight. I feel like I am not really there. Invisible and unrecognized. I feel like a monster. Alienated. And humiliated. Again.

I hold the feelings like they are a plate of 20 candles burning, hot wax dripping onto my hands and pooling on the floor. I don't know how to not hold the feelings, the candles, the fire. I am used to it. A lifetime of learning how to hold burning candles. Not knowing how to put them down, how to ask someone else to hold them, how to put them out. We order drinks, and the server flits away. My friend asks: "Do you want me to kick her ass?"

It is only the server. She has no idea she has caused me discomfort. She didn't mean any harm. I do not want to draw attention to myself. I do not know how to tell her that the rules of gender ascription just failed with me. She made a mistake. I do not want her to feel embarrassed. Even though I do. My female socialization is driving. So I say: "It's not worth it."

I stop by the drugstore to buy some last minute groceries. Standing at the checkout, the cashier looks at me. He hesitates. Searching my face, my body for cues. "That'll be $5.45," he tells me. As a guy, I estimate that he normally interacts with men and women in different ways: in a collegial way with men, and in a reserved, polite way with women. He cannot categorize me, so he does not know how to interact with me. Collegial? Reserved? He does not know how to address me. Am I a "sir" or a "ma'am"? The rules for gender attribution that usually help him are not working now. I pay. "Thanks, have a good day," he opts for a neutral salutation at a moment when "sir" or "ma'am" is customary. I say gruffly, "You too." I hope that he can tell by my voice how I want to be read.

On Thursday, in my gender class, we discuss transgender issues and possibilities for "undoing" gender in order to undermine gender inequality (Deutsch, 2007). My students share with me how anxious they feel when they see someone they cannot categorize as male or female. They want to interact with them appropriately, but they do not know how.

After feeling so much pain when experiencing others' fumbling treatment of me, I soften. Many people are doing their best. They do not mean to be disrespectful. They just do not know how to follow rules of gender attribution when people break rules of gender performance. I ask them how we might be able to undo gender if we are constantly trying to categorize people. Is there a way we can interrupt our own process of wanting to place people in binary gender categories?

Rage. Joy. Astonishment. Realization. Insight.

And

| Still |

Subjugation.

The origin of the word "humility" is the Latin "humus," which means earth. "Humility," "humiliation," "human" all come from "humus": bringing to earth through different journeys, different affectivities. I am privileged: I have access to resources to transform myself. Many do not. I am humbled, even as I am angered, experiencing the privileges accorded to White maleness. I am humbled by my encounters with people who do their best, but are still confused, interacting with me.

Rejection and Reconnection in New Bodies

It has been almost a year that I have been on T. I am about to turn 32, about to finish my 3rd year of doctoral study. I walk across the space, my luggage rolling behind me. Sunlight streaming in through the floor-to-ceiling windows. I am looking for her. A part of me fears seeing people I used to know. I wonder whether they would recognize me. I hope I do not see anyone because I do not want to deal with their awkwardness. I am slightly afraid that she will not recognize me.

I spot her. She is smiling, sparkling. She recognizes me. I smile too. Her small body looks more faded than it used to. More wispy. She stands with her hands clasped. "Hi! How was your flight?" she asks. I say, "Not too bad." I hug her. She feels older to me. We walk to the car. She asks what I want to eat, where I want to go, what I want to do when I am in town. I am not sure.

"We're going to Steve and Maureen's for Christmas Eve," she says. I picture the scene at Steve and Maureen's. Dainty White women in sundresses, long bleached blonde hair, paint visible on their faces, painting their faces with smiles. Chatting about polite things: families, children, events at the church. Acting interested. Making their bodies small, perching uncomfortably on chairs, moving calculatedly, holding themselves the way they hold their plates of food: tentatively, carefully, precariously. Aware of the space around them. The group of men moves more deliberately, standing as if they own the place, gesturing with sweeping hands, seeming at ease. Equally interested in the ball game on TV as they are in interacting with each other. They hold their beers and their bodies as if they mean it, as if they are meant to be there. As if the action in the space moves around them. Exclaiming collectively when something of consequence happens on the screen. A moving body of bodies.

This scene, this place, these people. I feel uncomfortable thinking about going to this event. There is no place for my reality there. This differently gendered transsexual I am. I do not see others like myself there. Others like my many selves. The places I go are foreign to these people. They do not ask about them. When I say I am in school, they ask which college? They call me "young man" and think I am that. No one sees that I am an adult. They erase my life history. The last 10 years, a third of my life. They ask how many years I have left before I finish. No one asks about what my work is about. No one asks about my personal life. Perhaps the idea makes them uncomfortable. They do not want to acknowledge that a queer transsexual exists in the midst of their middle class, White, straight, Christian life. I feel invisible and conspicuous at the same time. I do not feel free to bring myself into the space. There, I try to hold my body in a way that does not impose on their culture, but I do no matter what. My very being is monstrous there. They tell me in indirect ways that I am a monster.

I jolt back to the present moment. We are getting in her car. She says, "We're going to the Christmas Eve service at Someone's church." I am not sure I want to go, but am curious, interested. But perhaps I will not have to go.

The next day she tells me when I wake up that we are not going to the new church for Christmas Eve. Why? I ask. She refuses to answer. I ask why several more times, and she does not look at me. She looks pained. She says, "Someone is worried." And I should talk to Someone about it. "OK," I say. I am surprised. I did not anticipate that this would happen.

My phone is on silent mode but I see it ring. Someone is calling me. I wonder how this conversation will go. I answer. "Hi," I brave it. Someone says, "Why do you want to come when you haven't wanted to in years?" No greeting. No hello. No "How are you?" No indication Someone wants to interact. Strictly business. Someone seems distrustful, defended, worried. I say, "I thought it would be easier, a new space. People will not know me. They wouldn't know anything about me." Someone says, "I am worried that people will give you dirty looks." Fear of my monstrosity. Fear of others' feelings, fear of my feelings. Fear that they will hurt me. And couching discomfort in a shield of other people.

"But no one would know anything about me." I try to reassure Someone. "People just see me as a guy now. They have no clue about my history." Someone does not tell me I am unwelcome. But Someone does not say I am welcome, either. Someone says, "I told people in the church you are a woman." I feel foggy. I thought I told Someone I was transitioning. Many times. I have told Someone for years about my identity. Someone saw me last summer after months of hormone therapy, Someone saw changes in my body. Why did Someone tell them I am a woman?

It is confusing to me when they act like I have not come out. It makes me feel like I have not come out yet. That I have to do it all over again. By refusing to recognize, they are hiding me. I feel erased. And now, though it is confusing because Someone seems to be asking for reassurance, I begin to understand the purpose of the call. Someone is telling me not to come. Like Frankenstein's monster, "Still I desired love and friendship, and I was still spurned" (Shelley, 2003, p. 211).

I feel pain, like tearing. My heart feels like it is slowly tearing from being stretched so much, from this distancing. The distance that I too create. I pull away because I do not feel at ease, I do not get acceptance here. I so fear their rejection that I withdraw from them, and then I feel alone. Feeling their pain, feeling my pain. Their feeling of loss makes me feel lost. Now they feel defensive.

I hear Someone say that I "should consider what I am doing to the family." Like Frankenstein's monster, I wonder, "Is there no injustice in this? Am I to be thought the only criminal, when all humankind sinned against me?" (Shelley, 2003, p. 211). I am at a loss. I do not feel like I am doing anything to anyone. I am not *doing* anything. What I am doing feels no different than eating—I must do it to nourish myself, to be healthy, to survive. I obviously eat; I obviously transition. Transitioning does not feel like transitioning as much as it feels like others are coming closer into seeing me the way I see myself. I feel hollow.

Why does Someone respond this way to me? Perhaps Someone sees my transition as a self-re-creation—as a challenge to God similar to how Victor Frankenstein's creation of life in his monster dispenses with God (Ozdemir, 2003). According to Stryker and others, "Frankenstein's monster is his own dark, romantic double, the alien Other he constructs and upon which he projects all he cannot accept in himself; indeed, Frankenstein calls the monster 'my own vampire, my own spirit set loose from the grave'" (Shelley, 2003, p. 74, cited in Stryker, 1994, p. 238). Is Someone projecting onto me her own gender complexity, which she cannot accept in herself? Does Someone see my transition as an abandonment of my parents, as a being they created? As an abandonment of Someone, herself? We were formed in parallel anatomical sex configuration, born to the same family. Certain aspects of my body appear different, now. Someone does not seem to see that this transition is me, that I am still me.

This conflict reflects the tensions between different knowledge about gender. According to scholars, gender is a social system of oppression and an interactive process involving performances and interpretations of bodies. Trans communities know gender as a sense of selfhood, which in some cases, may shift. However, Someone appears to understand gender in the culturally conventional way—as an individual's essence, equivalent to anatomical sex. For Someone, by transitioning, I have become an entirely different person. Perhaps Someone sees my transition as a rejection of myself, and thus, of our relationship. And so Someone is rejecting me. This is what transgender oppression feels like. Though I am hurt, I try again.

"Would you like to get together while I'm in town?" I venture an invitation. Even after the rejection. "We're all booked." Someone is cold. Like ice. I wonder how Someone is feeling underneath the ice. I say, "I understand. I won't come." And I hang up the phone. There is no space for me in this part of myself, this part of my family's self, this space between us, anymore. The glimmer of belonging I once felt, momentarily, in this community, is gone. I did feel welcome there one time. No longer. I must run away from this part of myself. I must save myself.

I did not know that leaving the girl I used to be also meant leaving relationships. I should have known. By transitioning, I alleviate the profound discomfort I feel being seen as female, and in so doing, I create profound discomfort in others. Displacing my dysphoria relocates it in them. But why? I feel exasperated. It is not their life. Why do they think I am becoming a different person? I am the same as I have been. I am just making it possible for them to see me. This crushes them because they have a fantasy of who I am. Otherwise it would not bother them.

But I am not only me. I am part of the space between us. And I am shifting that space. And that space is part of them too. In transitioning, I am transitioning them. I am monstering us all. Writing this, I question whether I should write these words. What right do I have, to fix these moments in time, to write about family in this way? How would you feel, if you read what I write? Why do I do this? I am searching for the parts of myself that are lost. Parts of you and me you do not let me see because you feel too much pain. Too much fear. Too much shame.

I go to spend the night with my friend, Rachel. We make latkes using my mother's mother's recipe. Light candles. Sing blessings over the candles. The light, the sound refract around the space, reorganizing the fragments of me that I cannot see. In this ritual, I reconnect to myself, to my past life, to all the lives before me, who made me, to our past life, when Rachel knew me as a girl. I bring our past connection into the present one. I ask my mother and my aunt to teach me. We make latkes using my mother's mother's recipe and the same grater that she used. And we sing blessings over the Chanukah candles.

This part of me I find again. This part of me I have never had. I find belonging here, in this forbidden part of myself. Am I an impostor? I wonder. The unfamiliar Hebrew words feel right, the feeling feels right. Kind of like my transition. New and unfamiliar, but old and right just the same. Always forthcoming and already past.

At the end of Shelley's story, Frankenstein dies of exhaustion after pursuing the monster with the goal of ending the life he created. With no hope of obtaining a female like himself to share his life, who he had asked Frankenstein to create, the monster departs, declaring his intent to take his own life, and finally find relief from his miserable isolation. As the monster appears to exist in this story as a projection of Frankenstein himself, not in his own right, and as self-destruction is a form of internalized oppression, I want to write an alternate ending to a story about monstrosity. I want to find selfhood, love, and resistance, and hope for justice within monstrosity. To find these things, I look to a contemporary transsexual work of art.

In *Hedwig and the Angry Inch*, Hedwig, a transsexual woman, and her band offer a take on love that we might consider in finding freedom. Their song "The Origin of Love" (Trask, 1999) adapts a story from Plato's *Symposium*, describing a time before love existed when there were three sexes—the female-female, the male-male, and the male–female or androgynous—doubled people with two faces, and two bodies in one. When they planned to revolt, Zeus severed them, dividing them into two separate beings: our current bodily configurations. The words describe the origin of what love is:

> Last time I saw you we had just split in two.
> You were looking at me. I was looking at you.
> You had a way so familiar, but I could not recognize,
> 'Cause you had blood on your face; I had blood in my eyes.
> But I could swear by your expression that the pain down in your soul was the same as the one down in mine.
> That's the pain, cuts a straight line down through the heart; we called it love.
> So we wrapped our arms around each other, trying to shove ourselves back together. We were making love. Making love.

Here, there is a familiarity between people who presumably see "their other half" and the pain of separation is the desire to be one person again, which draws people to love. Thus, separation is where love comes from. Besides the origin of love, the trauma of severance in this story can also represent the creation of and segregation between socially differentiated groups: racial groups, social classes, sexual beings, colonizers and indigenous, able-bodied and disabled people, gendered beings—cis men and women, trans and cis people, and any other combination of those.

We experience social and collective traumas in our bodies in forms of chronic stress and at times, in gaps in memory or consciousness—

disconnection from ourselves, and at times from each other. Perhaps blood on the face symbolizes social subjugation; perhaps blood in the eyes symbolizes the inability to see the Other's humanity or one's role in perpetuating oppression, such as is often the case for people in privileged positions. Though the speaker here cannot "recognize" the Other, she senses a familiarity. Through the difference between the two, the speaker feels a resonance with the same pain of separation that they both feel, and the pain of separation is itself love. The potential for love is created by the *pain* of separation, manifest in oppression, and taking place in interpersonal rejection, intrapsychic fragmentation, and institutionalized social devastation, even war. Love itself is an *antidote to the pain* of separation. The original androgynous doubled being is love between men and women embodied in the form of singular trans beings; the all-male and all-female beings are love between men and between women, embodied in the forms of singular male and female beings, respectively.

This story speaks to the pain of oppression that all involved experience—both oppressors and oppressed—perhaps speaking to our status as betweeners. Uniting in love is a response to the deep pain we feel in our separation, and is an attempt to merge again to repair the wounds of separation. Trans people, by integrating different gendered parts of ourselves, perhaps regenerate some of the power Zeus aimed to immobilize when he separated the androgynous being into two. Thus, the monstrosity of androgyny exists in every being—as being formerly joined to another gender if not in current multigendered form—and can be a cathartic form of resistance. Perhaps we can find freedom from pain through attaching again—to the fragmented parts of ourselves and to those who are separated from us. Perhaps we can claim the Others within ourselves, in our own betweennesses, and claim other Others through restoring their place within us and our place within them to reconnect and rebuild our/themselves.

I want to claim all the rejected parts of me. All the disdain, all of the shame. Claim all the ways I am Other. Bring them into my full being. I claim friends as family. I try to connect, as much as we both will allow, with my blood family. Fighting the legacies of institutional trauma. Growing my fragmented selves and fragmented relationships together.

A New Belonging

I have been on T for a year and 6 weeks. I am 32 now. I have just finished my doctoral coursework and my 3rd year in graduate school. I run, in the crisp, warm morning air. As I lope past a jogging track, a man rounding the bend smiles and waves at me, calling out, "Take care, brother!"

I am floored by my feeling. I have never been called "brother" by a stranger. I never knew how it could be, how it could feel, in relation with him. A new sensation of belonging. He does not know the feelings this evokes in me. Recognition as male. Embodied feeling of brotherhood. Connection across color lines. When I read as female to others in the world, Black men—or any men—did not greet me as warmly. Probably because they have been taught not to. In the U.S. historical context of race relations, White people punish Black men for giving attention to White women. In sometimes murderous ways. Can being read as a White male perhaps open up a feeling of relative safety between myself and men of color? Where they might feel more comfortable being friendly with me, because no one would claim they tried to rape me? In transitioning gender, I feel that I am transitioning race, because White maleness is socially different from White femaleness. I am learning more about the intricacies of male Whiteness and the devastating manifestations of racism and sexism. I feel in my body the pain of separation between White women and Black men. I only notice this extent of pain because I can compare it to the connection that I am now feeling, being seen as a young, White man by an older, Black man. Connection and belonging is what White male privilege feels like.

There is loss and gain in this becoming. I am still a betweener, though my positionalities are shifting. I am moving into a heightened, at times visible, embodied monstrosity. With it come inclusions and fears. With this sometimes less visible monstrosity comes a sometime privilege of being enveloped back into "humanity"—knowing so recently and intimately the feeling of not belonging.

I must always hold my many experiences with different subjugations close to my heart. My gender that refuses assimilation is my home, a wound that runs down the length of my body.

My gendered body is a wound that runs down the length of society, embodying the trauma of gender, and the separation that cisgender normativity and all systems of oppression create. The assumptions that cisgender people are normal, and that trans people simultaneously do not exist and are "crazy" and inferior plays out on my body and through my interpersonal interactions. My body "wounds" society, disrupting normative ideas of gender, challenging the system. My body, in its ambiguity, brings the separation between binary genders to the fore. And I feel the effects of these social disruptions in my body in the emotional wounds of traumatic stress.

Cisgender normativity creates separation. Separation from myself. Separation from you. Your own separation from the gendered complexity within you. We are not separate beings. We are a living, breathing collectivity, we are a body. The idea of difference is a trauma both on our gendered selves and on our collective body. My gendered body is a wound; it is also a suture healing itself. I am trying to put myself back together. I am trying to sew us back together. The betweenness between us. Our betweenness, what separates us and what joins us. Our common wound of separation. And you? Are you also trying?

I am writing into the spaces between us. I speak through the wound in my mouth. The shape of my mouth is changing, though the shape of the wounds are not. They are speaking up in their own bodies. These wounds, our body.

Speaking through the wound in my mouth gives me back my power as the monster I am becoming. Always forthcoming and already past, the wounds of my gendered life are rebirthing me and reshaping themselves. And now, I move into new movements. I make new monstrosities, new sensations. Rage, joy, insight, humility. Ever-shifting relationalities. We find connection and reconnection. And we make—and we take—new places.

Declaration of Conflicting Interests

The author(s) declared no potential conflicts of interest with respect to the research, authorship, and/or publication of this article.

Funding

The author(s) received no financial support for the research, authorship, and/or publication of this article.

references

Adams, T. E. (2011). *Narrating the close: An autoethnography of same-sex attraction*. Walnut Creek, CA: Left Coast Press.

Adams, T. E., & Jones, S. H. (2011). Telling stories. Reflexivity, queer theory, and autoethnography. *Cultural Studies and Critical Methodologies, 11,* 108–116.

Anzaldua, G. (2007). *Borderlands/La Frontera: The new Mestiza*. San Francisco, CA: Aunt Lute Books.

Botting, F. (1991). *Making monstrous: Frankenstein, criticism, theory*. Manchester, UK: Manchester University Press.

Butler, J. (2004). *Undoing gender*. New York, NY: Routledge.

Collins, P. H. (1986). Learning from the outsider within: The sociological significance of Black feminist thought. *Social Problems, 33*(6), S14–S31.

Deleuze, G. (1990). *The logic of sense.* New York, NY: Columbia University Press.

Deleuze, G., & Guattari, F. (1987). *A thousand plateaus: Capitalism and schizophrenia.* Minneapolis: University of Minnesota Press.

Deutsch, F. M. (2007). Undoing gender. *Gender & Society, 21,* 106–127.

Diversi, M., & Moreira, C. (2009). *Betweener talk: Decolonizing knowledge production, pedagogy, and praxis.* Walnut Creek, CA: Left Coast Press.

Foucault, M. (1978). *The history of sexuality: Volume 1.* New York, NY: Vintage.

Garland-Thomson, R. (2005). Feminist disability studies. *Signs: Journal of Women in Culture and Society, 30,* 1557–1587.

Garland-Thomson. R. (2009). *Staring: How we look.* New York, NY: Oxford University Press.

Goffman, E. (1963). *Stigma: Notes on the management of spoiled identity.* New York, NY: Simon & Schuster.

Halberstam, J. J. (2005). *In a queer time and place: Transgender bodies, subcultural lives.* New York, NY: New York University Press.

Kaufman, M. (2001). The construction of masculinity and the triad of men's violence. In M. Kimmel & M. Messner (Eds.), *Men's lives* (pp. 4–16). Boston, MA: Allyn & Bacon.

Kidd, J. D., & Witten, T. M. (2008). Transgender and transsexual identities: The next strange fruit—Hate crimes, violence and genocide against the global trans-communities. *Journal of Hate Studies, 6,* 31–63.

Minh-ha, T. T. (1989). *Woman, native, other.* Indianapolis: Indiana University Press.

Ozdemir, E. (2003). Frankenstein: Self, body, creation and monstrosity. *Ankara Universitesi Dil ve Tarib Cografya. Fakultesi Dergisi, 43,* 127–155.

Serano, J. (2007). *Whipping girl: A transsexual woman on sexism and the scapegoating of femininity.* Emeryville, CA: Seal Press.

Shelley, M. (2003). *Frankenstein* (Republication of the text of 1818). New York, NY: Bantam Dell.

Solorzano, D., Ceja. M., & Yosso, T. (2000). Critical race theory, racial microaggressions, and campus racial climate: The experiences of African American college students. *Journal of Negro Education, 69,* 60–73.

Spivak, G. C. (1988). *Can the subaltern speak?* In C. Nelson & L. Grossberg (Eds.), *Marxism & the interpretation of culture* (pp. 271–313). London, UK: Macmillan.

Stryker, S. (1994). My words to Victor Frankenstein above the village of Chamounix: Performing transgender rage. *GLQ, 1,* 237–254.

Trask, S. (1999). The origin of love [Recorded by John Cameron Mitchell]. In *Hedwig and the Angry Inch* [Film]. New York, NY: Atlantic/Wea.

Weems, M. E. (2003). *Public education and the imagination-intellect: I speak from the wound in my mouth.* New York, NY: Peter Lang Publishing.

Wittman, E. H. (1998). Mary Shelley's Daemon. In M. Lowe-Evans (Ed.), *Critical essays on Mary Wollstonecraft Shelley* (pp. 88–100). New York, NY: G.K. Hall.

Yoshino, K. (2006). *Covering: The hidden assault on our civil rights.* New York, NY: Random House.

12

white-blindness

The Dominant Group Experience

Ashley "Woody" Doane*

What does it mean to be a member of the dominant group? My claimed ancestry is English American or "Yankee" (in the sense of a multigenerational
inhabitant of New England). For many in my ethnic group, the strongest
identity is simply "American." As Stanley Lieberson (1985) discovered in
an analysis of US Census data, white Protestant Americans whose families have lived in the United States for many generations are most likely to
self-identify as just "American." Indeed, as I will discuss later, the ability to
claim "American" identity is an important marker of dominant-group status. More recently, since the 1950s, the label "WASP" (White Anglo-Saxon
Protestant) has often been applied to my group, reflecting the assimilation
of other European ethnic groups into the Anglo-American core and the
broadening of group boundaries (Glazer & Moynihan, 1963: 15). Whatever the label, the important point is, as John Myers (2003: 44) has put it,
that "the White Anglo-Saxon Protestant group is the quintessential dominant group in our society."

Like many of the dominant-group students in my race and ethnic relations classes (for whom I assign an "ethnicity as personal experience" or
"family background" project), I would have had difficulty writing this essay

*Doane, Ashley "Woody." "White-Blindness: The Dominant Group Experience." Reprinted
from Myers, John P., *Minority Voices: Linking Personal Ethnic History and the Sociological
Imagination*, 1st Ed., ©2005, pp. 187–199. Reprinted by permission of Pearson Education
Inc., New York.

as a college student. Growing up, I never thought of myself as ethnic. I was "just like everyone else," an "American," as opposed to those who were "different" and could claim a specific ethnic affiliation. Most sociologists would not have seen me as ethnic either. The then-popular term "white ethnic," which was applied to such groups as Irish Americans, Italian Americans, or Jewish Americans, implied that there were white "nonethnics"—people who were just part of the "mainstream" or "larger society." Consequently, very little attention has been paid to the nature of dominant-group identity (Feagin & Feagin, 1996: 71–72; Doane, 1997a), as opposed to dominant-group treatment of racial and ethnic minorities. As I have argued elsewhere (Doane, 1997a), this "hidden" nature of dominant-group identity has assisted the dominant group in maintaining its position of power and influence. For me, developing an understanding of dominant-group identity has helped me to understand the history of my family.

Marking the Center: The Doane Family

On my father's side of the family, which is where I locate my ethnic identity, I am a twelfth-generation English American. Other branches of the family tree contain later immigrants from England and, on my mother's side, nineteenth-century immigrants from Scotland. All evidence, however, suggests that they assimilated rapidly into the Anglo-American group as what Charlotte Erickson (1972) has called "invisible immigrants." In any event, it is through my father's family that I take both my surname and my sense of heritage.

My first-generation ancestor, John Doane, migrated from England to the Plymouth Colony in Massachusetts around 1630 (Doane, 1960 [1902]; unless otherwise noted, all historical family information in this section is taken from this work). Interestingly, the family history refers to him as having "settled" in Plymouth, as opposed to more accurate terms such as *colonized* or even *invaded*. I do think that it is important to recognize that my ancestor, along with others of his time, were immigrants, even though their immigrant experience was different from that of other groups. While little is known as to where John Doane came from or why he migrated, I must assume that it was for economic opportunity, religious freedom, or both. Because he almost immediately came to occupy a position of relative prominence in Plymouth Colony (a 1633 document lists him as a member of the Governor's Council, along with Myles Standish and William Bradford), he clearly did not experience life at the bottom of the stratification system (e.g., as a hired laborer or as an indentured servant). As a very early immigrant, he also would not have had the experience of having to adapt to a dominant group within the emerging colonial society.

In 1644 or 1645, dissatisfied with the lack of prosperity and economic opportunity in Plymouth, John Doane and many others relocated to Nauset (later Eastham) on Cape Cod. The land in Nauset is listed as being "purchased" from Native Americans for "moose skins, boats, wampum, and little knives." As we now know, Native American and English notions of land ownership and use were dramatically different. Native Americans viewed land as a resource to be used, while the English treated land as a "commodity" with perpetual ownership rights (Richter, 2001: 54). What is clear is that my ancestor (and his descendants) certainly benefited from the transaction. From all accounts, John Doane appeared to have at least a comfortable economic status after the move to Eastham, as his original land purchase was 200 acres. He also had considerable local influence as a deacon, selectman, and deputy to the Colony Court until his death in 1685 at the age of 95.

For the next five generations, my ancestors remained in Eastham, living as relatively prosperous farmers and frequently serving as town officials. Living on Cape Cod, my family was not on the front lines of armed conflict with Native Americans in New England, conflicts such as King Philip's War in 1675 and 1676. While it is difficult to say for certain, I suspect that they would have shared the prevailing attitude of New Englanders, which was to view Native Americans as inherently heathen, lazy, barbaric, and a threat to civilized Christian society. Historian Ronald Takaki (1993: 38) has termed this the "racialization of savagery," the perspective that Native Americans were incapable of civilization. These attitudes justified the conquest and taking of Native American land and enabled Europeans to view the devastating epidemics (probably smallpox) that decimated Native American communities as "God's divine intervention." Even though the "frontier" soon moved far away from my ancestors, the conflicts between English colonists and Native Americans set the stage for two centuries of conflict across the American continent. While my family was increasingly removed from later conflict with and the removal of Native Americans, they were members of a racial-ethnic group that clearly benefited from the territorial expansion of the United States.

Once Native American communities had been eliminated, evidence suggests that my ancestors would have encountered little ethnic or racial diversity during their first two centuries in the United States. As Vincent Parillo (1994: 528) has observed, the initial population of colonial America in 1689 was about 80 percent English. Even though the population of the colonies became more diverse (by the 1790 census English Americans were about 49 percent of the population) with the involuntary immigration of enslaved Africans and the immigration of non-English Europeans (e.g., Germans, Scots-Irish), New England remained the most English area and Massachusetts the most English state (Parillo, 1994). Out on Cape Cod, my ancestors probably would have had little exposure to the increasing diversity of the colonies; there would have been little to dissuade them from the belief that English culture and customs were universal.

What emerged from colonial America was what can be called the Anglo-Protestant "core" of American society (Feagin & Feagin, 1996). As the United States became an independent nation, its culture and institutions had a distinct English influence. More significantly, its ideologies and policies concerning race and ethnic relations have reflected the perspectives and interests of Anglo-Americans (Marger, 2003). Throughout US history, other ethnic and racial groups have been expected to adhere to these practices, a phenomenon Milton Gordon (1964) has referred to as "Anglo-conformity." As "old stock" Americans, my ancestors had the advantage of navigating in familiar social and cultural waters.

In the sixth generation, my ancestor Samuel Dill Doane died and was buried at sea during a voyage to the West Indies in 1809. While I cannot say for certain whether he participated in the slave trade, we do know that the growth of the Atlantic trade and the maritime industry in New England was due in large part to the economic activity generated by the slave trade. Vessels from New England participated in the "Triangle Trade," which involved bringing slaves from Africa to the Americas, raw materials to Europe, and finished goods to the American colonies. Ships from New England carried farm products and manufactured goods (bricks, candles, building materials) to the West Indies and returned with molasses, sugar, spices, and even a few enslaved Africans. This trade stimulated the New England economy and enabled the growth of farming, manufacturing, shipbuilding, and distilling—to the extent that New England in 1770 had perhaps the highest standard of living in the world (Bailyn, cited in Lang, 2002: 9). Thus, whether my ancestors participated in the slave trade is immaterial. All of New England (and the United States) profited either directly or indirectly.

While there is the temptation for white Americans with roots in New England or the North to seek to distance themselves from slavery, the historical reality is more complicated. Slavery did exist in the North; it was legalized in Massachusetts in 1641 (Feagin & Feagin, 1996: 239) and persisted in New England until after the Revolutionary War. According to the *Hartford Courant* (2002: 19), the first US Census in 1790 recorded 3,763 slaves in New England, the majority of whom were in Connecticut. I cannot say definitively whether any of my ancestors owned slaves, although higher status (e.g., a deacon or a more prosperous farmer) increased the likelihood of an individual being a slave owner. A recent listing of Connecticut slave owners in 1790 (*Hartford Courant*, 2002: 18) included a Seth Doan (*sic*) of Chatham as owning two slaves; he appears to be a descendant of John Doane and, hence, a relative (another part of my family tree, involving my maternal grandfather, disappears in Texas in the early twentieth century and I have no knowledge of what their involvement with slavery may have been). Ultimately, whether any of my direct ancestors owned slaves is almost beside the point. They participated in a society that condoned slavery and benefited from the economic contributions of slaves.

After the death of Samuel Dill Doane at sea, his widow remarried and moved to the small town of Dana in central Massachusetts. My great-great-great-grandfather, Leonard Doane, was a sailor and later a sea captain. Upon leaving the sea, he engaged in an unsuccessful business (with Charles Goodyear and others) to place rubber upon cloth. After losing all of his money in this venture, he returned to Dana and made his living by manufacturing palm leaf hats. According to the family history (Doane, 1960 [1902]: 279), Leonard Doane was an abolitionist, opposed to slavery, and an active member (a state representative) of the Free-Soil Party, which was against the expansion of slavery into the western territories acquired from Mexico (I think that it is also important to recognize antiracist traditions among white Americans). He was also described as an active supporter, along with his son, my great-great-grandfather George Wood Doane, of the Temperance movement and in favor of prohibition of alcohol. While I do not know what motivated them to support this movement, I do know that there was a historical relationship between Protestantism, antislavery, temperance, and nativism—negative attitudes toward immigrants (Roediger, 1991: 152). One of the forces that propelled the Temperance movement was the association (stereotype) in the minds of many Americans between drunkenness and immigrant groups, most notably the Germans and the Irish (Billington, 1963 [1938]: 195).

While my great-great-grandfather worked initially as a salesman (for patent medicines), he returned to Dana and made his living first as a manufacturer of palm leaf goods, and then later as a farmer and carpenter. Subsequent generations—my great-grandfather and my grandfather—also lived in Dana and worked as farmers and carpenters. In fact, my father was born while the family was still living in Dana. During this period, from the 1850s through the 1920s, my family members lived in relative isolation in a small, racially and ethnically homogeneous town in rural Massachusetts. It would be easy to describe them as removed from the ethnic and racial issues of this era: emancipation, reconstruction, and the emergence of formal racial segregation; increased European immigration (especially from Southern and Eastern Europe); the rise of anti-immigrant sentiment and the eventual imposition of immigration quotas; the debate over and eventual restriction of immigration from China and Japan; and the final conflicts with Native Americans in the western United States and the creation of the reservation system. At the same time, their lives were shaped by—and they directly or indirectly benefited from—the evolution of American society, including industrialization and economic growth facilitated by immigrant labor and by the exploitation of African American, Mexican American, and Chinese American labor. I do not know what my ancestors' opinions were on these questions; however, I suspect that, like most people, they were products of their times and either supported or did not oppose these developments. In any event, there is no record of strong advocacy on either side of these issues.

What is important to emphasize here is that generations upon generations of dominant-group members—including my family—have benefited from the social and institutional practices of American society. Exclusion, segregation, and the failure to enforce treaties and ensure equal protection under the law certainly reduced competition and created economic opportunities for dominant-group members. Political and social practices, from voting access to citizenship requirements to educational opportunities, all served to reproduce group power from generation to generation. Government policies, from fugitive slave laws to New Deal legislation to welfare policy to tax policy (e.g., the mortgage interest deduction), have generally given disproportionate benefits to dominant-group members. In contemporary terms, the dominant group has always enjoyed a home field advantage.

Following the flooding of Dana in the mid-1930s to create the Quabbin Reservoir (the water supply for metropolitan Boston), my grandfather moved his family to the mill town of Springfield, Vermont. There he worked in a variety of industrial positions, eventually rising to some sort of supervisory position in one of the factories. From my father's accounts, and my own research on ethnic relations in northern New England, Springfield would have been a much more ethnically diverse environment than any place in which my family had previously lived. I recall from my father's stories an awareness of the ethnic backgrounds of his high school classmates and some sense of low-level intergroup conflict. These decades (the 1930s and 1940s) would have been the time of the gradual but uneven incorporation and assimilation of European immigrant groups (Irish Americans, French Canadians, German Americans, Polish Americans, and so on) amidst the struggles of the Depression and World War II. I had limited contact with my grandparents' generation; however, I do recall hearing occasional ethnic or racial slurs in adult conversations. As I was to learn later in life, one dilemma for dominant-group members is how to respond when racist statements are made by family members or close friends.

My father left Springfield to attend a seminary in Maine, and then joined the army near the end of World War II (he served with a medical unit in Alaska). After the war, aided by his veteran's benefits, he attended first the state university and then a theological seminary. I do not recall any specific discussion of the topic, yet I would assume that his environment was both mostly white, yet more diverse than that of previous generations. My mother, whom my father met while in college, had a broader range of intergroup experiences. She spent her early childhood in Texas, then, after her mother married her stepfather, who was a career army officer, moved with her parents through a variety of postings including Panama, a series of bases in the United States, and then high school experiences in postwar Beijing and Japan. Her classmates at the Peking American School came from a variety of nations, including local Chinese students. I would describe both of my parents as broadminded and antiracist, as evident in my father's ministry and my mother's work in community organizations. They certainly encouraged my siblings and me to be inclusive and to see diversity as positive.

Nevertheless, the world in which my siblings and I grew up was not a diverse one. The small New Hampshire towns in which we first lived and the Maine coastal town in which I spent summers were extremely homogeneous in terms of race and ethnicity. Even later, when my father's pastoral career led us to three different communities in suburban Boston in the 1960s and early 1970s (late elementary school through high school), race and ethnicity played a very limited role. There was no meaningful residential integration in any of these communities. I do vaguely recall identification and verbal jousting between Irish American and Italian American classmates, and ethnic slurs directed toward the latter group, but by the late 1960s, ethnic divisions among middle-class white Americans were becoming increasingly symbolic. In terms of my own ethnic identity, I only had a sense of just being present—of being "just like everybody else." This seemed also to be true for my Protestant European American classmates: They had either assimilated or were members of the dominant group to begin with.

Those intergroup experiences that I did have were somewhat unique in nature and linked to my father's work as a Congregational minister. We had missionaries and divinity students from sub-Saharan Africa and India stay with us at times, which certainly encouraged me to be aware of the diversity of the population of the world. I dimly recall my parents discussing events in the civil rights movement (I was only eight at the time of the March on Washington) or guest speakers coming to the church to talk about their role in the civil rights movement, but everything seemed very far away. Most of the events of the mid- and late 1960s (e.g., the later events in the civil rights movement, the urban rebellions) were merely headlines on the newspapers that I delivered on my afternoon paper route.

By high school, I began to become more aware of the scope of racial injustice in the United States. My parents' conversations began to have more impact. I remember, for example, their disgust upon moving to a new community and learning that some influential members of the church had been involved in discouraging a prominent African American athlete from purchasing a home in their neighborhood. I recall them successfully encouraging the church to provide office space for a former divinity school classmate of my father's who had left the ministry to work as an antiracist activist and consultant. Through the church, and at the encouragement of my mother, I spent a number of Saturdays in high school as a volunteer with a Boston community organization that rehabilitated housing in a low-income, predominantly African American neighborhood. This gave me firsthand exposure to the effects of residential segregation and concentrated poverty: It was clear that the neighborhood was very different from the suburban community in which we lived. I even recall coming home with copies of Nation of Islam and Black Panther Party newspapers that I picked up on the street. While I was becoming aware of some of the "costs" of being black in American society, I never really thought about the implications of being white.

One particular event does stand out in my memory. While volunteering with the community organization, I occasionally spent the lunch hour eating my bag lunch and answering the telephone while the office staff took a break. One day, a middle-aged African American man came into the office and inquired about employment possibilities. When I informed him that I had no knowledge of any openings and that he should return when the full-time staff members were available, I was shocked by his clear skepticism and repeated questioning of my statement. It was only later in the day that I realized that the communication gap between us was undoubtedly shaped by race. I think that it was the first time that I was ever aware that social interactions were affected by race. As a white American, I had the privilege of living for sixteen years before facing this reality.

After high school, new experiences continued to expand my awareness of ethnic and racial diversity. Before entering college, I spent six months working in one of the last textile mills (historically a significant employer of new immigrants) in Manchester, New Hampshire. Compared to my previous experiences in school and in my home communities, this was like entering the United Nations. My co-workers included, among others, Mexican Americans, French Canadians, Greek Americans, and Polish Americans. As I encountered linguistic barriers and cultural differences, and observed ethnic rivalry and conflict (verbal jousting), I began to appreciate the impact of group identities on everyday life. My own identity, however, remained unexamined as I focused upon the "differences" of others.

My undergraduate college experience did little to encourage examination of this issue, as the small liberal arts institution that I attended was not diverse. The first time that I ever recall thinking about my own ethnic identity in any concrete manner was near the end of my college career. By this time I had been exposed to "ethnic food," which was always the cuisine of "someone else." One week I happened to glance at the food section of the *Boston Globe* and saw an article on "Yankee food"—New England boiled dinner, codfish cakes, red flannel hash, smoked finnan haddie, "Indian pudding," and the like—dishes that regularly appeared on our family dinner table during my childhood. For the first time, I remember thinking, "I'm ethnic, too." This insight also encouraged me to think about how other aspects of small-town New England life, the stuff of Norman Rockwell paintings, were not universal but represented a particular ethnic and cultural heritage. I began to appreciate the ways in which dominant-group experiences were embedded or hidden in what was presented as "American" traditions. We "see" St. Patrick's Day, Columbus Day, Cinco de Mayo, Kwanzaa, and Rosh Hashanah as "ethnic" holidays, but we generally fail to recognize the ethnic origins of Thanksgiving, even though the story and symbols are part of an Anglo-American origin myth (Loewen, 1992, 1995).

My first professional position after college, as a researcher on a one-year study of the occupational and educational status of Franco-Americans in New Hampshire, represented another step in my education. As part of this research, I delved into the literature on assimilation, the experiences of immigrant groups, issues of ethnic stratification, and the history of French Canadians and Franco-Americans (see Doane, 1979, 1983). This enabled me to begin to understand issues of ethnic change and assimilation, as well as the impact of pressures for assimilation, pressures that I realized emanated from my group. Through my interactions with Franco-American scholars and activists, I also came to appreciate the "costs" of assimilation, the struggle to preserve group customs and heritage, and the greater sense of solidarity that goes along with being part of a nondominant ethnic group. In contrast, I began to realize that my dominant-group status did not revolve around these types of experiences, but instead focused on the "differences" of others. To a significant degree, dominant-group identity is grounded in *not* being a member of a minority group.

Throughout my graduate studies in sociology and the early years of my teaching career, I continued to study issues of race and ethnicity. My doctoral dissertation (Doane, 1989) was an in-depth study of the historical evolution of ethnic and racial identities and inequality in the United States and South Africa. This work left me convinced that power and economic competition are at the core of race and ethnic relations and intergroup conflict, and that dominant groups use society's institutions in order to reinforce and maintain their advantages. On a personal level, I came to a fuller understanding of how the history of my group was inextricably connected to relations of domination and subordination—that much of our "success" had come at the expense of other groups. Since then, I have reexamined many of the cultural and historical images that I grew up with, from the "settling" of New England and the American West, to the realities of life in small-town or suburban middle-class white communities, to the redefinition of what it means to be an "American." This process has not always been easy, since being a member of a dominant group in many ways limits our ability to see the nuances of race and ethnic relations. It is much easier to see social and institutional practices as "normal" instead of examining them for ways in which they reflect and reinforce the position of the dominant group.

During the past decade, one major focus for my research and writing has been to analyze the social role of dominant-group ethnic and racial identities. I began with a paper titled "The Myth of WASP Non-Ethnicity" (Doane, 1992), in which I explored the ways dominant-group identities were different from nondominant identities and how these differences affected race and ethnic relations. Since then, I have written a number of pieces analyzing dominant-group ethnicity and "whiteness" (Doane, 1997a, 1997b, 2003). I have also incorporated these issues into my teaching, and over the years I have encouraged students to confront the nature of whiteness. Despite all of this work, however, I find that it still takes me additional effort to "see" racial issues and the role of whiteness. Being a member of the dominant group makes it that much more difficult to see race relations clearly. White-blindness continues to affect intergroup relations.

Over the past few decades, many things have changed. Part of my family has moved geographically from our northern New England base. We have married and adopted across ethnic and racial lines that would have been impermeable a couple of generations ago. The old ethnic divisions among European Americans appear to be largely irrelevant. Our workplaces are in some cases considerably more diverse than those of our ancestors. We have friendships or relationships with neighbors and co-workers that are more diverse than ever before. At the same time, we all live in predominantly white neighborhoods, work in predominantly white workplaces, and move in a largely white social environment. Our intergroup interactions are largely on "home fields," and we generally have the option of becoming involved or not in the racial issues of our community and our society. In a lot of ways, many things have not changed.

Dominant-Group Identity and the Twenty-First Century

So what does it mean to be a member of the dominant group in the United States at the beginning of the twenty-first century? In general, there is still a lower level of self-awareness when it comes to race and ethnicity. White Americans tend not to think about being white because they do not have to; Anglo-Americans still have a tendency to think of themselves as "American" when they consider issues of ethnicity. At the same time, I believe that there is an increasing debate about what it means to be an "American." Past assumptions that "American" is equivalent to white or Anglo-American are still prevalent, but they are being challenged by ideas such as multicultural-ism, a rethinking of history, and a reevaluation of what constitutes "American" literature, art, or music. Perhaps this debate is particularly evident in the university environment where I work, but it is also making its way into the larger society.

The dominant group itself has undergone change. Over the centuries, the boundaries of the dominant group have expanded to include British Americans (Scots, Scots-Irish, Welsh), then Protestant European groups, and now to where it has become a generalized "white European American" identity. This has involved not only the assimilation of non-English groups, but also the evolution of the "Anglo core culture" into a more generalized European American culture. As I have argued elsewhere, this has been to the advantage of the dominant group, for by absorbing other European groups, it has been able to maintain its social, political, and economic ad-vantages in the face of substantial immigration (Doane, 1997a: 388).

Dominant-group status has served to benefit its members over the years in a variety of ways. While some whites and English Americans have ben-efited more than others (social class *does* make a difference), as a group we have enjoyed easier access to social resources and less competition from groups who have been excluded from full participation. For example, my siblings and I have all attained middle- to upper-middle-class positions in society. On one hand, it would be easy to attribute our relative success to individual effort—our education was through our own efforts and we have all worked hard in our chosen fields. On the other hand, we have been beneficiaries of a system that for members of our group was more likely to reward effort. We were able to attend better than average schools; we had easier access to college, housing, and mortgage loans; and we benefited from assumptions of individuality and trustworthiness. While life has had its struggles, we never had to confront the kinds of obstacles faced by peoples of color in the United States. As Melvin Oliver and Thomas Shapiro have noted in their book *Black Wealth, White Wealth* (1995), this has translated into higher levels of wealth for white Americans, even when compared with African Americans of the same income level. Higher levels of wealth in turn create more opportunities for the future—and for future generations.

What can we say about the present state of the dominant side of dominant-minority relations? In some, but not all, cases, there appears to be a greater sense of inclusiveness. According to survey researchers, attitudes of white Americans toward peoples of color have become more egalitarian and inclusive (e.g., Schuman et al., 1997). I see this when I look at my family—my parents' generation and my own generation. Yet we also know that behavior (and in-depth ideologies, as opposed to attitudes) is more problematic. For example, research shows that whites will still move out of neighborhoods once the percentage of black residents reaches a certain tipping point (Farley & Frey, 1994). Follow-up interviews with white survey respondents find that initial inclusive attitudes (e.g., acceptance of interracial marriage) are qualified or contradicted when explored in depth (Bonilla-Silva, 2001). Racial stereotypes have evolved, often including more complex combinations of race and class. We are also becoming more aware that even unconscious attitudes may have an impact; for example, the response to "black-sounding" names on a resume (Associated Press, 2003).

Seemingly changing attitudes may be problematic in another sense. Dominant-group members may "talk the talk" of equality by supporting equal opportunity in the abstract, but fail to "walk the walk" by supporting specific measures to attain racial equality. It is hard to change a system from which one is the beneficiary. Recently, we have seen the emergence of a new dominant-group racial ideology, "color-blind racism" (Bonilla-Silva, 2001), one that claims that race no longer "matters" and that racism no longer exists save in individual acts of discrimination. It is too easy for whites as a group to claim that slavery was 140 years ago and that "the past is the past" (Bonilla-Silva, 2001: 158). When we say "not today" or "it wasn't me" (Myers, 2003: 538), we ignore the persistent racial inequality built into American institutions—what Joe Feagin (2000: 6) has termed "systemic racism." I do not say this as an exercise in white-bashing, but instead to assert that a realistic accounting of the past and examination of the present leads to the inescapable conclusion that dominant-group members (white European Americans) *continue* to benefit from existing social arrangements.

Unfortunately, the "color-blind" worldview makes change more difficult. If dominant-group members are relatively unaware of their group advantages, then it is even more difficult to see systemic racism and the obstacles facing peoples of color. This then makes it easier to say that racial inequality is the result of circumstance, or the lack of effort or ability on the part of subordinate groups. It even becomes possible to make the claim, as increasing numbers of dominant-group members are doing, that racism *against* whites (e.g., "reverse discrimination") is an emerging social problem and that dominant-group members are increasingly becoming the "victims" in race relations in the United States (Gallagher, 1995; Doane, 1996). To the extent that color-blind racism becomes a dominant racial ideology, I believe that it will become a significant obstacle to addressing racial inequality and pursuing racial justice.

What will be the nature of the dominant group in the future? We know that the United States is becoming more diverse. New immigration from Asia, Latin America, the Caribbean, Africa, the Middle East, and Eastern Europe is creating an even more complex ethnic and racial mosaic. US Census Bureau projections suggest that white European Americans will be a bare majority of the population by 2050. How will the dominant group respond to these changes? Will we see increased white assertion and defensiveness, as has happened in the past when the dominant group has felt itself to be threatened? Will we see, as some have predicted, a new expansion of the boundaries of the dominant group to include selected Latinos, Asian Americans, and multiracial persons, thereby once again increasing dominant-group numbers and power (Bonilla-Silva, 2003; Yancey, 2003)? Or will circumstances lead whites to become more willing to address systemic racism, share power, and work to make the American dream truly open to all? I do know that my son, my nieces, and my nephews will grow up and live their lives in a world that will be significantly different from the one that I experienced. What I do not know is what will be the nature of dominant-minority relations in this society.

references

Associated Press. 2003. "White-Sounding Names Open Job Search Doors." *Hartford Courant,* January 15. Available at www.ctnow.com/business/hc-whitenames.artjan15.story.

Billington, Ray A. 1963 [1938]. *The Protestant Crusade, 1800–1860: A Study of the Origins of American Nativism.* Gloucester, MA: Peter Smith.

Bonilla-Silva, Eduardo. 2001. *White Supremacy and Racism in the Post–Civil Rights Era.* Boulder, CO: Lynne Rienner.

———. 2003. "New Racism, Color-Blind Racism, and the Future of Whiteness in America." In *White Out: The Continuing Significance of Racism,* Ashley Doane and Eduardo Bonilla-Silva, eds. New York: Routledge.

Doane, Alfred Adler. 1960 [1902]. *The Doane Family,* 2nd ed. Boston: Doane Family Association.

Doane, Ashley W., Jr. 1979. "Occupational and Educational Patterns for New Hampshire's Franco-Americans." Report prepared for the New Hampshire Civil Liberties Union, Concord.

———. 1983. "The Franco-Americans of New Hampshire: A Case Study of Ethnicity and Social Stratification." Master's thesis, University of New Hampshire.

———. 1989. "Ethnicity and Nationality: Towards a Class-Based Theoretical Framework." Ph.D. dissertation, University of New Hampshire.

———. 1992. "The Myth of WASP Non-Ethnicity." Paper presented at the annual meeting of the Association for Humanist Sociology, Portland, ME, October 22–24, 1992.

———. 1996. "Contested Terrain: Negotiating Racial Understanding in Public Discourse." *Humanity and Society* 20(4): 32–51.

———. 1997a. "Dominant Group Ethnic Identity in the United States: The Role of 'Hidden' Ethnicity in Intergroup Relations." *Sociological Quarterly* 38: 375–397.

———. 1997b. "White Identity and Race Relations in the 1990s." In *Perspectives on Current Social Problems,* Gregg Lee Carter, ed. Boston: Allyn and Bacon, pp. 151–159.

———. 2003. "Rethinking Whiteness Studies." In *White Out: The Continuing Significance of Racism,* Ashley Doane and Eduardo Bonilla-Silva, eds. New York: Routledge.

Erickson, Charlotte. 1972. *Invisible Immigrants: The Adaptation of English and Scottish Immigrants in Contemporary America.* Coral Gables, FL: University of Miami Press.

Farley, Reynolds, & William H. Frey. 1994. "Changes in the Segregation of Whites from Blacks in the 1980s: Small Steps Toward a More Integrated Society." *American Sociological Review* 59: 23–45.

Feagin, Joe. 2000. *Racist America: Roots, Current Realities, and Future Reparations.* New York: Routledge.

Feagin, Joe, & Clairece Booher Feagin. 1996. *Racial and Ethnic Relations,* 5th ed. Upper Saddle River, NJ: Prentice-Hall.

Gallagher, Charles A. 1995. "White Reconstruction in the University." *Socialist Review* 94 (1–2): 165–187.

Glazer, Nathan, & Daniel Patrick Moynihan. 1963. *Beyond the Melting Pot: The Negroes, Puerto Ricans, Jews, Italians, and Irish of New York City.* Cambridge, MA: MIT Press.

Gordon, Milton M. 1964. *Assimilation in American Life: The Role of Race, Religion, and National Origins.* New York: Oxford University Press.

Hartford Courant. September 29, 2002. "Connecticut Slave Owners in 1790," pp. 16–19.

Lang, Joel. September 29, 2002. "The Plantation Next Door: How Salem Slaves, Wethersfield Onions, and West Indies Sugar Made Connecticut Rich." *Hartford Courant*, pp. 6–13.

Lieberson, Stanley. 1985. "Unhyphenated Whites in the United States." *Ethnic and Racial Studies* 8: 159–180.

Loewen, James W. 1992. "The Truth About the First Thanksgiving." *Monthly Review* 44(6): 12–25.

———. *Lies My Teacher Told Me: Everything Your American History Textbook Got Wrong.* New York: New Press.

Marger, Martin N. 2003. *Race and Ethnic Relations: American and Global Perspectives*, 6th ed. Belmont, CA: Wadsworth.

Myers, John P. 2003. *Dominant-Minority Relations in America*. Boston: Allyn and Bacon.

Oliver, Melvin L., & Thomas M. Shapiro. 1995. *Black Wealth, White Wealth: A New Perspective on Racial Inequality*. New York: Routledge.

Parillo, Vincent. 1994. "Diversity in America: A Socio-historical Analysis." *Sociological Forum* 9: 523–546.

Richter, Daniel K. 2001. *Facing East from Indian Country: A Native History of Early America*. Cambridge, MA: Harvard University Press.

Roediger, David R. 1991. *Wages of Whiteness: Race and the Making of the American Working Class*. London: Verso.

Schuman, Howard, Charlotte Steeh, Lawrence Bobo, & Maria Krysan. 1997. *Racial Attitudes in America: Trends and Interpretations*. Cambridge, MA: Harvard University Press.

Takaki, Ronald. 1993. *A Different Mirror: A History of Multicultural America*. Boston: Little, Brown.

Yancey, George. 2003. *Who Is White? Latinos, Asians, and the New Black/Nonblack Divide*. Boulder, CO: Lynne Rienner.

13

class

Still Alive and Reproducing in the United States

Diana Kendall*

*Elites are elites not because of who they are but because of
who they are in relation to other social actors and institutions.
Elites are made.*

—SHAMUS RAHMAN KHAN (2011)

Many of us are fascinated by elites and how they fit into the United States class structure. My larger research has focused on members of the upper class and documented how this top class possesses a distinct demographic identity and routinely engages in boundary maintenance activities that help preserve their elite status. In this article, I describe how elites maintain and perpetuate their social location in society through their relations to other social actors and institutions in the US class hierarchy.

Although the concept of class is employed in a variety of ways by social scientists, it is most frequently applied in an economic context which refers to levels of income and/or wealth that an individual or family has accumulated. From this approach, in the twenty-first century, income inequality and class divisions have intensified. The rising standard of living in the West basically concealed increasing inequality until the 1980s, when the most

* Kendall, Diana. "Class: Still Alive and Reproducing in the United States." Adapted from "Class in the United States: Not Only Alive but Reproducing" by Diana Kendall, originally published in *Research in Social Stratification and Mobility* 24, no. 1 (2006): 89–104. Reprinted by permission of the author.

affluent US households began earning a larger and larger share of overall income to the extent the top 1 percent earns about one-sixth of all income and the top 10 percent earns about half, leaving the bottom 90 percent with about half of all earned income. Similarly, the distribution of wealth has become more concentrated as well. Wealth refers to the value of a person's or family's economic assets, including income, personal property, and income-producing property (Kendall, 2013). Today in the United States, the top 20 percent owns at least 85 percent of all privately held wealth, leaving the bottom 80 percent with less than 15 percent of such wealth.

However, class is not always used as a strictly objective criteria based on measurable amounts of money or other financial resources: Class can also be used to identify a person's more subjective location in a "social pecking order" based on factors such as one's family background, level of prestige, and social networks. As such, all classes, from the highest to the lowest, are constantly being socially reproduced. Although social reproduction of class occurs across class lines, this process is particularly found among elites who desire to maintain their privilege and pass it on to their children and grandchildren. A key point highlighted is that the US upper class not only exists economically but also socially and in terms of identity and class consciousness. My study of social reproduction shows that many people in local and regional upper classes form stable identities in class terms and that these identities remain features of contemporary life.

Class exists as a salient factor when people think in terms of "us" and "them" in society. The us-versus-them mentality of class-based relations in the local community has been a topic of sociological interest for many years. In the 1950s, scholars showed how members of the upper class created a set of exclusive clubs, luxury residential enclaves, and private social occasions unique to the upper class to ensure that many elites had a protective inner social circle that provided them with proximity to each other and a shield against having to deal with those who were "not our kind of people." There was also elaboration on how the upper-class debutante presentation served as a mechanism by which elites not only introduced their daughters to eligible bachelors but also introduced the young women to high society. This "coming out" ritual indicated that the daughters of privileged families were now full-fledged members of a restricted and exclusive group for which they and their families had fulfilled certain class-based prerequisites. This is an example of stratification by status based on a positive or negative social estimation of honor that is associated with a particular lifestyle expected of people in a specific social circle (Gerth and Mills, 1958). Implicit in these early studies of the upper class was the idea that elites were in the "inner circle," whereas people in other classes were outsiders, not only socially but also in the opportunity structure of the community and perhaps the larger society. In addition to these earlier studies of the upper class, a number of well-known community-based studies have addressed the issue of how class is reproduced not only biologically, but socially.

My research took place over a ten-year period in which I interviewed and observed privileged women in Texas (see Kendall, 2002). The participants generally are from wealthy, old-guard families who share not only an interest in the arts but also an interest—whether or not openly acknowledged—in the social reproduction of the upper class. Almost all of the women in the groups I studied are members of households with an annual income that would place them in the top 1–5 percent of households in this nation. I found that social elites across cities typically engage in similar behavior and have somewhat similar outlooks.

Maintenance and Social Reproduction of the Upper Class

Long-established elite families are in a unique economic and social position to perpetuate the advantages they hold because they have possessed wealth and privilege for several generations. They are not newcomers to privilege and exclusivity, and, for many of them, their primary goal is to maintain the boundaries that protect their elite position and that make it possible for them to pass their advantages on to their children.

My study focused on privileged women because, throughout the history of elite social reproduction, women have played a significant role in maintaining class-based boundaries and fostering cohesion among members of the upper class (Daniels, 1988; Domhoff, 1970, 1998; Odendahl, 1990; Ostrander, 1984; Ostrower, 1995, 2002). Boundary maintenance involves both geographic and social dimensions. In Texas, there is a distinct social geography of the upper class that is reflected in residential housing patterns, exclusive private schools many privileged children attend, by-invitation-only clubs and organizations, and seemingly archaic rituals such as debutante presentations that bring members of the upper class (and some who aspire to the inner circles of the upper class) together as a class-conscious, socially cohesive group.

The Upper-Class Residence, Children's Peer Groups, and "The Bubble"

One of the most significant ways that social class boundary maintenance occurs is through the selection of the family residence, an activity in which privileged women play a major role. The establishment of an upper-class home within a proper upper-class neighborhood is one key way in which both visible and invisible barriers can be created to keep others out and to provide the right social environment for the socialization of the next generation. Another mechanism of boundary maintenance is the highly selective nature of children's peer groups, which I also examine.

Whether stay-at-home moms, full-time community volunteers, or professional women, the women in my study typically indicated that they had been actively involved in the choice of residential location and style for their families. Based on location, type, and quality, an elite family's residence may be both a showplace of conspicuous consumption and a part of the social "bubble": a safe haven that provides the family with comfort, safety, and isolation from those of other social classes. Geographic isolation and exclusivity may be seen by elite parents as related to safety issues and often are described to the children as such. A number of women in my study recalled being repeatedly told during their childhood not to stray outside their own residential area without the protection and supervision of their own or a friend's parents or household employees. For example, "Nancy," a white woman in her mid-30s from a wealthy family, learned the importance of remaining in the "bubble" at an early age:

> We lived in a large brick house on a tree-lined street, but several blocks away there were smaller, wood-frame houses with families living in them. I wanted to play with a child who lived in one of those houses, but my mother repeatedly said, "We don't play with the children who live on [name of street]." When I asked, "Why?" I always got the same answer, "Well, they are different from you and me, and there are plenty of children that you can be friends with on our own street." When I pressed her further, one day Mother blurted

out, "Nancy, I wish you'd quit asking me about that. I've told you time after time that 'They are not our kind of people,' so will you kindly hush up about that?" (Kendall, 2006: 95)

Patterns of residential selection and segregation are found among elites in all major cities: Elite residences tend to be in exclusive urban enclaves, affluent suburbs, and multi-million-dollar gated communities where housing costs prohibit all but the wealthiest families from acquiring a home. As a result, no middle- or lower-income families and few families of color will be the neighbors of elite white families.

Although anyone with sufficient financial resources can acquire a residence in one of the affluent neighborhoods, the goal of elites—particularly those with children—is sufficient social distance and geographical isolation to separate themselves from people of other classes, races, or ethnic groupings and to be in the proximity of others from their own social group. This separation becomes part of the social reproduction of the upper class; whether parents explicitly use such terms or not, elite children quickly learn that some people are "our kind of people" and all others are not. Members of the upper class and the more affluent members of the upper-middle class seek, perhaps above all else, to purchase a home in a prestigious urban neighborhood or a wealthy suburban enclave. Social science literature affirms that residential choice patterns of elites and others are not strictly individual choices: Other practices are also at work at the macro, social structural, level of society that keep people in divergent class groupings segregated.

Residential boundary maintenance is a powerful force in perpetuating class distinctions because upper-class children are taught to have pride in their neighborhoods, and they do not realize that these neighborhoods are not representative of the larger social world. For the most part, elite children are surrounded by others (except for household help) who are similar to themselves. As one respondent stated, "When I was a kid, I thought everybody lived like we did." Preserving the social bubble for children in settings such as these is especially important to elite women because it provides a safe and protective environment from which the children only emerge in supervised and special circumstances.

To further insulate and isolate children in the "bubble," privileged women are careful about their children's play groups. Building social networks and controlling outsiders' access to these networks begins in early childhood for the typical upper-class child, and one early manifestation of such networks is the play group. Consider, for example, why one elite woman in my study believed it was extremely important for her to help her children choose their friends and play groups:

> My children don't really select their own friends. They decide who they like most or have the most fun with in playgroups that we set up for them. Young children don't really know how to go out and find friends of their own, but they enjoy doing activities together that the mothers have set up or that are like playday in the summer at the country club. . . . There are so many sad things that happen to children today, and as a parent, I have a responsibility to keep my kids away from anyone who might harm them. Sometimes I think children with nice things are victimized by other children, like those who come from the "wrong side of the tracks" [holding up the index and third finger of each hand to make visual quotation marks], if you know what I mean. (Kendall, 2006: 96)

Although play groups and play dates are popular ideas among middle- and upper-middle-class parents, elite mothers appear to be uniquely fond of this approach for building their children's social networks. For most of these women, the intended function of the play group has nothing to do with excluding outsiders but rather is based on the belief that children should interact with "others like us who share our family values and act like we want our kids to behave." However, the result of parental play-group management is largely one of promoting upper-class segregation.

Taking control of play groups is also a mechanism used by upper-class parents to ensure that their children will receive the appropriate socialization for an upper-class lifestyle and will not come to question their family's wealth or social position. For upper-class parents, careful selection of members of their child's play group is the key to building social networks for the child, but also has the effect of instilling notions of entitlement in the children. When upper-class children interact only with other privileged children, they compare themselves to others on a within-economic-class basis rather than looking across class lines where invidious distinctions in wealth and opportunity are highly visible. For example, children come to assume that the ownership of multiple luxury vehicles or possession of extravagant amenities in their homes is not unusual.

Prep Schools, Universities, and Upper-Class Reproduction

Children of the upper classes typically attend either private preparatory schools or even highly regarded public schools located within wealthy residential enclaves. The importance of elite private schools in the lives of the privileged is shown by the fact that women like "Gay," an upper-class white woman who was in her mid-20s at the time of these remarks, often seek to secure a position for their offspring in such schools even before the children are born:

> After the obstetrician told me I was pregnant, the first phone call I made was to my husband to tell him. The second call I made was to [an elite private school] to put my [unborn] child on the school's waiting list for four years down the road. I've been extremely happy with my choice and have enrolled my other children in the same school because they learn values that are in keeping with what we try to teach the children at home, and they develop playgroups and friendships with other children like themselves. (Kendall, 2002: 81)

As Gay's statement suggests, upper-class beliefs and values initially taught at home are strengthened in elite private schools and prestigious public schools primarily populated by elites, where students are encouraged to develop a sense of collective identity that involves school, peers, and one's place within the larger society.

As privileged young people create a web of affiliations in dormitories, sporting events, classrooms, and other settings within their schools, they establish ties that, because they are interwoven in such a way as to become indistinguishable from the students' individual identity, will grow and become even more important after graduation. Consequently, to develop solidarity with one's classmates is to develop a form of class solidarity because of the commonalities in beliefs and lived experiences shared over a period of time, frequently without the students being exposed to countervailing belief systems or social networks. Over time, identity with others in the same class is a stronger link than merely some vague perception that they share similar values. Additionally, and most importantly, elite schools convey to students the idea that their privilege is justified (Cookson and

Persell, 1985; Gaztambide-Fernández, 2009; Khan, 2011); this attitude is essential for maintaining an upper-class outlook.

Do Upper-Class Mechanisms of Social Reproduction Work?

Because of the need to socially (as well as biologically) reproduce the upper class in each new generation, elite women use the mechanisms set forth in this article to maintain class-based boundaries and to convey to their children social and cultural capital not as easily available to those in other classes. Do the class reproduction strategies described in this article actually work? I believe the answer is "yes." The social reproduction processes engaged in by privileged women do, in fact, help elite young people become class actors who support upper-class ideologies, and those same processes deny many other children the opportunities that might be available for them in a true democracy.

Do the advantages of the upper class disadvantage other people? Any form of exclusionary practice based on class (or race/ethnicity and gender), even in voluntary organizations and charitable activities, reproduces inequality in the United States. Exclusionary practices provide an unfair advantage to those elites who assume that it is their *right* to possess the most wealth in society, to hold the top positions, and to create a world of advantage for their children while showing little concern for those in the bottom tiers of society, whose labor often helps privileged elites to maintain their dominant position in a capitalist economy where they enjoy a consumer-oriented, leisure-class lifestyle.

references

Cookson, Peter W., Jr., and Caroline Hodges Persell. 1985. *Preparing for Power: America's Elite Boarding Schools.* New York: Basic Books.

Daniels, Arlene Kaplan. 1988. *Invisible Careers.* Chicago: University of Chicago Press.

Domhoff, G. William. 1970. *The Higher Circles.* New York: Random House.

———. 1998. *Who Rules America? Power and Politics in the Year 2000.* Mountain View, CA: Mayfield.

Gaztambide-Fernández, Rubén A. 2009. *The Best of the Best: Becoming Elite at an American Boarding School.* Cambridge, MA: Harvard University Press.

Gerth, H. H., and C. Wright Mills. 1958. *From Max Weber: Essays in Sociology.* New York: Oxford University Press.

Kendall, Diana. 2002. *The Power of Good Deeds: Privileged Women and the Social Reproduction of the Upper Class.* Lanham, MD: Rowman & Littlefield.

———. 2006. "Class in the United States: Not Only Alive but Reproducing." *Research in Social Stratification and Mobility* 24: 89–104.

———. 2013. *Sociology in Our Times*, 9th ed. Belmont, CA: Wadsworth/Cengage.

Khan, Shamus Rahman. 2011. *Privilege: The Making of an Adolescent Elite at St. Paul's School*. Princeton, NJ: Princeton University Press.

Odendahl, Teresa. 1990. *Charity Begins at Home: Generosity and Self-Interest Among the Philanthropic Elite*. New York: Basic Books.

Ostrander, Susan. 1984. *Women of the Upper Class*. Philadelphia: Temple University Press.

Ostrower, Francie. 1995. *Why the Wealthy Give: The Culture of Elite Philanthropy*. Princeton, NJ: Princeton University Press.

———. 2002. *Trustees of Culture: Power, Wealth, and Status on Elite Arts Boards*. Chicago: University of Chicago Press.

14

the everyday impact of christian hegemony

Paul Kivel*

*There is no country in the world where the Christian religion retains
a greater influence over the souls of men than in America.*
— ALEXIS DE TOCQUEVILLE (1831)[1]

Introduction

Historically, there is no shortage of evidence of Christian power and influence. Though Christianity often portrays itself as benign, as a force for
good in the world, the actual story is much more complex than that. What
is at stake here is not just the impact of Christianity but also the role of
Christianity as a determinant of institutions, culture, and behavior through
its centralizing and hierarchical authority structures, its alignment with
political elites, and its militant values.

For the last seventeen centuries ruling elites have used Christian institutions and values to control, exploit, and violate people in many regions
throughout the world. Claiming Christianity to be the only true source
of spiritual salvation, Christian leaders used their religion to sanction
and to justify participation in genocide, colonialism, slavery, cultural ap-
propriation, and other forms of violence and exploitation. Today, in the

---

* "Living in the Shadow of the Cross: Understanding and Resisting the Power and Privilege of Christian Hegemony," by Paul Kivel. www.christianhegemony.org, 2005. Used by
permission of the author.

twenty-first century, can we really speak about Christianity as a dominant force in our lives?

Buried even deeper than the political, military, and economic policies and actions of Christian institutions and individuals there seems to be a dominant Christian worldview which has shaped western culture so profoundly that it is difficult to delineate fully. The dominant form of western Christianity calls for a transcendence of the material world. It gives suffering and death a particular meaning and proclaims that salvation and eternal life are possible, contingent, and exclusively available to some and not to others based on God's judgment. A single person, Jesus, suffered and died to redeem humankind and make this possible. This western Christian story of transcendence, salvation, the purpose of suffering, and the possibility of redemption, as well as a number of related concepts and beliefs, have provided some of the core framework for western languages, art, music, literature, philosophy, architecture, politics, and ritual.

Within this framework there have been a thousand years of crusades against evil, terrorism, and Islam, including US wars in Iraq, Afghanistan, and Pakistan. Within this framework multinational corporate capitalism, colonialism, slavery, and various forms of genocide have ravaged the world, leading us to the brink of ecological destruction. Within this framework women, men and women of color, people who are queer, people who have disabilities, immigrants, and everyone who is not Christian—all those labeled "Other" by dominant Christianity—have been and remain marginalized, exploited, and vulnerable to violence.

What Is Christian Hegemony?

I define Christian hegemony as the everyday, pervasive, and systematic set of Christian values and beliefs, individuals, and institutions that dominate all aspects of our society through the social, political, economic, and cultural power they wield. Nothing is unaffected by Christian hegemony including our personal beliefs and values, our relationships to other people and to the natural environment, and our economic, political, education, health care, criminal/legal, housing, and other social systems.

Christian hegemony as a system of domination is complex, shifting, and operates through the agency of individuals, families, church communities, denominations, parachurch organizations, civil institutions, and through decisions made by members of the ruling class and power elite.

Christian hegemony benefits all Christians, all those raised Christian, and those passing as Christian. However, the concentration of power, wealth, and privilege under Christian hegemony accumulates to the ruling class and the predominantly white male Christian power elite that serve its interests.

At one level Christian hegemony operates through the internalization of dominant western Christian beliefs and values by individuals. Concepts such as original sin, manifest destiny, there is only one truth and Christianity holds it, and man (*sic*) was given dominion over the earth influence the behavior and voting patterns of tens of millions of people in the US.

The power that individual preachers, ministers, and priests have on people's lives is another level of influence. This influence often condones US expansionism abroad, missionary activity towards those who are not Christian, and exclusion and marginalization for groups or behaviors deemed sinful or dangerous by Christians.

Particular churches and some Christian denominations wield very significant political and economic power in our country. For example, the Mormon and Catholic churches and many individual religious leaders and particular churches raised millions of dollars, organized public campaigns, and mobilized constituents to vote for Proposition 8 on the California ballot—a ballot measure that would have made gay marriage illegal.[2]

There is a vast network of parachurch organizations, general tax-supported non-profits such as hospitals, broadcasting networks, publishing houses, lobbying groups, and organizations like Focus on the Family, Prison Fellowship, The Family, World Mission, and thousands of others which wield influence in particular spheres of US society and throughout the world. As just one example, the Child Evangelism Fellowship runs Good News Clubs in *public* schools across the country teaching hundreds of thousands of children to find Jesus and to proselytize to other children.[3]

Another level of Christian dominance is within the power elite, the network of 7,000 to 10,000 predominantly white Christian men who control the largest and most powerful social, political, economic, and cultural institutions in the country. The Koch brothers, Rupert Murdoch, and Bill Gates are examples of power elite members who wield this kind of power.

And finally there is the level that provides the foundation for all the others—the long and deep legacy of Christian ideas, values, practices, policies, icons, and texts that have been produced within dominant western

Christianity over the centuries. That legacy continues to shape our language, culture, and beliefs, and to frame public and foreign policy decisions.

These levels of Christian dominance have substantial personal, interpersonal, institutional, and structural effects in our society. The personal impact shows up in beliefs about heaven and hell, the apocalypse, sin and salvation, and the way that many Christians internalize feelings of superiority, entitlement, judgment, and narrow-mindedness while those who are not Christian may internalize feelings of inferiority, inadequacy, and low self-worth.

The interpersonal effects include the specific acts of discrimination, harassment, and violence directed at those who are not Christian or Christian of the wrong sort, e.g., Muslims or lesbians and gays.

The institutional effects show up in the ways that the policies, practices, and procedures of the health care, educational, and criminal/legal systems favor Christians and Christian values and treat those who are not Christian as abnormal, dangerous, and outside society's circle of caring. The interweaving and cumulative impact of Christian dominance in our institutions create an overall *structure* that is dense, pervasive, and devastating to our society.

The pervasive nature of Christian dominance can be seen in the way that, regardless of our awareness, certain words, symbols, and practices have resonances that influence our thinking and behavior. Words such as "crusade," "inquisition," or even "Christian" symbols like the cross, concepts like evil or hell, practices like public prayer, the torture of prisoners, or the public shaming of women—these and so many more can be triggered and manipulated by ruling elites because of our history of Christian dominance.

Frequently, discussions of Christian power or Christian values focus on the Christian right or other extreme versions of Christianity that are both visible and explicitly Christian. Evangelicals and fundamentalists constitute a powerful force. However, focusing on Christian Evangelicals and fundamentalists without reference to mainstream Christian dominance is similar to talking about the KKK and neo-Nazi groups without talking about institutional racism and white power. Defining the extremists and extreme versions of Christianity as aberrations leaves unexamined the institutions, policies, and practices of mainstream forms of Christianity and gives dominant Christianity itself a deceptively benign status.

Although it may seem confusing, in this discussion we are not talking about Christianity but about western Christian dominance. Christians and Christian institutions have done many beneficial things over the centuries. For example, some Christians and Christian institutions have fed the hungry, set up housing programs, provided medical care, and fought for social justice.

Nor are we talking about individual Christian beliefs and spiritual practices. If you are Christian you might feel a need to defend your religion or religious practice. You might want to say that "that" Christianity is not "my" Christianity. Just as I, as a man who respects women, work to end male violence, and challenge male dominance, might be tempted to say that I have rejected patriarchy and now stand against it. But I still benefit from male privilege, I still (often unwittingly) collude with the exploitation of women (Who made my clothes? Who made my computer?), and I still have to continually challenge internalized forms of male entitlement and superiority in myself. As social justice educator Mamta Motwani Accapadi wrote, "Christians cannot willingly dissolve and disown their Christian privilege because of their individual relationship with their Christian identity."[4]

A hegemonic system provides a worldview—an intellectual framework, a language, and a set of values—that is promoted as common sense, as just the way things are, as unchallengeable. Many of the everyday manifestations of Christian hegemony are often mistaken as non-Christian or secular. See the checklist at the end of the article for many examples of how it plays out in our lives.

Original Christians

The original Christians were West Asian and North African Jews, predominantly Arab. Jesus, Mary, the Apostles, and all of the early leaders in the church were Jewish Arabs of varying ethnic and cultural identities, and with diverse but certainly not white skin tones.

Since then, dominant western Christianity has produced another kind of "original" Christian—one who is white, male, European, and contrasted with and juxtaposed with *Others* such as Jews, pagans, Muslims, white Christian women, heretics, homosexuals, heathens, and people who were lepers, people with disabilities, and those with other physical "conditions." Women, people of color, and many others could become Christians of a sort but they were inferior imitations of the "real" thing because they were contaminated by their difference from the white, male, physically and morally perfect images of God, Adam, Jesus, the Apostles, and a long line of church leaders continuing into the current day. A person from any of these groups was considered more likely to revert to non-Christian ways, more likely to tempt good, i.e., white Christian men and women, away from virtue, and more likely to subvert Christian community norms and thus be a danger to community health and safety in their very being. On the other hand, as a group and taking into account differences in class, this system accords straight, white, male Christians power, prestige, political and economic representation, respect, protection, and credibility.

Key Concepts

There are six key concepts that have come to dominate Christian institutions and shape western culture. Christianity is based on a *binary framework* with a belief in a *cosmic battle between good and evil.* It embraces *love within a theology of hierarchy, dominance, and obedience.* It has a core belief that *people are innately sinful individuals who need to be saved* and they have available to them *one truth, one way to God.* There is *a linear, temporal focus*—God set things going in the beginning, gave us guidelines and a timeline in the Bible, revealed his plan in the natural world, and history is the unfolding of that plan. These powerful concepts frame our foreign and domestic policy—how we think about the world.

Foreign and Domestic Policy

The belief that "you're either with us or against us"[5] is the foundation of a Christian-based foreign policy. Early Christians offered pagans and Jews a choice: "convert or die."[6] Centuries later, Crusaders offered Jews and Muslims the same choice. Later still, indigenous peoples in the Western Hemisphere were told to convert and give up their land or be killed. Today US crusaders for freedom and "free" markets offer similar conditions to countries like Vietnam, Cuba, Iraq, or Afghanistan.

Manifest destiny is the belief that God has a plan for the world moving forward in time towards the final judgment and that the Christian-inspired United States has a special role in the unfolding of that plan. Along with a crusader mentality, belief in the manifest destiny of the US keeps the public supporting the invasion of other countries and a vast network of missionary organizations involving tens of thousands of individuals and billions of dollars of support for proselytizing around the world as well as in our local communities.

Examples of Christian dominance in the public policy arena are everywhere and include:

- Good News Clubs, athletic prayer programs, and other proselytizing efforts in our public schools
- The lack of reproductive rights for women, such as limits on access to contraception alternatives, severe limitations on access to safe abortion options
- Government funding for purity-based programs, such as abstinence-only sex education, zero tolerance, and prohibition campaigns instead of for the proven effectiveness of safer sex, needle-sharing, and other harm-reduction programs
- An economic system based on the invisible hand (whose hand?) of the market
- A criminal/legal morality system that rewards the wealthy (considered to be virtuous) and punishes those who are poor, are sexually active, or use substances deemed to be illegal (considered to be sinful)
- Lack of civil, worker, and human rights in Christian institutions and organizations
- Large-scale Christian Zionist support for the Israeli occupation of Palestine
- Intervention by groups such as The Family in the internal affairs of other countries
- Widespread ecological destruction based on the belief that God gave humans dominion over the earth
- Lack of full civil and human rights for lesbians, gays, bisexuals, and people who are transgender
- Widespread support and use of corporal punishment by parents and school personnel

Christian Allies

An ally is someone who uses their privilege and their resources to stand with those under attack and to dismantle systems of oppression. There have always been Christian dissidents—those individuals and groups who rejected dominant interpretations of the meaning of Christianity or the political, economic, and social role of the church.

There is also a long and honorable social justice tradition in Christianity, derived from the Jewish prophetic tradition in the Bible, which has challenged injustice in its many manifestations. This resistance has continued in the role of black churches, the development of the social gospel, and the liberation theology movement. There are many Christians today working for peace and justice.

In contemporary times, some Christian churches have challenged US wars of aggression, supported majority world liberation struggles, worked for economic, racial, and gender justice, fought for civil and human rights, and worked diligently to challenge Christian hegemony within Christian organizations. They have also created alternative feminist-, black-, Native American-, Latino-, gay-, and social justice–focused churches and organizations. Christian dissidents and liberation theologians[7] continue to try to reclaim Christianity.

What's a Christian Ally to Do?

If you are Christian or were raised Christian, there are many concrete things you can do to counter Christian hegemony.

- Learn the history of Christianity and its impact on other peoples.
- Learn the history of the denomination that you belong to and/or grew up in.
- Understand and acknowledge the benefits you gain from being Christian in the United States.
- Use your privilege to support the struggles of non-Christian peoples throughout the world for land, autonomy, independence, reparations, and justice.
- Notice the operation of Christian hegemony in your everyday life.
- Learn how to raise these issues with other Christians.
- Challenge organizational and institutional policies that perpetuate Christian hegemony.
- Challenge public exhibitions of Christianity.
- Respect other peoples' sacred places, rituals, sacred objects, and culture—don't appropriate them in any way.

- Support the First Amendment separation of church and state and work for religious pluralism.
- Challenge missionary programs.
- Challenge attempts to justify US imperialism by appeals to the special, superior, or righteous role that the US should play as a Christian, civilized, democratic, free-market, or human rights–based society.
- Examine the ways that you may have internalized feelings of superiority or negative judgment of others, especially those from marginalized or non-Christian groups based on Christian teachings.
- Examine the ways that you may have internalized judgments about yourself based on Christian teachings.
- Examine the ways that you may have cut yourself off from your body, from natural expressions of your sexuality or spirituality, from connections to the natural world, or from particular groups, ethnicities, behaviors, or cultures because of Christian teachings.
- Avoid excusing hurtful behavior or policies because of the good intent of their perpetrators.
- Look for the complexity in situations and people and avoid reducing things to an artificial either/or dynamic.
- Don't assume that other people you meet are Christian—or should be.

No living Christian created the system of Christian hegemony that we live within. In that sense none is guilty. But Christians are responsible for their response to it, for the way that they show up as allies in the struggle to build a just society.

All of us, Christian or not, working to create a world without hate, terror, exploitation, and violence must identify the internalization of Christian ideology in our thinking and eliminate its negative consequences from our behavior. In addition, we must learn effective techniques for educating people about Christian hegemony and for organizing to challenge its power.

Finally, we must free ourselves from the restraints it has imposed on our imaginations so that we can establish relationships with ourselves, other people, and all living things built on values of mutuality, cooperation, sustainability, and interdependence with all life.

Living in a Christian-Dominant Culture Checklist[8]

Please check the following that apply to you:

1. You have ever attended church regularly.
2. You ever attended Sunday school as a child, or attended church periodically, e.g., during Christian holidays.
3. You ever attended a Christian-based recreational organization as a young person, such as the YMCA or YWCA, or church-based summer camp, or participated in a program of a nonreligious youth organization that was based in Christian beliefs, such as the Girl Scouts and Boy Scouts.
4. You were ever told or instructed by a Christian or by a Christian authority figure, such as a minister, priest, teacher, parent, public official, or counselor, that things that you do with your body, sex with others, or sex by yourself was sinful or unclean.
5. You were ever told by a Christian or Christian authority figure that sexual acts other than intercourse between a man and a woman, or sexual orientations other than heterosexual, are sinful or unclean.
6. You were ever told or instructed by a Christian or Christian authority figure that women are unclean, that women are the source of temptation, or that they are the source of sin or evil.
7. You have ever heard heaven and good described as light or white and hell and evil described as dark or black.
8. You have ever been told something you did was sinful or evil, or that you were sinful or evil.
9. You have ever noticed that a Christian theological either/or framework of good/evil, black/white, sinner/saved is used by you, people around you, or is prominent in mainstream culture.
10. You have ever been approached by family members, friends, or strangers trying to convince you to become Christian or a Christian of a particular kind.
11. You have ever been rejected in any way by family or community members because you were not Christian or were not Christian enough.
12. You have ever found that, in your community, the church is a major center of social life that influences those around you and is difficult to avoid.
13. You have ever taken Christian holidays such as Christmas or Easter off, whether you practice them as Christian holidays or not, or have taken Sunday off or think of it, in any way, as a day of rest.
14. You have ever been given a school vacation or paid holiday related to Christmas or Easter when school vacations or paid holidays for

non-Christian religious celebrations, such as Ramadan or the Jewish High Holidays, were not observed.

15. The public institutions you use, such as offices, buildings, banks, parking meters, the post office, libraries, and stores, are open on Fridays and Saturdays but closed on Sundays.

16. When you write the date, the calendar of time you use calculates the year from the birth of Jesus and is divided into two segments, one before his birth and one after it.

17. You have ever seen a public institution in your community, such as a school, hospital, or city hall, decorated with Christian symbols, e.g., Christmas trees, wreathes, Jesus, nativity scenes, or crosses.

18. If you wanted to, you could easily find Christian music, TV shows, movies, and places of worship.

19. You can easily access Christmas- or Easter-related music, stories, greeting cards, films, and TV shows at the appropriate times of the year.

20. You have ever received public services—medical care, family planning, food, shelter, or substance-abuse treatment—from a Christian-based organization or public services that were marked by Christian beliefs and practices, e.g., Alcoholics Anonymous or other 12-step programs, pro-life family planning, hospitals, etc.

21. You daily use currency that includes Christian words or symbols, such as the phrase "in God we trust" (the "god" in this phrase does not refer to Allah, Ogun, Shiva, the goddess, or the great spirit).

22. You have ever received an educational, job training, job, housing, or other opportunity where Jews, Muslims, Buddhists, or other non-Christians were screened out or discriminated against.

23. You have ever been told that a war or invasion, historical or current, was justified because those who were attacked were heathens, infidels, unbelievers, pagans, terrorists, evil, sinners, or fundamentalists of a non-Christian religion.

24. Your foreparents or ancestors were ever subject to invasion, forced conversion, or the use of missionaries as part of a colonization process either in the US or in another part of the world.

25. In your community or metropolitan area, there have been hate crimes against Jews, Muslims, gays, people who are transgender, women, or others based on the perpetrator's Christian beliefs.

26. You have ever attended public nonreligious functions, such as civic or governmental meetings, which were convened with Christian blessings, references, or prayers.

27. You have ever been asked or commanded to sing or recite, in public, material which had Christian references, such as the Pledge of Allegiance, "The Battle Hymn of the Republic," or "America, the Beautiful."

28. You have ever heard the US referred to as a Christian or God-fearing country.

29. As a young person you were ever read or told to read Christian-themed stories that were not identified as such, for example, *The Chronicles of Narnia, The Last of the Mohicans, Little House on the Prairie, Doctor Doolittle, Charlie and the Chocolate Factory, Babar, Indian in the Cupboard*, or the Grimm Brothers' fairy tales.

30. You or young people you know have ever played video games in which white people colonized, attacked, killed, or "converted" darker-skinned people, games in which women were physically brutalized or sexually assaulted, or games where there were "implicit stereotypes of colonial domination."[9]

31. You have ever viewed Christian-themed movies that were not identified as such, for example, *Star Wars; The Matrix; The Lion, the Witch, and the Wardrobe; Tarzan.*

32. You have ever thought of yourself as non-Christian or not religious, but when you think about it have had a Christian upbringing or have been influenced by Christian rituals and values.

33. You have any feelings of discomfort, reluctance, fear, or defensiveness in talking about the major impact Christianity has had on you and on our society.

notes

1. Alexis de Tocqueville, "Democracy in America," trans. Henry Reeve (London: Saunders and Otley, 1835), chapter 17. Quoted in Stephen Prothero, *American Jesus: How the Son of God Became a National Icon* (New York: Farrar, Straus, and Giroux, 2003), 6.

2. ProtectMarriage, the official proponent of Proposition 8, estimates that about half the donations it received came from Mormon sources, and that LDS church members made up somewhere between 80% and 90% of the volunteers for early door-to-door canvassing. Jesse McKinley and Kirk Johnson, "Mormons Tipped Scale in Ban on Gay Marriage," *New York Times,* November 14, 2008, www.nytimes.com/2008/11/15/us/ politics/15marriage. html?_r=3&pagewanted=1&hp&oref=slogin.

3. Katherine Stewart, *The Good News Club: The Christian Right's Stealth Assault on America's Children* (New York: PublicAffairs, 2012), 45.

4. Mamta Motwani Accapadi, "Christmas in a Cultural Center," in Warren Blumenfeld et al., *Investigating Christian Privilege and Religious Oppression in the United States* (Dordrecht, Netherlands: Sense Publishers, 2008), 26.

5. This is a phrase that George W. Bush used just days after the 9/11 attacks.

6. Conversion did not mean acceptance or safety but was simply less life-threatening.

7. Such as Cornel West, Matthew Fox, Rita Nakashima Brock, Mary Radford Reuther, James Cone, Howard Thurmond, Tricia West, Karen Armstrong, Catherine Keller, and thousands of others, as well as the multitude of majority world cohorts.

8. © 2004. Adapted from Allan Creighton by Paul Kivel with input by Luz Guerra, Nell Myhand, Hugh Vasquez, and Shirley Yee.

9. The phrase is from Ziauddin Sardar, *Postmodernism and the Other: The New Imperialism of Western Culture* (London: Pluto Press, 1998), 116.

15

just because it's ableist doesn't mean it's bad

Cara Liebowitz*

I see the word ableism getting flung around a lot lately. Most of the time, it's justified ableism. But people toss it at others like a knife. Like a weapon. Like it's a word that's meant to hurt. And then the recipients, the ones who are being informed of their ableism, get offended and very hurt, because the connotation associated with all these -isms is that they're **bad, very bad** and if you're an ableist, then you're a horrible horrible person who needs to go sit in a corner and shut up.

Ableism doesn't mean you hate disabled people. It doesn't mean you're an evil person. It doesn't even mean you think disabled people aren't capable of anything, although all of those qualifiers can certainly fall under ableism. Ableism is the **system of oppression** that faces disabled people in our society, a system that marks disabled people as inferior and most importantly, **other**. It doesn't have to be done with malice to be ableism. It doesn't even have to be done with conscious intent. Ableism is separating society into *us* and *them*, sequestering disabled people into this category of not-entirely-human, mythical type people that are: a) *so sad and tragic* and/or b) *sooo inspiring!!*

Ableism is dictating that there is a right, a "normal" way to be, and disabled people aren't it. Ableism is merely "tolerating" us instead of accepting

---

* Liebowitz, Cara . "Just because it's ableist doesn't mean it's bad." Originally published at http://thatcrazycrippledchick.blogspot.com/2012/03/just-because-its-ableist-doesnt-mean .html and later at https://disabilityrightnow.wordpress.com/2012/03/28/just-because-its -ableist-doesnt-mean-its-bad/. Reprinted by permission of the author.

us for who we are and embracing the differences that make us unique. Ableism is preaching that diversity makes us stronger, and then conveniently leaving disability out of that equation. Ableism is believing that we have a lesser life, that we suffer, because we are disabled.

Ableism is "otherizing" us. Ableism is using language that *really has* been used over generations to attack disabled people, to tell us that we are not normal and as such, we are less than human. And ableism is using that language without any idea what it has done, how many people it's hurt, because society doesn't want us to know how, in a society that's supposed to have conquered discrimination the way we conquered countries, millions and millions of people were systematically threatened, bullied, and slaughtered. Ableism is never speaking about disability history, never even *knowing* that there *is* a history, because our history is not considered history. At best, our struggle for rights is largely viewed as a cute little adolescent rebellion, complete with whining protests and stomping of feet. At worst, it is completely wiped from the collective consciousness, because the world doesn't want to see us, hear us, acknowledge our existence beyond using us, our stories, as a tool to make the privileged feel better about themselves. Ableism is using us as scare tactics, as examples of what you don't want to be. Ableism is assuming that our lives are inherently less worth living than yours.

Ableism is having only one definition of disability, and only viewing a disabled person as one way. Ableism is calling the rest of us fakers and benefit scroungers, because we don't fit *your* definition of disability. Ableism is cutting the services that we need to survive. Ableism is putting disabled people in a box, a box that is never opened and has very clear edges. Ableism is never recognizing that you or someone you know may be disabled, because they have a productive life. Ableism is thinking that it is okay, even commendable, for disabled people to want to die, because our lives are not worth living. Ableism is killing us before we have the chance to live, all because of a pre-conceived notion of what our lives will be like.

Ableism is warping the public notion of an *entire group of people* as "so smiley and happy all the time!" Ableism is reducing us to a caricature of human beings, painting us all as one shade of a color, when in fact we are as diverse as any other group of people. Ableism is dividing a diverse community into "high functioning" and "low functioning" and deciding that only those who fit your idea of "high functioning" can possibly have anything to say. Ableism is defining disability as solely an unfortunate happening, and not recognizing the social and cultural factors that oppress us. Ableism is denying that you have privilege, that you can feel safe, because you are non-disabled. Ableism is a world that is centered on the nondisabled, instead of being welcoming for everyone. And truth be told? Ableism is claiming that there *is* no ableism.

You don't have to know that ableism exists to be an ableist. Nor does being an ableist mean that you are a horrible, soulless person. Being an ableist just means that you have privilege you need to acknowledge, and patterns of thought that you need to change. So what should you do if someone calls you out on your ableism? Take a step back. Reflect on your privilege and what you said or did. Recognize why someone may take offense at that. If you don't understand why it's ableist, don't start pointing fingers at the other person, claiming that they are oversensitive. Ask politely, and think on their answer. Apologize, and learn a lesson. You are not evil because you are an ableist. You are simply an ableist. So take the opportunity to learn about your own privilege. Hopefully, you'll come away knowing more than you did before.

discussion questions and activities

Discussion or Journal Questions

1. What were some of the most powerful and memorable insights you gained? In the first section, you examined some of the forms of privilege you benefit from. We all share the experience of benefitting from some form of privilege. Is it possible to opt out? To refuse to benefit from your privilege?
2. What is intersectionality? How does examining intersectionality change our understanding of our privilege?
3. Re-read and respond to the three questions posed by Messner at the end of his chapter.
4. Each chapter in this section examines examples of the ways in which privilege is reproduced and maintained. Identify examples of how this occurs at the individual level as well as at the level of social systems.
5. Individual behaviors both shape and are shaped by social systems. Identify examples in this section of how this occurs in terms of the maintenance of privilege.
6. Kendall examines the reproduction of class privilege. How does gender shape the ways in which women are involved in perpetuating class privilege?
7. Select another social identity, and examine some of the ways in which is it reproduced and maintained over generations.
8. Identify examples of resistance found in these readings.

Personal Connections

The following questions and activities are designed to be completed either on your own or in class and then discussed as a group with others. As you share your insights with others, think about the patterns and similarities that emerge, as well as the differences among your answers.

A. The Messages We Learn

- Identify three of the most significant socializing institutions in your life, such as family, education, religion, media, sports, law, criminal justice, and so forth. For each institution, list the key messages you received about the following social identities and specific identity groups: race, gender, class, sexual identity, religion, and ability. Have the messages been consistent? Have you heard more about some classifications than others?
- Examining the messages identified above, what are some of the ways in which you have experienced or witnessed the reproduction and maintenance of privilege? Discuss one example for each of the institutions you examined.

B. Abandoning the Path of Least Resistance

- Identify at least five specific moments/examples throughout your life when you have taken the path of least resistance, and why.
- Now identify one specific example in your life today where you see yourself taking the path of least resistance. Why? How does it contribute to the status quo of inequality?
- What makes it difficult to **not** choose the path of least resistance? What are we afraid of? What are the risks? What can we do to make alternative paths more visible? More appealing or compelling?
- Try **not** taking the path of least resistance. How can you change your behavior in one specific case? Select an example where you can change your behavior right now (for example, if you hang out with a group of friends that make racist, sexist, or anti-Semitic jokes, and you usually just ignore it, choose to say something next time).
- After making this change, discuss the experience and describe what it felt like. What were the results? Did it have any immediate impact on you or others? Depending upon what you have changed, is this a change you think you can continue to embrace? Work on responding to this question as you work through the next two sections of this text.

part three

intersections: the complicated reality

The essays in this section further complicate our understanding of privilege by inviting us to hold aloft multiple dimensions at the same time. For example, although we know that men are privileged over women, Michael Kimmel and Bethany Coston ask: What about gay men or working-class men or disabled men? What sort of strategies do these men use to neutralize their marginality, and do they do it at the expense of women in one area in which they are privileged?

And what about white gay men, asks Alan Bérubé? Do they not benefit from racial privilege even as they suffer from heterosexism? Kortney Ziegler introduces another dimension into the discussion. By looking specifically at black transmen, Ziegler reveals just how entangled these webs of privilege and marginalization really are. And what of gay Jewish men, asks Seth Goren—doubly marginalized by sexuality and religion, yes, but also, still privileged by gender?

Sometimes privilege based on one status ends up looking like privilege based on something else. For example, although Muslims are marginalized by religion, this is often "read" as ethnicity and nationality—that is, as racial privilege as all people from the Middle East are assumed to be Muslim. John Tehranian asks, what about Middle Eastern Christians?

16

seeing privilege where it isn't

Marginalized Masculinities and the Intersectionality of Privilege

Michael S. Kimmel and Bethany M. Coston*

"Privilege is invisible to those who have it" has become a touchstone epigram for work on the "super-ordinate"—that is, white people, men, heterosexuals, and the middle class. When one is privileged by class, or race or gender or sexuality, one rarely sees exactly how the dynamics of privilege work. Thus, pedagogical tools such as Peggy McIntosh's (1988) "invisible knapsack" and the Male Privilege Checklist or the "heterosexual questionnaire" have become staples in college classes.

Yet sometimes these efforts posit a universal and dichotomous understanding of privilege: one either has it or one does not. The notion of intersectionality complicates this binary understanding. Occasionally a document breaks through those tight containers, such as Jewel Woods's (2010) Black Male Privileges Checklist, but such examples are rare.

We propose to investigate sites of inequality within an overall structure of privilege. Specifically, we look at three groups of men—disabled men, gay men, and working-class men—to explore the dynamics of having privilege in one sphere but being unprivileged in another arena. What does it

*Kimmel, Michael, and Bethany M. Coston. "Seeing Privilege Where It Isn't: Marginalized Masculinities and the Intersectionality of Privilege," Article first published online: March 19, 2012. *Journal of Social Issues* 68, no. 1, March 2012, pp. 97–111. DOI: 10.1111/j.1540-4560.2011.01738.x. © 2012 The Society for the Psychological Study of Social Issues. Reprinted by permission of John Wiley and Sons.

161

mean to be privileged by gender and simultaneously marginalized by class, sexuality, or bodily status?

This is especially important, we argue, because for men, the dynamics of removing privilege involve assumptions of emasculation—exclusion from that category that would confer privilege. Gender is the mechanism by which the marginalized are marginalized. That is, gay, working-class, or disabled men are seen as "not-men" in the popular discourse of their marginalization. It is their masculinity—the site of privilege—that is specifically targeted as the grounds for exclusion from the site of privilege. Thus, though men, they often see themselves as reaping few, if any, of the benefits of their privileged status as men.

And yet, of course, they do reap those benefits. But often such benefits are less visible, since marginalized men are less likely to see a reduced masculinity dividend as much compensation for their marginalization. This chapter will explore these complex dynamics.

Doing Gender and the Matrix of Oppression

In the United States, there is a set of idealized standards for men. These standards include being brave, dependable, and strong, emotionally stable, as well as critical, logical, and rational. The ideal male is supposed to be not only wealthy, but also in a position of power over others. Two words sum up the expectations for men: hegemonic masculinity (cf. Connell, 1995)—that is, the predominant, overpowering concept of what it is to be a "real man."

The idealized notion of masculinity operates as both an ideology and a set of normative constraints. It offers a set of traits, attitudes, and behaviors (the "male role"), as well as organizing institutional relationships among groups of women and men. Gender operates at the level of interaction (one can be said to "do" gender through interaction) as well as an identity (one can be said to "have" gender, as in the sum total of socialized attitudes and traits). Gender can also be observed within the institutionally organized sets of practices at the macro-level—states, markets, and the like all express and reproduce gender arrangements. One of the more popular ways to see gender is as an accomplishment; an everyday, interactional activity that reinforces itself via our activities and relationships. "Doing gender involves a complex of socially guided perceptual, interactional, and micropolitical activities that cast particular pursuits as expressions of masculine and feminine 'natures'" (West & Zimmerman, 1987).

These "natures," or social *norms* for a particular gender, are largely internalized by the men and women who live in a society, consciously and otherwise. In other words, these social norms become personal identities. Moreover, it is through the intimate and intricate process of daily interaction with others that we fully achieve our gender, and are seen as valid and appropriate gendered beings. For men, masculinity often includes preoccupation with *proving* gender to others. Indeed, "in presenting ourselves as a gendered person, we are making ourselves accountable—we are purposefully acting in such a way as to be able to be recognized as gendered" (West & Fenstermaker, 1995).

Society is full of men who have embraced traditional gender ideologies—even those who might otherwise be marginalized. While the men we discuss below may operate within oppression in one aspect of their lives, they have access to alternate sites of privilege via the rest of their demographics. A working-class man, for example, may also be white and have access to white privilege and male privilege. What is interesting is how these men choose to navigate and access their privilege within the confines of a particular social role that limits, devalues, and often stigmatizes them as "not-men."

Marginalization requires the problematization of the category (in this case masculinity) so that privilege is rendered invisible. And yet, at the same time, marginalization also frames power and privilege from an interesting vantage point; it offers a seemingly existential choice: to over-conform to the dominant view of masculinity as a way to stake a claim to it or to resist the hegemonic and develop a masculinity of resistance.

The commonalities within the somewhat arbitrary categories (race, class, sexuality, etc.) are often exaggerated and the behavior of the most dominant group within the category (e.g., rich, straight, white men) becomes idealized as the only appropriate way to fulfill one social role. "This conceptualization is then employed as a means of excluding and stigmatizing those who do not or cannot live up to these standards. This process of 'doing difference' is realized in constant interpersonal interactions that reaffirm and reproduce social structure" (West & Fenstermaker, 1995).

It is important to realize that masculinity is extremely diverse, not homogenous, unchanging, fixed, or undifferentiated. Different versions of masculinities coexist at any given historical period and can even coexist within different groups. However, it is this diversity and coexistence that creates a space for marginalization. "The dominant group needs a way to justify its dominance—that difference is inferior" (Cheng, 2008).

Dynamics of Marginalization and Stigma

Marginalization is both gendered and dynamic. How marginalized groups respond to the problematization of masculinity as the dynamic of their marginalization is the central interest of this chapter. How do marginalized men respond to the problematization of their masculinity as they are marginalized by class, sexuality, or disability status?

Goffman's (1963) understanding of stigma may be of use to explicate this dynamic. Stigma is a stain, a mark, and "spoiled identity," Goffman writes, an attribute that changes you "from a whole and usual person to a tainted and discounted one." People with stigmatized attributes are constantly practicing various strategies to ensure minimal damage. Since being stigmatized will "spoil" your identity, you are likely to attempt to alleviate it.

Goffman identified three strategies to neutralize stigma and revive a spoiled identity. He listed them in order of increased social power—the more power you have, the more you can try to redefine the situation (these terms reflect the era in which he was writing, since he obviously uses the civil rights movement as the reference). They are:

Minstrelization: If you're virtually alone and have very little power, you can overconform to the stereotypes that others have about you. To act like a minstrel, Goffman says, is to *exaggerate* the differences between the stigmatized and the dominant group. Thus, for example, did African Americans overact as happy-go-lucky entertainers when they had no other recourse. Contemporary examples might be women who act "ultrafeminine"— helpless and dependent—in potentially harassing situations, or gay men who really "camp it up," like Carson Kressley on *Queer Eye for the Straight Guy*. Note that minstrels exaggerate difference in the face of those with more power; when they are with other stigmatized people, they may laugh about the fact that the powerful "actually think we're like this!" That's often the only sort of power that they feel they have.

Normification: If you have even a small amount of power, you might try to *minimize* the differences between the stigmatized groups. "Look," you'll say, "we're the same as you are, so there is no difference to discriminate against us." Normification is the strategy that the stigmatized use to enter institutions formerly closed to them, like when women entered the military or when black people ran for public office. Normification is the process that gays and lesbians refer to when they argue for same-sex marriage, or that women use when they say they want to be engineers or physicists. Normification involves exaggerating the similarities and downplaying the differences.

Militant chauvinism: When your group's level of power and organization is highest, you may decide to again *maximize* differences with the dominant group. But militant chauvinists don't just say "we're different," they say "we're also better." For example, there are groups of African Americans ("Afrocentrists" or even some members of the Nation of Islam) who proclaim black superiority. Some feminist women proclaim that women's ways are better than the dominant "male" way. These trends try to turn the tables on the dominant group. (Warning: Do not attempt this if you are the only member of your group in a confrontation with members of the dominant group.)

These three responses depend on the size and strength of the stigmatized group. If you're alone, minstrelizing may be a lifesaving technique. If there are many of you and you are strong, you might try to militantly turn the tables.

However, we might see these three strategic responses to stigma through a somewhat different lens. It's clear that normification is a strategy of conformity, a strategy that minimizes the differences between the dominant group and the stigmatized group. Normifiers, therefore, are likely to accept the dominant group's definition of the situation; their only strategy is to demonstrate that there is no reason for them to be excluded from the dominant category. By contrast, both minstrels and militant chauvinists can be said to be resisters. Minstrelizing exaggerates the differences between the dominant and marginalized groups, by seeming to accept the terms of marginalization as legitimate. Minstrels say, in effect, "Yes, you are right to marginalize us. We are not real men as you define masculinity." However, behind the scenes, with other similarly marginalized men, they may also critique the criteria by which they are judged and found wanting. Militant chauvinists likewise resist dominant conceptions by exaggerating the differences between the dominant group and the marginalized group. However, with greater resources, the marginalized can also assert that the dominant group cannot actually approximate the traits and behaviors of the marginalized; indeed, the marginalized may be so precisely because the dominant group fears the marginalized's power.

In this sense, the overconformity of normification accepts the criteria that the dominant group uses to maintain its power; normifiers simply want to be included. By contrast, both minstrelizers and militant chauvinists resist their marginalization by rejecting the criteria by which they are marginalized.

We realize that it might also seem to be arguable in the exact opposite frame—that, for example, normifiers may be seen to be resisting their own marginalization, while minstrelizers and militant chauvinists accept their marginalization and overconform to those stereotypic characterizations that the dominant culture may hold about them. However, we argue that resistance comes in the posture toward those criteria themselves: normifiers accept the criteria and make efforts to demonstrate their legitimate claim for inclusion. Minstrelizers and militant chauvinists turn the criteria on their head, play with them paradoxically, and even suggest that the dominant culture is impoverished for being unable to express those traits.

In this way, marginalized men may present to us overconformity to hegemonic masculinity and resistance to it.

Disabled Men

Discrimination against men with disabilities is pervasive in American society, and issues of power, dominance, and hegemonic masculinity are the basis. Over time, hegemonic masculinity has grown to encompass all aspects of social and cultural power, and the discrimination that arises can have an alarmingly negative effect on a man and his identity. Disabled men do not meet the unquestioned and idealized standard of appearance, behavior, and emotion for men. The values of capitalist societies based on male dominance are dedicated to warrior values, and to a frantic ablebodiedness represented through aggressive sports and risk-taking activities that do not make room for those with disabilities.

For example, one man interviewed by Robertson (2011) tells the story of his confrontations with those who discriminate against him. Frank says,

If somebody doesn't want to speak to me 'cause I'm in a chair, or they shout at me 'cause I'm in a chair, I wanna know why, why they feel they have to shout. I'm not deaf you know. If they did it once and I told them and they didn't do it again, that'd be fair enough. But if they keep doing it then that would annoy me and if they didn't know that I could stand up then I'd put my brakes on and I'd stand up and I'd tell them face-to-face. If they won't listen, then I'll intimidate them, so they will listen, because it's important. (p. 12)

Scholars seem to agree that terms such as "disability" and "impairment" refer to limitations in function resulting from physiological, psychological, and anatomical dysfunction of bodies (including minds), causing restrictions in a person's ability to perform culturally defined normal human activities (World Health Organization, 1980). Normal life activities are defined as walking, talking, using any of the senses, working, and/or caring for oneself.

Men with physical disabilities have to find ways to express themselves within the role of "disabled." Emotional expression is not compatible with the aforementioned traits because it signifies vulnerability; in this way, men, especially disabled men, must avoid emotional expression. If they fail in stoicism, discrimination in the form of pejorative words ("cripple," "wimp," "retard") is sometimes used to suppress or condemn the outward expressions of vulnerability.

But men with disabilities don't need verbal reminders of their "not-men" status. Even without words, their social position, their lack of power over themselves (let alone others), leads them to understand more fully their lacking masculinity. One man, Vernon, detailed these feelings specifically:

Yeah, 'cause though you know you're still a man, I've ended up in a chair, and I don't feel like a red-blooded man. I don't feel I can handle 10 pints and get a woman and just do the business with them and forget it, like most young people do. You feel compromised and still sort of feeling like "will I be able to satisfy my partner." Not just sexually, other ways, like DIY, jobs round the house and all sorts. (Robertson, 2011, pp. 8–9)

It seems that in the presence of their disability, these men are often left with three coping strategies: they can reformulate their ideas of masculinity (minstrelize); rely on and promote certain hegemonic ideals of masculinity (normify); or reject the mass societal norms and deny the norms' importance, creating another set of standards for themselves (militant chauvinism) (Gerschick & Miller, 1995).

When reformulating ideas of masculinity, these men usually focus on personal strengths and abilities, regardless of the ideal standards. This can include maneuvering an electric wheelchair or driving a specially equipped vehicle, tasks that would be very difficult for other people. Men who rely on hegemonic ideals are typically very aware of others' opinions of masculinity. These men internalize ideals such as physical and sexual prowess, and athleticism, even though it can be nearly impossible for them to meet these standards. Then there are men who reject hegemonic masculinity. These men believe that masculine norms are wrong; they sometimes form their own standards for masculinity, which often go against what society thinks is right for men. Some men even try devaluing masculinity's importance altogether. The operative word is "try," because despite men's best efforts to reformulate or reject hegemonic masculinity, the expectations and ideals for men are far more pervasive than can be controlled. Many men trying to reformulate and reject masculine standards often end up "doing" gender appropriately in one aspect of life or another.

Indeed, some men find that hypermasculinity is the best strategy. Wedgwood (2011) interviewed disabled men and Carlos was certainly one who appreciated gender conformity:

> The thrill you get out of doing it [playing contact sports] because I'm an adrenaline junkie! [laughs] Contact for me, gets your adrenaline going, gets your blood going and it's a rush. . . . If I have a really hard match and I'm getting bruised and getting smashed in there and I'm still trying to go for the ball and I keep getting hit—that's what I love about contact sports—I keep getting hit and everything and still getting up. (p. 14)

Scott Hogsett, a wheelchair rugby player, detailed this feeling as well in the movie *Murderball* when he discussed some people's perceptions that their Special Olympics sport wasn't difficult or a "real" sport. He said, "We're not going for a hug. We're going for a fucking gold medal."

However, as Erving Goffman (1963) writes, "The stigmatized individual tends to hold the same beliefs about identity that we do. . . . His deepest feelings about what he is may be his sense of being a 'normal person,' a human being like anyone else" (p. 116). Failing to maintain the hegemonic norms for masculinity has a direct, sometimes negative psychological effect. People tend to judge themselves and measure their worth based upon an intersubjective, sometimes impossible reality. Goffman (1963) goes on to say any man who fails to meet the social standards for masculinity is "likely to view himself—during moments at least—as unworthy, incomplete, and inferior" (p. 128). Identity, self-worth, and confidence depend on whether he accepts, conforms to, or relies on the social norms.

Men with disabilities are no strangers to accepting and relying upon social norms of masculinity. Despite their sometimes stigmatized status, they do have access to sites of privilege. For instance, disability has emerged as an important niche for expansion by prostitution industries. In some countries, giving the disabled access to open and free sexual rights has been argued as a way to make prostitution respectable and to suggest that it serves a noble purpose. As a matter of fact, in February 2008 the sex-industry lobby group Sexual Freedom Coalition, in the UK, staged a demonstration of disabled men against proposed legislation that would have restricted men's rights to access prostituted women.

Another example of the normification of disabled men has been around sexuality. Recently narratives of how disabled men utilize prostitutes as sex tourists and within their own countries have emerged. For example, a 2008 documentary, *Real Life: For One Night Only,* aired in the UK and Australia, is described in an Australian newspaper review as a "charming documentary on the sexuality of disabled people" (Jeffreys, 2008). Here, a disabled man is taken on a trip to Spain by his parents to access prostituted women in a special brothel for "people with various disabilities" (Schwartz, 2008). In this way, he claims male privilege—the ability to use economic resources to gain access to women's bodies—and we, the viewers, see his masculinity—his sexual needs, rights, and entitlements—as validated.

This normalization of prostitution in the interests of servicing disabled men's "sexual rights" is supported by the rhetoric about the sexual rights of people with disabilities that is common to much academic and practitioner literature on disability (Earle, 2001). Much of the material on sexuality and disability is composed of reasonable arguments for information and training to be supplied to persons with disabilities so that they may understand sexuality, pleasure themselves, develop relationships, and, in the case of men and boys, learn not to engage in unacceptable behaviors such as masturbation in public.

But the sexual-rights argument goes further and leads to demands that men with disabilities, though gender is never referred to in this literature, which is carefully neutral, should not only be able to access pornography and prostitution, but be helped by their caregivers, including nurses, to do so. The argument has gone so far, under the title of "facilitated sexuality," that it appears that nurses may be expected to become adjuncts to the sex industry or even a part of it, by directly "sexually facilitating" men with disabilities themselves (Earle, 2001).

Yet, the desire to maintain a disabled man's masculinity does not just stem from within that man. The model of rehabilitation of people with disabilities, the medical model of disability, has a male body and male sexuality in mind. "Rehabilitation programs seek to cultivate 'competitive attitudes' and address 'concerns about male sexuality'" (Jeffreys, 2008). They are about "enabling men to aspire to dominant notions of masculinity" (Begum, 1992).

In today's world, men with disabilities fight an uphill battle against hegemonic masculinity—their position in the social order—and its many enforcers. Men with disabilities seem to scream, "I AM STILL A MAN!" They try to make up for their shortcoming by exaggerating the masculine qualities they still have, and society accommodates this via support of disabled men's sexual rights and the sexist nature of medical rehabilitation programs and standards.

Robert David Hall is an actor on the hit television show *CSI* and walks on two artificial legs due to having both of his legs amputated in 1978 after an eighteen-wheeler crushed his car. His character is not defined by his disability. "I used to hate the word 'disability,'" he says. "But I've come to embrace the fact that I'm one of more than 58 million Americans with some kind of physical or learning disability. After the accident, I realized I had more strength than I knew," he says. "I was forced to face up to reality, but facing such a reality helped me face any fears I had of taking risks" (Skrhak, 2008, p. 1).

Gay Men

Male homosexuality has long been associated with effeminacy (i.e., not being a real man) throughout the history of Western societies; the English language is fraught with examples equating men's sexual desire for other men with femininity: "molly" and "nancy-boy" in eighteenth-century England; "buttercup," "pansy," and "she-man" of early twentieth-century America; and the present-day "sissy," "fairy," "queen," and "faggot" (Edwards, 1994). Moreover, the pathologization of male homosexuality in the early twentieth century led to a rhetoric of de-masculinization. By the

1970s, a number of psychiatric theorists referred to male homosexuality as "impaired masculine self-image" (Bieber, 1965), "a flight from masculinity" (Kardiner, 1963), "a search for masculinity" (Socarides, 1968), and "masculine failure" (Ovesey & Person, 1973).

Today in the United States, gay men continue to be marginalized by gender—that is, their masculinity is seen as problematic. In a survey of over 3,000 American adults (Levitt & Klassen, 1976), 69 percent believed homosexuals acted like the opposite sex and that homosexual men were suitable only to the "unmasculine" careers of artist, beautician, and florist, but not the "masculine" careers of judges, doctors, and ministers. Recent studies have found similar results, despite the changing nature of gay rights in America (Blashill & Powlishta, 2009; Wright & Canetto, 2009; Wylie, Corliss, Boulanger, Prokop, & Austin, 2010).

The popular belief that gay men are not real men is established by the links among sexism (the systematic devaluation of women and "the feminine"), homophobia (the deep-seated cultural discomfort and hatred toward same-sex sexuality), and compulsory heterosexuality. Since heterosexuality is integral to the way a society is organized, it becomes a naturalized, "learned" behavior. When a man decides he is gay (if this "deciding" even occurs), he is rejecting the *compulsion* toward a heterosexual lifestyle and orientation (Rich, 1980).

More than this, though, compulsory heterosexuality is a mandate; society demands heterosexuality. And in response, men find that one of the key ways to prove masculinity is to demonstrate sexual prowess. Thus, a normifying process can be discerned among gay men of the pre-HIV, post-Stonewall era.

The ideological turn in the 1970s made by gay men, away from camp and drag, and toward a more hypermasculine affective style, dominated mainstream gay male culture through the 1980s. Hypermasculine men began to emerge in many major Western cities in the 1970s (Levine, 1995; Messner, 1997). "Like the less visible queer movement of the early 1900s, the hypermasculine appearance and sensibility announced a new masculine gay identity to replace the 'limp-wristed swish' stereotype of the previous eras" (Taywaditep, 2001).

Levine's classic ethnography of clone culture makes clear that among gay men, hypermasculine display—clothing, affective styles, fashion, and above all, sexual promiscuity—consisted of a large promissory note to the larger culture—a culture that was both heterosexist and sexist in its anti-gay sentiments (Levine, 1995). "We are real men!" that note read. "We not only perform masculinity successfully, but we embrace the criteria that denote and confer masculinity. And so we want you, the larger dominant culture, to confer masculinity on us."

But larger dominant culture has not, generally, conferred masculinity on gay men. Indeed, one study found that "the stereotype of gay men as more feminine and less masculine than other men appears robust" (Mitchell & Ellis, 2011). This research found that simply labeling a man gay, despite the man's presenting as gender-typical, made the man more likely to be rated as effeminate. Gender-nonconforming gay men may often feel marginalized *within gay culture itself* from other gay men, who are most likely to have experienced stigmatization and may have been effeminate earlier in their lives. Writing about gay men's feminine stereotype, Lehne (1989) notes that "effeminacy itself is highly stigmatized in the homosexual subculture" (p. 417).

In the wake of the liberation movement, gay men seemed to rely on similar coping strategies as the disabled men detailed earlier: they reformulated their ideas of masculinity; relied on and promoted certain hegemonic ideals of masculinity; or rejected the mass societal norms and denied the norms' importance, creating another set of standards for themselves (Gerschick & Miller, 1995). But such a move also opened up an oppositional culture within the gay community—a culture of resistance to masculinist overconformity. It consisted in reclaiming the nelly queen, the camp and drag affective styles that the mainstream had discarded.

Sociologist Tim Edwards detailed this type of rejection and reliance: on one hand, there are the *effeminists,* who express gender nonconformity and/or seek to denounce traditional masculinity because of their personal style or a commitment to feminism—in other words, they reject mass social norms and deny their importance or very foundation. On the other hand, there are the *masculinists,* who are proponents of gay male "machismo" and seek to challenge the long-held effeminate stereotype of gay men—they rely heavily on the hegemonic ideals.

This reliance is, interestingly, the main site of access to privilege for these gay men. Gay men's misogyny in humor and argot, as well as some politico-ideological departures from feminism, have been well documented (Goodwin, 1989). As noted by Astrachan (1993), though it would seem beneficial for gay men and women to unite under their common experiences within the oppressive gender system, some gay men oppress and dominate women by "searching for people they can define as inferior—and finding women. A gay man told me, 'We want to be the equals of straight men, and if that means screwing women—figuratively—we'll do it'" (p. 70).

The gay men who conform to hegemonic norms secure their position in the power hierarchy by adopting the heterosexual masculine role and subordinating both women and effeminate gay men. Having noted that hypermasculine gay men have been accused of being "collaborators with patriarchy," Messner (1997) points out the prominence of hegemonic masculinity in gay culture: "It appears that the dominant tendency in gay culture eventually became an attempt to claim, eroticize, and display the dominant symbols of hegemonic masculinity" (p. 83).

Historically, camp and drag were associated with minstrelizers, those who exaggeratedly expressed stereotypic constructions of homosexual masculinity. The 1950s hairdresser, interior decorator, and florist of classic cultural stereotype were embraced as lifestyle choices, if not yet a political position. Minstrelizers embraced the stereotypes; their effeminacy asked the question "who wants to be butch all the time anyway? It's too much work."

On the other hand, there was a group of effeminists who were explicitly political. As a political movement, effeminism emerged in the first years of the modern post-Stonewall gay liberation movement, but unlike their normifying brethren, effeminists explicitly and politically rejected mainstream heterosexual masculinity. Largely associated with the work of Steve Dansky, effeminists published a magazine, *Double F*, and three men issued "The Effeminist Manifesto" (Dansky, Knoebel, & Pitchford, 1977).

The effeminists thrilled to the possibilities for a liberated masculinity offered by feminism. Effeminism, they argued, is a positive political position, aligning anti-sexist gay men with women, instead of claiming male privilege by asserting their difference from women. Since, as Dansky et al. (1977) argued, male supremacy is the root of all other oppressions, the only politically defensible position was to renounce manhood itself, to refuse privilege. Dansky and his effeminist colleagues were as critical of mainstream gay male culture (and the denigration of effeminacy by the normifiers) as was the hegemonic dominant culture.

This position was also taken up by John Stoltenberg, in his book *Refusing to Be a Man* (1989). Refusing manhood meant refusing privilege out of solidarity with women and in opposition to women's oppression. Though little observed today in mainstream gay male culture's uncritical embrace of mainstream masculinity, effeminacy was a most politicized form of gendered resistance to male privilege.

Working-Class Men

Working-class men are, perhaps, an interesting reference group when compared to disabled men and gay men. The way(s) in which they are discriminated against or stigmatized seem very different. These men, in fact, are often seen as incredibly masculine; strong, stoic, hard workers—there is something particularly masculine about what they have to do day in and day out. Indeed, the masculine virtues of the working class are celebrated as the physical embodiment of what all men should embrace (Gagnon & Simon, 1973).

Working-class white males may work in a system of male privilege, but they are not the main beneficiaries; they are in fact expendable. The working class is set apart from the middle and upper classes in that the working class is defined by jobs that require less formal education, sometimes (not always) less skill, and often low pay. For men, these jobs often include manual labor, such as construction, automotive work, or factory work. The jobs these men hold are typically men-dominant.

If the stereotypic construction of masculinity among the working class celebrates their physical virtues, it also problematizes their masculinity by imagining them as dumb brutes. Working-class men are the male equivalent of the "dumb blonde"—endowed with physical virtues, but problematized by intellectual shortcomings. Minstrelizing might be the sort of self-effacing comments such as "I'm just a working stiff." It can be a minstrelizing strategy of low-level resistance because these behaviors actually let the working-class man off the hook when it comes to accountability or responsibility. He exempts himself from scrutiny because he clearly isn't capable of such deep analytic thought.

We can also see this type of minstrelization in men who overemphasize their adherence to strict gender roles—being rough, uncivilized, brave, or brutish. Like Oliver Mellors in *Lady Chatterley's Lover*, these men want it to be known that they are the epitome of masculinity. By some standards, though, Mellors is the ultimate nightmare boyfriend: socially isolated and isolating; highly critical of others; the type to spitefully pick fights with others; with an attitude problem, making him highly likely to quit jobs or be fired. And yet Connie Chatterley is obsessed with him. She finds his vulnerabilities entrancing; she can't wait to have his child.

Here is a sociological example of minstrelizing. In their classic work, *The Hidden Injuries of Class*, Sennett and Cobb (1993) document a difference between working-class and middle-class men as they view the relationships between fathers and sons. Middle-class men see themselves as role models, Sennett and Cobb found. They want their sons to grow up to be "just like me." Such a posture requires a certain accountability and probity on the part of the middle-class father. Being a role model is a responsibility.

However, by contrast, the working-class fathers saw themselves as *negative* role models.

"If you grow up to be like me," they said, "I'll feel like a failure." "Don't make the same mistakes I made." Or as one of the chapter authors' own father used to say all the time: "If a son does not surpass his father, then both are failures." Such sentiments remove responsibility and actually place the onus for acting responsibly on the son, not the father. "It's too late for me, but not for thee." Thus, working-class men, by conforming to the dumb-brute stereotype, offer a modest resistance to the dominant mode of masculinity as upwardly mobile striver. Giving up can also imply not actually giving in.

Of course, there are elements of militant chauvinism in the proclamation of those stereotypes as well. For men in these positions, sexism and patriarchy are key features of their masculine dominance. When the workforce is all or mostly male, relationships are often "built through a decidedly male idiom of physical jousting, sexual boasting, sports talk, and shared sexual activities" (Freeman, 1993). Here, what is key for men is how they can effectively "compensate" for being underlings in the eyes of the managers who rule over them and the families they go home to. Using physical endurance and tolerance of discomfort, required by their manual labor, they signify a truer masculinity than even their office-working bosses can embody. They somehow signify a truer masculinity than their effeminate, "yes-men," paper-pushing managers can lay claim to (Collinson, 1992).

Moreover, those in the working, or blue-collar, class form a network of relationships with other blue-collar workers that serves to support them and give them a sense of status and worth, regardless of actual status or worth in the outside world (Cohen & Hodges Jr., 1963). In fact, because those in the working class cannot normally exercise a great amount of power in their jobs or in many other formal relationships, they tend to do so in their relationships with other working-class members. "To a greater extent than other classes, [the lower-lower class] will tend to measure status by power, and to validate his own claim to status, where he feels entitled to it, by asserting a claim to power" (Cohen & Hodges Jr., 1962).

However, for those who want to minimize the apparent differences between them and the more dominant masculine ideal, a site of normification could be the focus on all men's general relationship to women and the family. Those involved in the union movement, for example, stake claims to manhood and masculinity by organizing around the principle of men as breadwinners. The basic job that all "real men" should share is to provide for their wives and children. This would explain the initial opposition to women's entry into the workplace, and also now the opposition to gay men's and lesbian women's entrance. There is a type of white, male, working-class solidarity that these men have constructed and maintained, that promotes and perpetuates racism, sexism, and homophobia—the nexus of beliefs that all men are supposed to value (Embrick, Walther, & Wickens, 2007).

This power in the workplace translates directly to the home, as well. In the absence of legitimated hierarchical benefits and status, working-class husbands and partners are more likely to "produce hypermasculinity by relying on blatant, brutal, and relentless power strategies in their marriages, including spousal abuse" (Pyke, 1996). However, violence can also extend outside the home. As Pyke (1996) points out, "The hypermasculinity found in certain lower-status male locales, such as on shop floors, in pool halls, motorcycle clubs, and urban gangs, can be understood as both a response to ascendant masculinity and its unintentional booster." Willis (1977) details how working-class boys refuse to submit to the "upper-class" imperatives of social mobility, knowledge, and skill acquisition, instead choosing to reproduce themselves as working class, despite the social and financial consequences. These students become agentic, rebellious even, but in doing so also become "uneducated" workers of manual labor.

Conclusion

Privilege is not monolithic; it is unevenly distributed. Even among members of one privileged class, other mechanisms of marginalization may mute or reduce privilege based on another status. Thus, a white gay man might receive race and gender privilege, but will be marginalized by sexuality. In this paper, we described these processes for three groups of men—men with disabilities, gay men, and working-class men—who see their gender privilege reduced and their masculinity questioned, not confirmed, through their other marginalized status. We described strategies these men might use to restore, retrieve, or resist that loss. Using Goffman's discussion of stigma, we described three patterns of response. It is through these strategies—minstrelization, normification, and militant chauvinism—that their attempts to access privilege can be viewed and, we argue, that we can better see the standards, ideals, and norms by which society measures a man and his masculinity, and the benefits or consequences of his adherence or deviance.

references

Astrachan, A. 1993. "Dividing Lines: Experiencing Race, Class, and Gender in the United States." In M. S. Kimmel and M. A. Messner, eds., *Men's Lives* (pp. 63–73). New York: Macmillan.

Begum, N. 1992. "Disabled Women and the Feminist Agenda." *Feminist Review* 40: 70–84.

Bieber, I. 1965. "Clinical Aspects of Male Homosexuality." In J. Marmor, ed., *Sexual Inversion: The Multiple Roots of Homosexuality* (pp. 248–267). New York: Basic Books.

Blashill, A. J., and K. K. Powlishta. 2009. "The Impact of Sexual Orientation and Gender Role on Evaluations of Men." *Psychology of Men & Masculinity* 10, no. 2: 160. doi:10.1037/a0014583

Cheng, C. 2008. "Marginalized Masculinities and Hegemonic Masculinity: An Introduction." *Journal of Men's Studies* 7, no. 3: 295–315.

Cohen, A. K., and H. M. Hodges Jr. 1963. "Characteristics of the Lower-blue-collar Class." *Social Problems* 10, no. 4: 303–334.

Collinson, D. 1992. *Managing the Shopfloor: Subjectivity, Masculinity, and Workplace Culture*. New York: Walter de Gruyter.

Connell, R. W. 1995. *Masculinities*. Berkeley: University of California Press.

Dansky, S., J. Knoebel, and K. Pitchford. 1977. "The Effeminist Manifesto." In J. Snodgrass, ed., *A Book of Readings: For Men Against Sexism* (pp. 116–120). Albion, CA: Times Change Press.

Earle, S. 2001. "Disability, Facilitated Sex, and the Role of the Nurse." *Journal of Advanced Nursing* 36, no. 3: 433–440. doi:10.1046/j.1365-2648.2001.01991.x

Edwards, T. 1994. *Erotics & Politics: Gay Male Sexuality, Masculinity, and Feminism*. New York: Routledge .

Embrick, D. G., C. S. Walther, and C. M. Wickens. 2007. "Working-class Masculinity: Keeping Gay Men and Lesbians Out of the Workplace." *Sex Roles* 56, no. 11: 757–766.

Freeman, J. B. 1993. "Hardhats: Construction Workers, Manliness, and the 1970 Pro-war Demonstrations." *Journal of Social History* 26, no. 4: 725–744; www.jstor.org.libproxy .cc.stonybrook.edu/stable/pdfplus/3788778.pdf.

Gagnon, J. H., and W. Simon. 1973. *Sexual Conduct: The Social Origins of Human Sexuality*. Chicago: Aldine.

Gerschick, T. J., and A. S. Miller. 1995. "Coming to Terms: Masculinity and Physical Disability." In D. Sabo and D. F. Gordon, eds., *Men's Health and Illness: Gender, Power, and the Body, Research on Men and Masculinities Series,* vol. 8 (pp. 183–204). Thousand Oaks, CA: Sage.

Goffman, E. 1963. *Stigma.* Englewood Cliffs, NJ: Prentice-Hall.

Goodwin, J. P. 1989. *More Man Than You'll Ever Be: Gay Folklore and Acculturation in Middle America.* Bloomington: Indiana University Press.

Jeffreys, S. 2008. "Disability and the Male Sex Right." *Women's Studies International Forum* 31, no. 5: 327–335. doi:10.1016/j.wsif.2008.08.001

Kardiner, A. 1963. "The Flight from Masculinity." In H. M. Ruisenbeck, ed., *The Problem of Homosexuality in Modern Society* (pp. 17–39). New York: Dutton.

Lehne, G. K. 1989. "Homophobia Among Men: Supporting and Defining the Male Role." In M. S. Kimmel and M. A. Messner, eds., *Men's Lives* (pp. 416–429). New York: Macmillan.

Levine, M. 1995. *Gay Macho.* New York: New York University Press.

Levitt, E. E., and A. D. Klassen. 1976. "Public Attitudes Toward Homosexuality." *Journal of Homosexuality* 1, no. 1: 29–43. doi:10.1300/J082v01n01_03

McIntosh, P. 1988. "White Privilege and Male Privilege: A Personal Account of Coming to See Correspondences Through Work in Women's Studies." Working paper no. 189, Wellesley College Center for Research on Women, Wellesley, MA.

Messner, M. A. 1997. *Politics of Masculinities: Men in Movements.* New York: Sage.

Mitchell, R. W., and A. L. Ellis. 2011. "In the Eye of the Beholder: Knowledge That a Man Is Gay Promotes American College Students' Attributions of Cross-gender Characteristics." *Sexuality & Culture* 15, no. 1: 80–100.

Ovesey, L., and E. Person. 1973. "Gender Identity and Sexual Psychopathology in Men: A Psychodynamic Analysis of Homosexuality, Transsexualism, and Transvestism." *Journal of the American Academy of Psychoanalysis and Dynamic Psychiatry* 1, no. 1: 53–72.

Pyke, K. D. 1996. "Class-based Masculinities: The Interdependence of Gender, Class, and Interpersonal Power." *Gender and Society* 10, no. 5: 527–549.

Rich, A. 1980. "Compulsory Heterosexuality and Lesbian Existence." *Signs* 5, no. 4: 631–660.

Robertson. 2011. Working paper for special issue of *Men and Masculinities,* forthcoming.

Schwartz, L. 2008. *For One Night Only.* Melbourne, Australia: The Age.

Sennett, R., and J. Cobb. 1993. *The Hidden Injuries of Class.* New York: W. W. Norton.

Skrhak, K. S. 2008. "*CSI*'s Robert David Hall Is Still Standing." *Success Magazine*; www.successmagazine.com/csi-robert-david-hall-is-still-standing/PARAMS/article/1134/channel/22.

Socarides, C. W. 1968. "A Provisional Theory of Aetiology in Male Homosexuality—A Case of Preoedipal Origin." *International Journal of Psychoanalysis* 49: 27.

Stoltenberg, J. 1989. *Refusing to Be a Man.* Portland, OR: Breitenbush Books.

Taywaditep, K. J. 2001. "Marginalization Among the Marginalized: Gay Men's Anti-effeminacy Attitudes." *Journal of Homosexuality* 42, no. 1: 1–28.

Wedgwood. 2011. Working paper for special issue of *Men and Masculinities,* forthcoming.

West, C., and S. Fenstermaker. 1995. "Doing Difference." *Gender and Society* 9, no. 1: 8–37.

West, C., and D. Zimmerman. 1987. "Doing Gender." *Gender and Society* 1, no. 2: 125–151.

Willis, P. E. 1977. *Learning to Labor: How Working-class Kids Get Working-class Jobs.* New York: Columbia University Press.

World Health Organization. 1980. *International Classification of Impairments, Disabilities, and Handicaps,* pp. 27–28.

Wright, S. L., and S. Canetto. 2009. Stereotypes of Older Lesbians and Gay Men. *Educational Gerontology* 35, no. 5: 424–452. doi:10.1080/03601270802505640

Wylie, S. A., H. L. Corliss, V. Boulanger, L. A. Prokop, and S. B. Austin. 2010. "Socially Assigned Gender Nonconformity: A Brief Measure for Use in Surveillance and Investigation of Health Disparities." *Sex Roles* 63, nos. 3–4: 264–276.

17

how gay stays white and what kind of white it stays

Allan Bérubé*

The Stereotype

When I teach college courses on queer history or queer working-class studies, I encourage students to explore the many ways that homosexuality is shaped by race, class, and gender. I know that racialized phantom figures hover over our classroom and inhabit our consciousness. I try to name these figures out loud to bring them down to earth so we can begin to resist their stranglehold on our intelligence. One by one, I recite the social categories that students have already used in our discussions—immigrant, worker, corporate executive, welfare recipient, student on financial aid, lesbian mother—and ask students first to imagine the stereotypical figure associated with the category and then to call out the figure's race, gender, class, and sexuality. As we watch each other conjure up and name these phantoms, we are stunned at how well each of us has learned by heart the same fearful chorus.

Whenever I get to the social category "gay man," the students' response is always the same: "white and well-to-do." In the United States today, the

* Bérubé, Allan. "How Gay Stays White and What Kind of White It Stays," in *The Making and Unmaking of Whiteness*, Brander Rasmussen et al., Eds., pp. 234–265. Copyright 2001, Duke University Press. All rights reserved. Republished by permission of the copyright holder. www.dukeupress.edu.

dominant image of the typical gay man is a white man who is financially better off than most everyone else.

My White Desires

Since the day I came out to my best friend in 1968, I have inhabited the social category "gay white man." As a historian, writer, and activist, I've examined the gay and the male parts of that identity, and more recently I've explored my working-class background and the Franco-American ethnicity that is so intertwined with it. But only recently have I identified with or seriously examined my gay male whiteness.[1]

Several years ago I made the decision to put race and class at the center of my gay writing and activism. I was frustrated at how my own gay social and activist circles reproduced larger patterns of racial separation by remaining almost entirely white. And I felt abandoned as the vision of the national gay movement and media narrowed from fighting for liberation, freedom, and social justice to expressing personal pride, achieving visibility, and lobbying for individual equality within existing institutions. What emerged was too often an exclusively gay rights agenda isolated from supposedly nongay issues, such as homelessness, unemployment, welfare, universal health care, union organizing, affirmative action, and abortion rights. To gain recognition and credibility, some gay organizations and media began to aggressively promote the so-called positive image of a generic gay community that is an upscale, mostly male, and mostly white consumer market with mainstream, even traditional, values. Such a strategy derives its power from an unexamined investment in whiteness and middle-class identification. As a result, its practitioners seemed not to take seriously or even notice how their gay visibility successes at times exploited and reinforced a racialized class divide that continues to tear our nation apart, including our lesbian and gay communities.

My decision to put race and class at the center of my gay work led me as a historian to pursue the history of a multiracial maritime union that in the 1930s and 1940s fought for racial equality and the dignity of openly gay workers.[2] And my decision opened doors that enabled me as an activist to join multiracial lesbian, gay, bisexual, and transgender groups whose members have been doing antiracist work for a long time and in which gay white men are not the majority—groups that included the Lesbian, Gay, Bisexual, and Transgender Advisory Committee to the San Francisco Human

Rights Commission and the editorial board of the now-defunct national lesbian and gay quarterly journal *Out/Look*.

But doing this work also created new and ongoing conflicts in my relationships with other white men. I want to figure out how to handle these conflicts as I extend my antiracist work into those areas of my life where I still find myself among gay white men—especially when we form new activist and intellectual groups that once again turn out to be white. To do this I need "to clarify something for myself," as James Baldwin put it, when he gave his reason for writing his homosexual novel *Giovanni's Room* in the 1950s.[3]

I wanted to know how gay gets white, how it stays that way, and how whiteness is used both to win and attack gay rights campaigns.

I want to learn how to see my own whiteness when I am with gay white men and to understand what happens among us when one of us calls attention to our whiteness.

I want to know why I and other gay white men would want to challenge the racist structures of whiteness, what happens to us when we try, what makes me keep running away from the task, sometimes in silent despair, and what makes me want to go back to take up the task again.

I want to pursue these questions by drawing on a gay ability, developed over decades of figuring out how to "come out of the closet," to bring our hidden lives out into the open. But I want to do this without encouraging anyone to assign a greater degree of racism to gay white men, thus exposed, than to other white men more protected from exposure, and without inviting white men who are not gay to more safely see gay men's white racism rather than their own.

I want to know these things because gay white men have been among the men I have loved and will continue to love. I need them in my life and at my side as I try to make fighting racism a more central part of my work. And when students call out "white" to describe the typical gay man, and they see me standing right there in front of them, I want to figure out how, from where I am standing, I can intelligently fight the racist hierarchies that I and my students differently inhabit.

Gay Whitening Practices

Despite the stereotype, the gay male population is not as white as it appears to be in the images of gay men projected by the mainstream and gay media, or among the "out" men (including myself) who move into the public spotlight as representative gay activists, writers, commentators, and spokesmen. Gay men of color, working against the stereotype, have engaged in long, difficult struggles to gain some public recognition of their cultural heritages, political activism, and everyday existence. To educate gay white men, they've had to get our attention by interrupting our business as usual, then convince us that we don't speak for them or represent them or know enough about either their realities or our own racial assumptions and privileges. And when I and other gay white men don't educate ourselves, gay men of color have done the face-to-face work of educating us about their cultures, histories, oppression, and particular needs—the kind of personal work that tires us out when heterosexuals ask us to explain to them what it's like to be gay. Also working against their ability to put "gay" and "men of color" together in the broader white imagination are a great many other powerful *whitening practices* that daily construct, maintain, and fortify the idea that gay male means white.

How does the category "gay man" become white? What are the whitening practices that perpetuate this stereotype, often without awareness or comment by gay white men? How do these practices operate, and what racial work do they perform?

I begin by mining my own experience for clues.[4] I know that if I go where I'm surrounded by other gay white men, or if I'm having sex with a white man, it's unlikely that our race will come up in conversation. Such racially comfortable, racially familiar situations can make us mistakenly believe that there are such things as gay issues, spaces, culture, and relationships that are not "lived through" race, and that white gay life, so long as it is not named as such, is not about race.[5] These lived assumptions, and the privileges on which they are based, form a powerful camouflage woven from a web of unquestioned beliefs—that gay whiteness is unmarked and unremarkable, universal and representative, powerful and protective, a cohesive bond. The markings of this camouflage are pale—a characteristic that the wearer sees neither as entirely invisible nor as a racial "color," a shade that allows the wearer to blend into the seemingly neutral background of white worlds. When we wear this everyday camouflage into a gay political arena that white men already dominate, our activism comes wrapped in a *pale protective coloring* that we may not notice but which is clearly visible to those who don't enjoy its protection.

I start to remember specific situations in which I caught glimpses of how other gay whitening practices work.

One night, arriving at my favorite gay disco bar in San Francisco, I discovered outside a picket line of people protesting the triple-carding (requiring three photo IDs) of gay men of color at the door. This practice was a form of racial *exclusion*—policing the borders of white gay institutions to prevent people of color from entering. The management was using this discriminatory practice to keep the bar from "turning," as it's called—a process by which a "generically gay" bar (meaning a predominantly white bar) changes into a bar that loses status and income (meaning gay white men with money won't go there) because it has been "taken over" by black, Latino, or Asian gay men. For many white owners, managers, and patrons of gay bars, only a white gay bar can be *just* gay; a bar where men of color go is seen as racialized. As I joined the picket line, I felt the fears of a white man who has the privilege to choose on which side of a color line he will stand. I wanted to support my gay brothers of color who were being harassed at the door, yet I was afraid that the doorman might recognize me as a regular and refuse to let me back in. That night, I saw a gay bar's doorway become a racialized border, where a battle to preserve or challenge the whiteness of the clientele inside was fought among dozens of gay men who were either standing guard at the door, allowed to walk through it, or shouting and marching outside. (The protests eventually made the bar stop the triple-carding.)

I remember seeing how another gay whitening practice works when I watched, with other members of a sexual politics study group, an antigay video, *Gay Rights, Special Rights*, produced in 1993 by The Report, a religious right organization. This practice was the *selling* of gay whiteness—the marketing of gays as white and wealthy to make money and increase political capital, either to raise funds for campaigns (in both progay and antigay benefits, advertising, and direct-mail appeals) or to gain economic power (by promoting or appealing to a gay consumer market). The antigay video we watched used racialized class to undermine alliances between a gay rights movement portrayed as white and movements of people of color portrayed as heterosexual. It showed charts comparing mutually exclusive categories of "homosexuals" and "African Americans," telling us that homosexuals are wealthy, college-educated white men who vacation more than anyone else and who demand even more "special rights and privileges" by taking civil rights away from low-income African Americans.[6] In this zero-sum, racialized world of the religious right, gay men are white; gay, lesbian, and bisexual people of color, along with poor or working-class white gay men, bisexuals, and lesbians, simply do not exist. The recently vigorous gay media promotion of the high-income, brand-loyal gay consumer market—which is typically portrayed as a population of white, well-to-do, college-educated young men—only widens the racialized class divisions that the religious right so eagerly exploits.

During the 1993 Senate hearings on gays in the military, I saw how these and other whitening practices were used in concentrated form by another gay institution, the Campaign for Military Service (CMS).

The Campaign for Military Service was an ad hoc organization formed in Washington, D.C., by a group composed primarily of well-to-do, well-connected, professional men, including billionaires David Geffen and Barry Diller, corporate consultant and former antiwar activist David Mixner (a personal friend of Bill Clinton's), and several gay and lesbian civil rights attorneys. Their mission was to work with the Clinton White House and sympathetic senators by coordinating the gay response to hearings held by the Senate Armed Services Committee, chaired by Sam Nunn. Their power was derived from their legal expertise, their access to wealthy donors, and their contacts with high-level personnel inside the White House, Senate, and Pentagon. The challenge they faced was to make strategic, pragmatic decisions in the heat of a rapidly changing national battle over what President Clinton called "our nation's policy toward homosexuals in the military."[7]

The world in and around the CMS that David Mixner describes in his memoir, *Stranger Among Friends,* is a network of professionals passionately dedicated to gay rights who communicated with Washington insiders via telephone calls, memos, and meetings in the White House, the Pentagon, and private homes. Wearing the protective coloring of this predominantly white gay world, these professionals entered the similarly white and male but heterosexual world of the US Senate, where their shared whiteness became a common ground on which the battle to lift the military's ban on homosexuals was fought—and lost.

The CMS used a set of arguments they called the *race analogy* to persuade senators and military officials to lift the military's antigay ban. The strategy was to get these powerful men to take antigay discrimination as seriously as they supposedly took racial discrimination, so they would lift the military ban on homosexuals as they had eliminated official policies requiring racial segregation. During the Senate hearings, the race analogy projected a set of comparisons that led to heated disputes over whether sexual orientation was analogous to race, whether sexual desire and conduct were like "skin color," or, most specifically, whether being homosexual was like being African American. (Rarely was "race" explicitly discussed as anything other than African American.) On their side, the CMS argued for a qualified analogy—what they called "haunting parallels" between "the words, rationale and rhetoric invoked in favor of racial discrimination in the past" and those used to "exclude gays in the military now." "The parallel is inexact," they cautioned, because "a person's skin color is not the same as a person's sexual identity; race is self-evident to many whereas sexual orientation is not. Moreover, the history of African Americans is not equivalent to the history of lesbian, gay and bisexual people in this country." Yet, despite these qualifications, the CMS held firm to the analogy. "The bigotry expressed is the same; the discrimination is the same."[8]

The military responded with an attack on the race analogy as self-serving, racist, and offensive. They were aided by Senator Nunn, who skillfully managed the hearings in ways that exploited the whiteness of the CMS and their witnesses to advance the military's antigay agenda. Working in their favor was the fact that, unlike the CMS, the military had high-ranking officials who were African American. The chairman of the Joint Chiefs of Staff, Gen. Colin L. Powell, who opposed lifting the ban, responded to the CMS with the argument that the antigay policy was not analogous to racial segregation because "skin color" was a "benign characteristic" while homosexuality constituted conduct that was neither benign nor condoned by most Americans.[9] Another African American army officer, Lt. Gen. Calvin Waller, Gen. Norman Schwarzkopf's deputy commander and the highest-ranking African American officer in Operation Desert Storm, attacked the race analogy with these words: "I had no choice regarding my race when I was delivered from my mother's womb. To compare my service in America's armed forces with the integration of avowed homosexuals is personally offensive to me."[10] Antigay white senators mimicked his outrage.

During the race analogy debates, the fact that only white witnesses made the analogy, drawing connections between antigay and racial discrimination without including people of color, reduced the power of their argument and the credibility it might have gained had it been made by advocates who had experienced the racial discrimination side of the analogy.[11] But without hearing these voices, everyone in the debate could imagine homosexuals as either people who do not experience racism (the military assumption) or as people who experience discrimination only as homosexuals (the progay assumption)—two different routes that ulti-mately led to the same destination: the place where gay stays white, the place where the CMS chose to make its stand.

According to Mixner's memoir, the Senate Armed Services Committee "had asked CMS to suggest witnesses."[12] As gay gatekeepers to the hearings, the CMS utilized another whitening practice—*mirroring*. This is a political strategy that reflects back the whiteness of the men who run powerful insti-tutions to persuade them to take "us" seriously, accept "us," and let "us" in because "we are just like you." From the witnesses they selected, it appears that the CMS tried to project an idealized image of the openly gay service member that mirrored the senators' racial makeup and their publicly es-poused social values and sexual mores—the image of the highly competent, patriotic, sexually abstinent, young, male officer who had earned the right to serve with a proud record and therefore deserved equality. The CMS se-lected for the gay panel a group of articulate and courageous veterans—all white men, except for one white woman.[13] Cleverly, Senator Nunn's staff selected a panel of African American ministers opposed to lifting the ban to precede the gay white panel, so that both sides constructed and partici-pated in a racialized dramatic conflict that reinforced the twin myths that gay is white and African Americans are antigay.

Missing was the testimony of service members whose lives bridged the hearings' false divide between black and gay—veterans who were both Af-rican American and lesbian, gay, or bisexual. In this context, a significant whitening practice at the hearings was the exclusion of Sgt. Perry Watkins as a witness. Watkins was an openly gay, African American veteran consid-ered by many to be a military hero. Kicked out of the army as a homosexual shortly before his retirement, he successfully appealed his discharge to the Supreme Court, becoming what one attorney called "the first out gay sol-dier to retire from the Army with full honors."[14]

To my knowledge, there is no public record of how or why the CMS did not invite Watkins to testify.[15] (This is another privilege that comes with whiteness—the ability to make decisions that seriously affect people of color and then protect that decision-making process from public scru-tiny or accountability.) Sabrina Sojourner, who recalls that she was the only African American at the CMS among the nonsupport staff, told me that she "got moved further and further from the decision-making process" be-cause she "brought up race," including the problem of the racial dynamic set up by presenting only white witnesses to testify.[16]

There was a moment when I was personally involved with this process. As the author of *Coming Out Under Fire: The History of Gay Men and Women in World War Two*, I was asked by the CMS to prepare to fly from California to Washington to testify, but my appearance was not approved by the Senate staff, who allowed no open homosexuals to testify as expert witnesses.[17] During a phone conversation with a white CMS staff member, I remember getting up the courage to ask him why Watkins wasn't a witness and was told that "Perry is a difficult personality." I didn't push my question any further, getting the message that I shouldn't ask for complicated explanations during the heat of battle and deferring to their inside-the-beltway tactical decisions, thus forfeiting an important opportunity to seriously challenge Watkins's exclusion. More instances of this painful struggle over Watkins's participation in and around the hearings must have been going on behind the scenes.[18] Watkins believed he was shut out because he was a "queeny" African American.[19]

It seems that the CMS considered Watkins to be the opposite of their ideal witness. His military story was indeed more complicated than the generic coming-out story. During his 1968 induction physical exam in Tacoma, Washington, he had openly declared his homosexuality, checking "Yes" to the written question "Do you have homosexual tendencies?" and freely describing his sexual experiences to the induction psychiatrist. But the army drafted him nevertheless because it needed him to fight in Vietnam, along with other mostly working-class African American men, who accounted for 20 percent of US combat deaths in that war by 1966, when African Americans made up 11 percent of the US population and 12.6 percent of US troops in Vietnam. Journalist Randy Shilts, who later interviewed Watkins, reported that Watkins believed "the doctor probably figured Watkins would . . . go to Vietnam, get killed, and nobody would ever hear about it again."[20] So Watkins's story was not a white narrative. "If I had not been black," he told Mary Ann Humphrey in an oral history interview, "my situation would not have happened as it did. . . . Every *white* person I knew from Tacoma who was gay and had checked that box 'Yes' did not have to go into the service."[21] Watkins's story resonated more with how men of color experience antigay racism in the military than with the story so many white servicemen tell. That white narrative begins with how a gay serviceman never experienced discrimination until he discovered his homosexuality in the service and ends with his fighting an antigay discharge, without referring to how he lived this experience through his whiteness. But Watkins explicitly talked about how he lived his gay military experience through race. "People ask me," he explained, "'How have you managed to tolerate all that discrimination you have had to deal with in the military?' My immediate answer to them was, 'Hell, I grew up black. Give me a break.'"[22] Watkins had also, while in the military, danced and sung on US Army bases as the flamboyant "Simone," his drag persona; as a veteran he was HIV-positive; and in some gay venues he wore body piercings in public.[23]

Nevertheless, Watkins's testimony at the hearings could have struck familiar chords among many Americans, including working-class and African American communities, as the experience of someone who was *real* rather than an *ideal*. His story was so compelling, in fact, that after the hearings he was the subject of two films and a segment of the television news magazine *20/20*.[24] But the story of his military career—which he so openly lived through race (as an African American), sexuality (had a sex life), and gender (performed in drag)—seems to have been considered by the CMS as too contaminated for congressional testimony and too distracting for the personal media stories that were supposed to focus only on the gay right to serve.

Watkins's absence was a lost opportunity to see and hear in nationally televised Senate hearings a gay African American legal hero talk about his victory over antigay discrimination in the military and expose the racist hypocrisy of how the antigay ban was in practice suspended for African Americans during wartime. The lack of testimony from any other lesbian, gay, or bisexual veteran of color was a lost opportunity to build alliances with communities of color and to do something about the "(largely accurate) perception of the gay activist leadership in Washington as overwhelmingly white."[25] Their collective absence reinforced another powerful myth that, even in a military population that is disproportionately African American and Latino, the representative gay soldier is a white officer, and the most presentable gay face of military competence is a white face.

As the hearings progressed, some CMS activists, speaking in public forums outside the hearings, took the race analogy a step further by promoting the idea that the gay rights movement was *like* the civil rights movement. During the hearings, those who argued the race analogy had drawn parallels between racist and antigay bigotry and discrimination. But those who extended the race analogy to the civil rights movement analogy had to take several more steps. First, they had to reconceptualize the civil rights movement. They took a multiracial movement for human equality and human rights, which included many lesbian, gay, and bisexual activists, and changed it into a nongay, black movement for African American racial equality. Next, they had to imagine the gay movement as a white movement for homosexual rights rather than as a multiracial movement that grew out of and continued the work of the civil rights movement. Then they could make the analogy between these two now-separated movements—one just about race, the other just about homosexuality. The last step was to symbolically recast gay white men in the roles of African American civil rights leaders. These moves tried to correct a problem inherent in such whitening practices as excluding people of color and the wearing, mirroring, and selling of gay whiteness. Because such practices draw directly on the privileges of whiteness, they do not on their own carry much moral weight. The extended race analogy compensates for this weightlessness by first invoking the moral authority of the civil rights movement (while erasing its actual history), and then transferring that unearned moral authority to a white gay movement, without giving anything back. At its worst, the race analogy can become a form of historical erasure, political cheating, and, ultimately, a theft of cultural capital and symbolic value.

David Mixner's memoir reveals how the extended race analogy was used in and around the Campaign for Military Service. When President Clinton, at a press conference, revealed that he wouldn't rule out separating homosexuals from heterosexuals within the military, Mixner first interpreted Clinton's comments as condoning gay segregation, then began equating it with racial segregation. Mixner's account of what happened next does not include attempts to seek advice from or build alliances with people whose histories include long struggles against legal segregation. This despite solid support for lifting the ban from civil rights veterans including Coretta Scott King and Roger Wilkins, the Black Lesbian and Gay Leadership Forum, the Congressional Black Caucus (including Ron Dellums, chairman of the House Armed Services Committee and a former marine who eventually held House hearings to counter Nunn's Senate hearings), and, in public opinion polls, a majority of African Americans (in contrast to a minority of white Americans).[26] Mixner instead describes a series of decisions and actions in which he invokes scenes from the history of racial segregation and the civil rights movement and appears to be reenacting those scenes as if he were a gay (white) version of a black civil rights leader.

A telling moment was when Mixner asked his friend Troy Perry, a gay white minister who founded and heads the gay Metropolitan Community Church, to let him use the Sunday pulpit at the MCC Cathedral in Dallas as a "platform from which to speak." Covered by network television, Mixner delivered a sermon to the nation about the gay "road to freedom." In his sermon he referred to the military's antigay policy as "ancient apartheid laws" and charged that "Sam Nunn is our George Wallace" and that "[b]igotry that wears a uniform is nothing more than a uniform with a hood." He angrily warned President Clinton, cast as antigay segregationist, that "with or without you we will be free . . . we will prevail!"[27] Shortly after the sermon, Tracy Thorne, a gay white Navy veteran who had courageously faced verbal abuse at the Senate hearings and who flew to Dallas to support Mixner, said out loud what had been implied by Mixner's words and actions. David Mixner "could be our Martin Luther King, no questions asked," Thorne told a reporter from a gay newspaper.[28]

Such dramatic race-analogy scenarios performed by white activists beg some serious questions. Are actual, rather than "virtual," people of color present as major actors in these scenarios, and if not, why not? What are they saying or how are they being silenced? How is their actual leadership being supported or not supported by the white people who are reenacting this racialized history? And who is the "we" in this rhetoric? Mixner's "we," for example, did not account for those Americans—including lesbian, gay, bisexual, and transgender activists from many racial backgrounds—who did not finally have or indeed need "our own George Wallace" or "our own Martin Luther King." "Martin Luther King is the Martin Luther King of the gay community," Dr. Marjorie Hill, board president of Unity Fellowship Church and former director of the New York City Mayor's Office for Lesbian and Gay Issues, has pointedly replied in response to those who were looking for King's gay equivalent. "His lesson of equality and truth and non-violence was for everyone."[29] If the gay rights movement is already part of the ongoing struggle for the dignity of all people exemplified in the activism of Dr. Martin Luther King Jr., then there is no need for gay equivalents of Dr. King, racial segregation, or the civil rights movement. If the gay rights movement is not already part of the civil rights movement, then what is it? Answering this question from a white position with the race analogy—saying that white gay leaders and martyrs are "our" versions of African American civil rights leaders and martyrs—can't fix the problem and ultimately undermines the moral authority that is its aim. This use of

192 ■ intersections: the complicated reality

the race analogy ends up reinforcing the whiteness of gay political campaigns rather than doing the work and holding onto the dream that would continue the legacy of Dr. King's leadership and activism.[30]

What would the gay movement look like if gay white men who use the race analogy took it more seriously? What work would we have to do to close the perceived moral authority gap between our gay activism and the race analogy, to directly establish the kind of moral authority we seek by analogy? What if we aspired to achieve the great vision, leadership qualities, grassroots organizing skills, and union solidarity of Dr. Martin Luther King Jr., together with his opposition to war and his dedication to fighting with the poor and disenfranchised against the deepening race and class divisions in America and the world? How could we fight, in the words of US Supreme Court Justice Harry A. Blackmun, for the "fundamental interest all individuals have in controlling the nature of their intimate associations with others," in ways that build a broad civil rights movement rather than being "like" it, in ways that enable the gay movement to grow into one of many powerful and direct ways to achieve race, gender, and class justice?[31]

These, then, are only some of the many whitening practices that structure everyday life and politics in what is often called the "gay community" and the "gay movement"—making *race analogies; mirroring* the whiteness of men who run powerful institutions as a strategy for winning credibility, acceptance, and integration; *excluding* people of color from gay institutions; *selling* gay as white to raise money, make a profit, and gain economic power; and daily wearing the *pale protective coloring* that camouflages the unquestioned assumptions and unearned privileges of gay whiteness. These practices do serious damage to real people whenever they mobilize the power and privileges of whiteness to protect and strengthen gayness—including the privileges of gay whiteness—without using that power to fight racism—including gay white racism.

Most of the time, the hard work of identifying such practices, fighting racial discrimination and exclusion, critiquing the assumptions of whiteness, and racially integrating white gay worlds has been taken up by lesbian, gay, bisexual, and transgender people of color. Freed from this enforced daily recognition of race and confrontation with racism, some prominent white men in the gay movement have been able to advance a gay rights politics that, like the right to serve in the military, they imagine to be just gay, not about race. The gay rights movement can't afford to "dissipate our energies," Andrew Sullivan, former editor of the *New Republic*, warned on the

Charlie Rose television program, by getting involved in disagreements over nongay issues such as "how one deals with race . . . how we might help the underclass . . . how we might deal with sexism."[32]

But a gay rights politics that is supposedly color-blind (and sex-neutral and classless) is in fact a politics of race (and gender and class). It assumes, without ever having to say it, that gay must equal white (and male and economically secure); that is, it assumes white (and male and middle class) as the default categories that remain once one discounts those who as gay people must continually and primarily deal with racism (and sexism and class oppression), especially within gay communities. It is the politics that remains once one makes the strategic decision, as a gay activist, to stand outside the social justice movements for race, gender, or class equality, or to not stand with disenfranchised communities, among whom are lesbian, bisexual, gay, or transgender people who depend on these movements for dignity and survival.

For those few who act like, look like, and identify with the white men who still run our nation's major institutions, for those few who can meet with them, talk to them, and be heard by them as peers, the ability to draw on the enormous power of a shared but unacknowledged whiteness, the ability never to have to bring up race, must feel like a potentially sturdy shield against antigay discrimination. I can see how bringing up explicit critiques of white privilege during high-level gay rights conversations (such as the Senate debates over gays in the military), or making it possible for people of color to set the agenda of the gay rights movement, might weaken that white shield (which relies on racial division to protect)—might even, for some white activists, threaten to "turn" the gay movement into something less gay, as gay bars "turn" when they're no longer predominantly white.

The threat of losing the white shield that protects my own gay rights raises even more difficult questions that I need to "clarify . . . for myself": What would *I* say and do about racism if someday my own whiteness helped me gain such direct access to men in the centers of power, as it almost did during the Senate hearings, when all I did was ask why Perry Watkins wasn't testifying and accept the answer I was given? What privileges would I risk losing if I persistently tried to take activists of color with me into that high-level conversation? How, and with whom, could I begin planning for that day?

Gay white men who are committed to doing antiracist activism *as* gay men have to work within and against these and other powerful whitening practices. What can we do, and how can we support each other, when we once again find ourselves involved in gay social and political worlds that are white and male?

Gay, White, Male, and HIV-Negative

A few years ago, in San Francisco, a friend invited me to be part of a new political discussion group of HIV-negative gay men. Arriving at a neighbor's apartment for the group's first meeting, I once again felt the relief and pleasure of being among men like me. All of us were involved in AIDS activism. We had supported lovers, friends, and strangers with HIV and were grieving the loss of too many lives. We didn't want to take time, attention, and scarce resources away from people with AIDS, including many people of color. But we did want to find a collective, progressive voice as HIV-negative men. We wanted to find public ways to say to gay men just coming out, "We are HIV-negative men, and we want you to stay negative, have hot sex, and live long lives. We don't want you to get sick or die." We were trying to work out a politics in which HIV-negative men, who are relatively privileged as not being the primary targets of crackdowns on people who are HIV-positive, could address other HIV-negative men without trying to establish our legitimacy by positioning ourselves as victims.

When I looked around the room, I saw only white men. I knew that many of them had for years been incorporating antiracist work into their gay and AIDS activism, so this seemed like a safe space to bring up the whiteness I saw. I really didn't want to hijack the purpose of the group by changing its focus from HIV to race, but this was important because I believed that not talking about our whiteness was going to hurt our work. Instead of speaking up, however, I hesitated.

Right there. That's the moment I want to look at—that moment of silence, when a flood of memories, doubts, and fears rushed into my head. What made me want to say something about our whiteness, and what was keeping me silent?

My memory took me back to 1990, when I spoke on a panel of gay historians at the first Out/Write conference of lesbian and gay writers, held in San Francisco. I was happy to be presenting with two other community-based historians working outside the academy. But I was also aware—and concerned—that we were all men. When the question period began, an African American writer in the audience, a man whose name I later learned was Fundi, stood up and asked us (as I recall) how it could happen, at this late date, that a gay history panel could have only white men on it. Awkward silence. I don't trust how I remember his question or what happened next—unreliable memory and bad thinking must be characteristics of inhabiting whiteness while it's being publicly challenged. As the other panelists responded, I remember wanting to distance myself from their whiteness while my own mind went blank, and I remember feeling terrified that Fundi would address me directly and ask me to respond personally. I kept thinking, "I don't know what to say, I can't think, I want to be invisible, I want this to be over, now!"

After the panel was over I spoke privately to Fundi. Later, I resolved never to be in that situation again—never to agree to be on an all-white panel without asking ahead of time why it was white, if its whiteness was crucial to what we were presenting, and, if not, how its composition might be changed. But in addition to wanting to protect myself from public embarrassment and to do the right thing, that writer's direct challenge made me understand something more clearly: that only by seeing and naming the whiteness I'm inhabiting, and taking responsibility for it, can I begin to change it and even do something constructive with it. At that panel, I learned how motivating, though terrifying, it can be as a white person to be placed in such a state of heightened racial discomfort—to be challenged to see the whiteness we've created, figure out how we created it, and then think critically about how it works.[33]

In the moment of silent hesitation I experienced in my HIV-negative group, I found myself imagining for the first time, years after it happened, what it must have been like for Fundi to stand up in a predominantly white audience and ask an all-white panel of gay men about our whiteness. My friend and colleague Lisa Kahaleole Hall, who is a brilliant thinker, writer, and teacher, says that privilege is "the ability not to have to take other people's existence seriously," the "ability not to have to pay attention."[34] Until that moment I had mistakenly thought that Fundi's anger (and I am not certain that he in fact expressed any anger toward us) was only about me, about us, as white men, rather than also about him—the history, desires, and support that enabled him to speak up, and the fears he faced and risks he took by doing it. Caught up in my own fear, I had not paid close attention to the specific question he had asked us. "The problem of conventional white men," Fundi later wrote in his own account of why he had decided to take the risk of speaking up, "somehow not being able, or not knowing how, to find and extend themselves to women and people of color had to be talked through. . . . My question to the panel was this: 'What direct skills might you share with particularly the whites in the audience to help them move on their fears and better extend themselves to cultural diversity?'"[35] I'm indebted to Fundi for writing that question down, and for starting a chain of events with his question that has led to my writing this essay.

I tried to remember who else I had seen bring up whiteness. The first images that came to mind were all white lesbians and people of color. White lesbian feminists have as a movement dealt with racism in a more collective way than have gay white men. In lesbian and gay activist spaces I and other gay white men have come to rely on white lesbians and people of color to raise the issue of whiteness and challenge racism, so that this difficult task has become both gendered as lesbian work and racialized as "colored" work. These images held me back from saying anything to my HIV-negative group. "Just who am I to bring this up?" I wondered. "It's not my place to do this." Or, more painfully, "Who will these men think I think I am? Will they think I'm trying to pretend I'm not a white man?"

Then another image flashed in my mind that also held me back. It was the caricature of the white moralist—another racialized phantom figure hovering in the room—who blames and condemns white people for our racism, guilt-trips us from either a position of deeper guilt or holier-than-thou innocence, claims to be more aware of racism than we are, and is prepared to catalog our offenses. I see on my mental screen this self-righteous caricature impersonating a person of color in an all-white group or, when people of color are present, casting them again in the role of spectators to a white performance, pushed to the sidelines from where they must angrily or patiently interrupt a white conversation to be heard at all. I understand that there is some truth to this caricature—that part of a destructive racial dynamic among white people is trying to determine who is more or less responsible for racism, more or less innocent and pure, more or less white. But I also see how the fear of becoming this caricature has been used by white people to keep each other from naming the whiteness of all-white groups we are in. During my moment of hesitation in the HIV-negative group, the fear of becoming this caricature was successfully silencing me.

I didn't want to pretend to be a white lesbian or a person of color, or to act like the self-righteous white caricature. "How do I ask that we examine our whiteness," I wondered, "without implying that I'm separating us into the good guys and bad guys and positioning myself as the really cool white guy who 'gets it' about racism?" I needed a way to speak intelligently from where I was standing without falling into any of these traps.

I decided to take a chance and say something.

"It appears to me," I began, my voice a little shaky, "that everyone here is white. If this is true, I'd like us to find some way to talk about how our whiteness may be connected to being HIV-negative, because I suspect there are some political similarities between being in each of these positions of relative privilege."

There was an awkward pause. "Are you saying," someone asked, "that we should close the group to men of color?"

"No," I said, "but if we're going to be a white group I'd like us to talk about our relationship to whiteness here."

"Should we do outreach to men of color?" someone else asked.

"No, I'm not saying that, either. It's a little late to do outreach, after the fact, inviting men of color to integrate our already white group."

The other men agreed and the discussion went on to other things. I, too, didn't really know where to take this conversation about our whiteness. By bringing it up, I was implicitly asking for their help in figuring this out. I hoped I wouldn't be the only one to bring up the subject again.

At the next month's meeting there were new members, and they all appeared to be white men. When someone reviewed for them what we had done at the last meeting, he reported that I'd suggested we not include men of color in the group. "That's not right," I corrected him. "I said that if we're going to be a white group, I'd like us to talk about our whiteness and its relation to our HIV-negative status."

I was beginning to feel a little disoriented, like I was doing something wrong. Why was I being so consistently misunderstood as divisive, as if I were saying that I didn't want men of color in the group? Had I reacted similarly when, caught up in my own fear of having to publicly justify our panel's whiteness, I had misunderstood Fundi's specific question—about how we could share our skills with other white people to help each other move beyond our fear of cultural diversity—as an accusation that we had deliberately excluded women and men of color? Was something structural going on here about how white groups respond to questions that point to our whiteness and ask what we can do with it?

Walking home from the meeting I asked a friend who'd been there if what I said had made sense. "Oh yes," he said, "it's just that it all goes without saying." Well, there it is. That *is* how it goes, how it stays white. "Without saying."

Like much of the rest of my gay life, this HIV-negative group turned out to be unintentionally white, although intentionally gay and intentionally male. It's important for me to understand exactly how that racial *unintentionality* gets *constructed,* how it's not just a coincidence. It seems that so long as white people never consciously decide to be a white group, a white organization, a white department, so long as we each individually believe that people of color are always welcome, *even though they are not there,* then we do not have to examine our whiteness because we can believe it is unintentional, it's not our *reason* for being there. That may be why I had been misunderstood to be asking for the exclusion of men of color. By naming our group as white, I had unknowingly raised the question of *racial intent*—implying that we had intended to create an all-white group by deliberately excluding men of color. If we could believe that our whiteness was purely accidental, then we could also believe that there was nothing to say about it because creating an all-white group, which is exactly what we had done, had never been anyone's intent, and therefore had no inherent meaning or purpose. By interrupting the process by which "it just goes without saying," by asking us to recognize and "talk through" our whiteness, I appeared to be saying that we already had and should continue to exclude men of color from our now very self-consciously white group.

The reality is that in our HIV-negative group, as in the panel of the Out/ Write conference and in many other all-white groupings, we each did make a chain of choices, not usually conscious, to invite or accept an invitation from another white person. We made more decisions whether or not to name our whiteness when we once again found ourselves in a white group. What would it mean to make such decisions consciously and out loud, to understand why we made them, and to take responsibility for them? What if we intentionally held our identities as white men and gay men in creative tension, naming ourselves as gay *and* white, then publicly explored the possibilities for activism this tension might open up? Could investigating our whiteness offer us opportunities for reclaiming our humanity against the ways that racial hierarchies dehumanize us and disconnect us from ourselves, from each other, and from people of color? If we took on these difficult tasks, how might our gay political reality and purpose be different?[36]

When I told this story about our HIV-negative group to Barbara Smith, a colleague who is an African American lesbian writer and activist, she asked me a question that pointed to a different ending: "So why didn't you bring up the group's whiteness again?" The easy answer was that I left the group because I moved to New York City. But the more difficult answer was that I was afraid to lose the trust of these gay men whom I cared about and needed so much, afraid I would distance myself from them and be distanced by them, pushed outside the familiar circle, no longer welcomed as white and not belonging among people of color, not really gay and not anything else, either. The big fear is that if I pursue this need to examine whiteness too far, I risk losing my place among gay white men, forever—and then where would I be?

Pale, Male—and Antiracist

What would happen if we deliberately put together a white gay male group whose sole purpose was to examine our whiteness and use it to strengthen our antiracist gay activism?

In November 1995, gay historian John D'Emilio and I tried to do just that. We organized a workshop at the annual Creating Change conference of activists put on that year in Detroit by the National Gay and Lesbian Task Force. We called the workshop "Pale, Male—and Anti-Racist." At a conference of over 1,000 people (mostly white but with a large number of people of color), about thirty-five gay white men attended.[37]

We structured the workshop around three key questions: (1) How have you successfully used your whiteness to fight racism? (2) What difficulties have you faced in doing antiracist activism as a gay white man? And (3) what kind of support did you get or need or wish you had received from other gay white men?

Before we could start talking about our successes, warning lights began to flash. You could sense a high level of mistrust in the room, as if we were looking at each other and wondering, "Which kind of white guy are *you?*" One man wanted to make sure we weren't going to waste time congratulating ourselves for sharing our white privilege with people who don't have access to it or start whining about how hard it is to work with communities of color. Someone else wanted to make sure we weren't going to guilt-trip each other. Another said, "I'm so much more aware of my failures in this area, I can't even see the accomplishments."

But slowly, once all the cautions were out in the open, the success stories came out. About fighting an anti–affirmative action initiative. About starting a racism study group. About getting a university department to study why it had no teaching assistants who were students of color. About persuading a gay organization in Georgia to condemn the state's Confederate flag. "What keeps me from remembering," I wondered, "that gay white men publicly do this antiracist work? Why can't I keep their images in my mind?"

One possible answer to my question appeared in the next success story, which midway made a sharp turn away from our successes toward how gay white men can discipline each other for standing on the "wrong" side of the color line. A man from Texas, Dennis Poplin, told us about what happened to him as the only white man on the board of the San Antonio Lesbian and Gay Assembly (SALGA), a progressive, multiracial lesbian and gay alliance. When SALGA mobilized support that successfully canceled a so-called gay community conference whose planning committee was all-white— this in a city that was 65 percent Latina/Latino—a "community scandal" exploded, as he put it, "about political correctness, quotas, [and] reverse racism." A local newspaper, which was run by gay white men, started attacking SALGA. When a white reporter asked a man of color from SALGA why the group's board had no white men on it, and he replied that Dennis was on the board, the reporter said, "He's not white."[38]

Right away the men in the workshop started talking about the difficulties they'd had with other gay white men. "I find myself like not even knowing who it's safe to bring it up with," one man said. When he tries to talk about race, another said, "I'm just met with that smug, flippant, 'I'm tired of hearing about [all that].'" Others talked about fears of being attacked as too "PC."

At the "risk of opening a whole can of worms," as he put it, another man moved the discussion away from us to our relationships with white lesbians and people of color. Some men talked about how tired they were of being called "gay white men," feeling labeled then attacked for who they were and for what they tried to do or for not doing enough; about having to deal with their racism while they didn't see communities of color dealing with homophobia; and about how, after years of struggling, they felt like giving up. Yet here they all were at this workshop. I began to realize that all our frustrations were signs of a dilemma that comes with the privileges of whiteness: having the ability to decide whether to keep dealing with the accusations, resentments, racial categorizations, and other destructive effects of racism that divide people who are trying to take away its power; or, because the struggle is so hard, to walk away from it and do something else, using the slack our whiteness gives us to take a break from racism's direct consequences.

Bringing this dilemma into the open enabled us to confront our expectations about how the antiracist work we do should be appreciated, should be satisfying, and should bring results. One man admitted that he didn't make antiracist work a higher priority because "I [would have to face] a level of discomfort, irritation, boredom, frustration, [and] enter a lot of [areas where] I feel inept, and don't have confidence. It would require a lot of humility. All these are things that I steer away from."

Over and over the men at the workshop expressed similar feelings of frustration, using such phrases as "We tried, but . . . ," "No matter what you do, you can't seem to do anything right," and "You just can't win." These seemed to reflect a set of expectations that grew out of the advantages we have because we are American men and white and middle class or even working class—expectations that we *can* win, that we should know how to do it right, that if we try we will succeed.

What do we—what do I—expect to get out of doing antiracist work, anyway? If it's because we expect to be able to fix the problem, then we're not going to be very satisfied. When I talk with my friend Lisa Kahaleole Hall about these frustrations, she tells me, "Sweet pea, if racism were that easy to fix, we would have fixed it already." The challenge for me in relation to other gay white men—and in writing this essay—is to figure out how we can support each other in going into exactly those areas of whiteness where we feel we have no competence yet, no expertise, no ability to fix it, where we haven't even come up with the words we need to describe what we're trying to do. For me, it's an act of faith in the paradox that if we, together with our friends and allies, can figure out how our own whiteness works, we can use that knowledge to fight the racism that gives our whiteness such unearned power.

And whenever this struggle gets too difficult, many of us, as white men, have the option to give up in frustration and retreat into a more narrowly defined gay rights activism. That project's goal, according to gay author Bruce Bawer, one of its advocates, is "to achieve acceptance, equal rights, and full integration into the present social and political structure."[39] It's a goal that best serves the needs of men who can live our gayness through our whiteness and whose only or most important experience with discrimination is as homosexuals. James Baldwin, who wrote extensively about whiteness in America, noticed long ago the sense of entitlement embedded in a gay whiteness that experiences no other form of systematic discrimination. "[Y]ou are penalized, as it were, unjustly," he said in an interview. "I think white gay people feel cheated because they were born, in principle, into a society in which they were supposed to be safe. The anomaly of their sexuality puts them in danger unexpectedly."[40]

The gay rights project that grows out of the shocking experience of being cheated unexpectedly by society because one is gay defines the gay political problem in its narrowest form. One solution is to get back the respect one has learned to expect as a white man. Some prominent, well-connected activists do this by educating the men who run our nation's powerful institutions, using reasoned arguments to combat their homophobia and expose discrimination as irrational—a strategy that sometimes does open doors but mostly to those who look and behave like the men in power. I have heard some of these activists express a belief that less privileged members of the "gay community" will eventually benefit from these high-level successes, but this would happen apparently without the more privileged having to do the work of fighting hierarchies that enforce race, class, and gender inequality. Their belief in a kind of "trickle-down" gay activism is based on the idea that powerful men, once enlightened, will generously allow equality to flow from the top to those near the top and then automatically trickle down to those down below. An alternative belief in "bottom-up activism" is based on the idea that, with great effort, democratic power must more slowly be built from the bottom up, and out, experimenting with more equal power relations along the way by creating links of solidarity across the divides of difference. Some gay white men explicitly reject, as nongay, this broader goal of joining activists who stand and work at the intersections of the many struggles to achieve social justice and to dismantle interlocking systems of domination. In the narrow world of exclusively gay "integrationist" activism, which its advocates privilege as the site of "practical" rather than "utopian" politics,[41] college-educated gay white men have a better chance of knowing what to say and how to be heard, what to do and how to succeed within existing institutions. Because when antigay barriers and attitudes are broken down but no other power relations are changed, we are the ones most likely to achieve "full integration into the present social and political structure." All it takes sometimes is being the white man at the white place at the white time.

When John and I asked the workshop participants our last question— "What would you need from each other to be able to continue doing anti-racist work?"—the room went silent.

When push comes to shove, I wondered, holding back a sense of isolation inside my own silence, do gay white men as *white* men (including myself) have a lasting interest in fighting racism or will we sooner or later retreat to the safety of our gay white refuges? I know that gay white men as *gay* men, just to begin thinking about relying on each other's support in an ongoing struggle against racism, have to confront how we've absorbed the antigay lies that we are all wealthy, irresponsible, and sexually obsessed individuals who can't make personal commitments, as well as the reality that we are profoundly exhausted fighting for our lives and for those we love through years of devastation from the AIDS epidemic. These challenges all make it hard enough for me to trust my own long-term commitment to antiracist work, let alone that of other gay white men.

Yet at this workshop we created the opportunity for us to see that we were not alone, to risk saying and hearing what we needed from each other in fighting racism, and to assess what support we could realistically hope to get. We wanted the opportunity to complain to another gay white man, to be held and loved when we get discouraged or feel attacked, whether justifiably or not. We wanted understanding for all the frustrations we feel fighting racism, the chance just to let them out with a gay white man who knows that it's not our racism he's supporting but the desire to see it and together figure out what to do next, so we won't give up or run away. We wanted other gay white men to take us seriously enough to call us on our racist shit in ways we could actually hear without feeling attacked. And we wanted to help each other lift at least some of the work and responsibility of supporting us from the shoulders of our friends and co-workers who are white women or people of color.

As time ran out at the workshop, I asked everyone to think about another difficult question: "Who is the gay white man who has had more experience than you in supporting other gay white men who are fighting racism, and who you can look to for advice on how to do it well?" "I think the more interesting question," one man answered, "is how many of us don't have anyone like that." We looked around at each other, wondering if any of us could name someone, until somebody said, "It's us."

Staying White

By trying to figure out what is happening with race in situations I'm in, I've embarked on a journey that I now realize is not headed toward innocence or winning or becoming not white or finally getting it right. I don't know where it leads, but I have some hopes and desires.

I want to find an antidote to the ways that whiteness numbs me, makes me not see what is right in front of me, takes away my intelligence, divides me from people I care about. I hope that, by occupying the seeming contradictions between the "antiracist" and the "gay white male" parts of myself, I can generate a creative tension that will motivate me to keep fighting. I hope to help end the exclusionary practices that make gay worlds stay so white. When I find myself in a situation that is going to stay white, I want to play a role in deciding what kind of white it's going to stay. And I want to become less invested in whiteness while staying white myself—always remembering that I can't just decide to stand outside of whiteness or exempt myself from its unearned privileges.[42] I want to be careful not to avoid its responsibilities by fleeing into narratives of how I have been oppressed as a gay man. The ways that I am gay will always be shaped by the ways that I am white.

Most of all, I want never to forget that the roots of my antiracist desires and my gay desires are intertwined. As James Baldwin's words remind me, acting on my gay desires is about not being afraid to love and therefore about having to confront this white society's terror of love—a terror that lashes out with racist and antigay violence. Following both my gay and antiracist desires is about being willing to "go the way your blood beats," as Baldwin put it, even into the heart of that terror, which, he warned, is "a tremendous danger, a tremendous responsibility."[43]

notes

This is an expanded version of a personal essay I presented at the Making and Unmaking of Whiteness conference at the University of California at Berkeley in April 1997. I want to acknowledge that my thinking has grown out of conversations with many friends and colleagues, including Nan Alamilla Boyd, Margaret Cerullo, John D'Emilio, Arthur Dong, Marla Erlein, Jeffrey Escoffier, Charlie Fernandez, Dana Frank, Wayne Hoffman, Amber Hollibaugh, Mitchell Karp, Jonathan Ned Katz, Judith Levine, William J. Mann, David Meacham, Dennis Poplin, Susan Raffo, Eric Rofes, Gayle Rubin, Sabrina Sojourner, Barbara Smith, Nancy Stoller, Carole Vance, and Carmen Vasquez; the editors of this collection, especially Matt Wray and Irene Nexica; the participants in the "Pale, Male—and

Anti-Racist" workshop at the 1995 Creating Change conference in Detroit; Lisa Kahaleole Hall and the students I joined in her San Francisco City College class on Lesbian and Gay Communities of Color; and the students in the courses I taught at the University of California at Santa Cruz, Portland State University, Stanford University, and the New School for Social Research.

1. "Caught in the Storm: AIDS and the Meaning of Natural Disaster," *Out/Look: National Lesbian and Gay Quarterly* 1 (fall 1988), 8–19; "'Fitting In': Expanding Queer Studies beyond the *Closet* and *Coming Out*," paper presented at Contested Zone: Limitations and Possibilities of a Discourse on Lesbian and Gay Studies, Pitzer College, 6–7 April 1990, and at the Fourth Annual Lesbian, Bisexual, and Gay Studies Conference, Harvard University, 26–28 October 1990; "Intellectual Desire," paper presented at La Ville en rose: Le premier colloque Québécois d'études lesbiennes et gaies (First Quebec Lesbian and Gay Studies Conference), Concordia University and the University of Quebec at Montreal, 12 November 1992, published in *GLQ: A Journal of Lesbian and Gay Studies* 3, no. 1 (February 1996): 139–57, reprinted in *Queerly Classed: Gay Men and Lesbians Write about Class*, ed. Susan Raffo (Boston: South End Press, 1997), 43–66; "Class Dismissed: Queer Storytelling Across the Economic Divide," keynote address at the Constructing Queer Cultures: Lesbian, Bisexual, Gay Studies Graduate Student Conference, Cornell University, 9 February 1995, and at the Seventeenth Gender Studies Symposium, Lewis and Clark College, 12 March 1998; "I Coulda Been a Whiny White Guy," *Gay Community News* 20 (spring 1995): 6–7, 28–30; and "Sunset Trailer Park," in *White Trash: Race and Class in America*, ed. Matt Wray and Annalee Newitz (New York: Routledge, 1997), 15–39.

2. *Dream Ships Sail Away* (forthcoming, Houghton Mifflin).

3. "'Go the Way Your Blood Beats': An Interview with James Baldwin (1984)," Richard Goldstein, in *James Baldwin: The Legacy*, ed. Quincy Troupe (New York: Simon and Schuster/Touchstone, 1989), 176.

4. Personal essays, often assembled in published collections, have become an important written form for investigating how whiteness works, especially in individual lives. Personal essays by lesbian, gay, and bisexual authors that have influenced my own thinking and writing about whiteness have been collected in James Baldwin, *The Price of the Ticket: Collected Nonfiction, 1948–1985* (New York: St. Martin's, 1985); Cherríe Moraga and Gloria Anzaldúa, eds., *This Bridge Called My Back: Writings by Radical Women of Color* (Watertown, Mass.: Persephone Press, 1981); Cherríe Moraga, *Loving in the War Years* (Boston: South End Press, 1983); Audre Lorde, *Sister Outsider* (Freedom, Calif.: Crossing Press, 1984); Elly Bulkin, Minnie Bruce Pratt, and Barbara Smith, *Yours in Struggle: Three Feminist Perspectives on Anti-Semitism and Racism* (Brooklyn: Long Haul Press, 1984); Essex Hemphill, ed., *Brother to Brother: New Writings by Black Gay Men* (Boston: Alyson, 1991); Mab Segrest, *Memoir of a Race Traitor* (Boston: South End Press, 1994); Dorothy Allison, *Skin: Talking about Sex, Class and Literature* (Ithaca, N.Y.: Firebrand, 1994); and Becky Thompson and Sangeeta Tyagi, eds., *Names We Call Home: Autobiography on Racial Identity* (New York: Routledge, 1996).

5. For discussion of how sexual identities are "lived through race and class," see Robin D. G. Kelley, *Yo' Mama's Dysfunktional!* (Boston: Beacon, 1997), 114.

6. Whiteness can grant economic advantages to gay as well as straight men, and gay male couples can sometimes earn more on two men's incomes than can straight couples or lesbian couples. But being gay can restrict a man to lower-paying jobs, and most gay white men are not wealthy; like the larger male population, they are lower middle class, working class, or poor. For discussions of the difficulties of developing an accurate economic profile

of the "gay community," and of how both the religious right and gay marketers promote the idea that gay men are wealthy, see Amy Gluckman and Betsy Reed, eds., *Homo Economics: Capitalism, Community, and Lesbian and Gay Life* (New York: Routledge, 1997).

7. David Mixner, *Stranger Among Friends* (New York: Bantam, 1996), 291. For accounts of how the Campaign for Military Service was formed, see Mixner's memoir and Urvashi Vaid, *Virtual Equality: The Mainstreaming of Lesbian and Gay Equality* (New York: Anchor, 1995). Preceding the ad hoc formation of the Campaign for Military Service in January 1993 was the Military Freedom Project, formed in early 1989 by a group composed primarily of white feminist lesbians. Overshadowed during the Senate hearings by the predominantly male Campaign for Military Service, these activists had raised issues relating the military's antigay policy to gender, race, and class; specifically, that lesbians are discharged at a higher rate than are gay men; that lesbian-baiting is a form of sexual harassment against women; and that African American and Latino citizens, including those who are gay, bisexual, or lesbian, are disproportionately represented in the military, which offers poor and working-class youth access to a job, education, and health care that are often unavailable to them elsewhere. Vaid, *Virtual Equality*, 153–59.

8. "The Race Analogy: Fact Sheet Comparing the Military's Policy of Racial Segregation in the 1940s to the Current Ban on Lesbians, Gay Men and Bisexuals," in *Briefing Book*, prepared by the Legal/Policy Department of the Campaign for Military Service, Washington, D.C. (1993).

9. Quoted from the *Legal Times*, 8 February 1993, in Mixner, *Stranger Among Friends*, 286. Professor of history and civil rights veteran Roger Wilkins, responding to Powell's statement, argued that "lots of white people don't think that being black is benign even in 1993." Mixner, *Stranger Among Friends*, 286.

10. Henry Louis Gates Jr., "Blacklash?" *New Yorker*, 17 May 1993.

11. For brief discussions of how the whiteness of those making the race analogy reduced the power of their arguments, see Gates, "Blacklash?" and David Rayside, *On the Fringe: Gays and Lesbians in Politics* (Ithaca, N.Y.: Cornell University Press, 1998), 243.

12. Mixner, *Stranger Among Friends*, 319.

13. The gay service members on this panel were former Staff Sgt. Thomas Pannicia, Sgt. Justin Elzie, and Col. Margarethe Cammermeyer. Margarethe Cammermeyer, with Chris Fisher, *Serving in Silence* (New York: Penguin, 1994), 299. Other former gay service members who testified at the hearings were Sgt. Tracy Thorne and PO Keith Meinhold. Active-duty lesbian, gay, or bisexual service members could not testify without being discharged from the military as homosexuals, a situation that existed under the former "don't ask, don't tell" military policy.

14. Mary Dunlap, "Reminiscences: Honoring Our Legal Hero, Gay Sgt. Perry Watkins 1949–1996," *Gay Community News* (winter 1996): 21.

15. In his memoir, *Stranger Among Friends*, Mixner makes no mention of Watkins.

16. Author's personal conversation with Sabrina Sojourner, 19 October 1998.

17. An expert witness who was white, male, and not a gay historian was allowed to introduce a brief written synopsis of historical evidence from my book. I was one of the white men working with the CMS behind the scenes and from afar. Early in the hearings, Senator Edward Kennedy's staff asked me to compile a list of questions for him to ask during the hearings. In July, after the hearings were over and the "don't ask, don't tell" policy had been adopted, I submitted to the House Armed Services Committee written testimony, titled "Historical Overview of the Origins of the Military's Ban on Homosexuals," that critiqued the new policy and identified heterosexual masculinity, rather than the competence or be-

havior of homosexual service members, as the military problem requiring investigation. And I sent the CMS a copy of a paper I had given in April, "Stripping Down: Undressing the Military's Anti-Gay Policy," that used historical documents and feminist analysis to argue for investigating the military's crisis in heterosexual masculinity. In all these writings, I was trying, unsuccessfully, to get the CMS and the Senate to adopt a gender and sexuality analysis of the military policy; I used race and class analysis only to argue that the antigay policies disproportionately affected service members who were people of color and/or working class.

18. After Watkins's death in 1996 from complications due to HIV, Mary Dunlap, a white civil rights attorney who for years had followed his appeal case, in a tribute addressed to him, called him a "generous, tireless leader" who expressed "open and emphatic criticism and unabashed indictment of the racism of those among us who so blatantly and hurtfully excluded your voice and face and words from the publicity surrounding the gaylesbitrans community's challenge to 'Don't Ask, Don't Tell' in the early 90s." Dunlap, "Reminiscences," 21.

19. Shamara Riley, "Perry Watkins, 1948–1996: A Military Trailblazer," *Outlines*, 8 May 1996.

20. Randy Shilts, *Conduct Unbecoming: Gays and Lesbians in the U.S. Military* (New York: St. Martin's, 1993), 60, 65; Mary Ann Humphrey, *My Country, My Right to Serve* (New York: HarperCollins, 1990), 248–57. Statistics are from D. Michael Shafer, "The Vietnam-Era Draft: Who Went, Who Didn't, and Why It Matters," in *The Legacy: The Vietnam War in the American Imagination*, ed. D. Michael Shafer (Boston: Beacon Press, 1990), 69.

21. Humphrey, *My Country*, 255–56.

22. Ibid.

23. Dunlap, "Reminiscences"; Shilts, *Conduct Unbecoming*, 155–56; Humphrey, *My Country*, 253–54.

24. A 1996 documentary film, *Sis: The Perry Watkins Story*, was coproduced by Chiqui Cartagena and Suzanne Newman. On the *20/20* segment and a feature film on Watkins that was in preproduction, see Jim Knippenberg, "Gay Soldier Story to Be Filmed," *Cincinnati Enquirer*, 23 December 1997.

25. Rayside, *On the Fringe*, 243.

26. Keith Boykin, *One More River to Cross: Black and Gay in America* (New York: Anchor, 1996), 186–92.

27. Mixner, *Stranger Among Friends*, 301–2, 308–10.

28. Garland Tillery, "Interview with Top Gun Pilot Tracy Thorne," *Our Own*, 18 May 1993.

29. Quoted from the documentary film *All God's Children*, produced by Dee Mosbacher, Frances Reid, and Sylvia Rhue (Women Vision, 1996). I wish to thank Lisa Kahaleole Hall, Stephanie Smith, and Linda Alban for directing me to this quotation.

30. One way to measure how much moral authority the race analogy tries to take from the civil rights movement and transfuse it into a predominantly white gay movement is to see what moral authority remains when the race analogy is removed. David Mixner would be the David Mixner of the gay movement, the military's antigay policy would be a form of antigay bigotry, and Sam Nunn would be "our" Sam Nunn. Or, to reverse the terms, other movements for social change would try to gain moral authority by using a "gay analogy," declaring that their movement was "like" the gay movement. These moves do not seem to carry the moral weight of the race analogy.

31. Quoted from Justice Blackmun's dissenting opinion in the US Supreme Court's 1986 *Bowers v. Hardwick* decision. "Blackmun's Opinions Reflect His Evolution of the 24 Court

Years," *New York Times*, 5 March 1999. I wish to thank Lisa Kahaleole Hall for the conversation we had on 24 October 1998, out of which emerged the ideas in this essay about how the civil rights movement analogy works and is used as a strategy for gaining unearned moral authority, although I am responsible for how they are presented here.

32. "Stonewall 25," *The Charlie Rose Show*, Public Broadcasting System, 24 June 1994. I wish to thank Barbara Smith for lending me her videotape copy of this program.

33. For Fundi's reports on this panel and the entire conference, see "Out/Write '90 Report, Part I: Writers Urged to Examine Their Roles, Save Their Lives," *San Diego GLN*, 16 March 1990, 7; "Out/Write Report, Part II: Ringing Voices," *San Diego GLN*, 23 March 1990, 7, 9; and "Out/Write Report, Part III: Arenas of Interaction," *San Diego GLN*, 30 March 1990, 7, 9.

34. Lisa Kahaleole Chang Hall, "Bitches in Solitude: Identity Politics and Lesbian Community," in *Sisters, Sexperts, Queers: Beyond the Lesbian Nation*, ed. Arlene Stein (New York: Plume, 1993), 223, and in personal conversation.

35. Fundi, "Out/Write Report, Part III," 7, 9.

36. I wish to thank Mitchell Karp for the long dinner conversation we had in 1996 in New York City during which we jointly forged the ideas and questions in this paragraph.

37. I have transcribed the quotations that follow from an audiotape of the workshop discussion.

38. I wish to thank Dennis Poplin for allowing me to use his name and tell his story.

39. Bruce Bawer, "Utopian Erotics," *Lambda Book Report* 7 (October 1998): 19–20.

40. Goldstein, "Go the Way," 180.

41. Bawer, "Utopian Erotics," 19–20.

42. I wish to thank Amber Hollibaugh for introducing me to this idea of "staying white" during a conversation about how a white person can be tempted to distance oneself from whiteness and escape the guilt of its privileges by identifying as a person of color. I was introduced to the idea that white privilege is unearned and difficult to escape at a workshop called White Privilege conducted by Jona Olssen at the 1995 Black Nations/Queer Nations Conference, sponsored by the Center for Lesbian and Gay Studies at the City University of New York. See also Peggy McIntosh, "White Privilege: Unpacking the Invisible Knapsack," *Peace and Freedom* (July/August 1989): 10–12.

43. Goldstein, "Go the Way," 177.

18

the peculiarity of
black trans male privilege

*Men of All Genders Benefit from the
Complicit Oppression of Black Women*

Kortney Ziegler*

In May, I journeyed to Dallas to spend a weekend of community building and love sharing with a group of black trans men, many of whom I call my chosen brothers, at the third annual Black Trans Advocacy Conference. As it is one of the few opportunities for black transgender people to collectively gather, each one of us traveled from different parts of the country with our significant others, with friends, or by ourselves to the annual gathering with the hopes of finding family.

Outside of panels that covered topics such as self-awareness and relationship building, our chats turned into late-night discussions in each other's hotel rooms. We openly shared our fears and insecurities around the expectations of black masculinity, the ways in which we are learning to accept our bodies, our successes and failures at dating while trans, and other intimate issues related to transition. Through all of our talks, however, we kept returning to the topic of navigating our newfound privilege as men

*Ziegler, Kortney. "Peculiarity of Black Trans Male Privilege." *The Advocate*, August/September 2014, p. 58. Available at http://www.advocate.com/print-issue/current-issue/2014/07/15/peculiarity-black-trans-male-privilege. Courtesy *The Advocate*/Here Media © 2014. All rights reserved.

who carry with us the emotional, mental, and physical memory of being perceived as women—a peculiar type of privilege that is both liberating and restrictive.

Shifted Privilege

One of the most obvious ways in which I benefit from male privilege is the reduction of public sexual assault from other men. When I walk down the street in this body, I can do so without the fear I once held as a victim of male harassment, such as the time a group of men hurled their fists and homophobic slurs at my friends and I at a bar in San Francisco. We were lucky to survive that and other similar situations, but I often think of black queer women who are not afforded the same. Women like Sakia Gunn whose masculinity causes men to kill them, and the ever-growing list of murdered black trans women whose femininity brings the same results.

Although I'm less likely to be sexually assaulted because of the ways in which I present my gender, this privilege is in exchange for becoming a visible target of racist practices designed to police young black manhood. Policies such as "stop and frisk" and the sanctioned citizen killings of young black men like Trayvon Martin and Jordan Davis have forced me to learn new ways to manage my body to attract the least amount of attention. I am constantly learning new social cues to present myself as less threatening, less aggressive, and less criminal, to challenge the irrational fear of black masculinity that can literally end my life.

I also experience male privilege in the economic realm. In employment situations I am more likely to earn a higher wage and to experience career advancements faster than black women, but this is only if my trans status does not become a point of contention. For black trans men who transition on the job or seek employment with a public trans status, the presence of both anti-trans and anti-black discriminatory practices is a primary reason why we make up a large portion of the 26% of black transgender people who are unemployed. Attorney Kylar Broadus, for example, has been very public about the discrimination he experienced at a successful corporate law firm that resulted in his being let go six months after he announced his medical transition.

Broadus's story is not unique—the same risk applies to black trans men who are stealth or private about their gender status. There are numerous stories of being outed in the workplace, leading to harassment from co-workers in the form of intentional misgendering, rescinded promotions, and even firing. Furthermore, stealth black trans men are not immune to negative views that perceive black men as being dishonest or unskilled or having a poor work ethic, no matter their level of education or professional credentials.

Another way in which my passing privilege, or my ability to be seen as a cisgender person, functions is that in most social situations I am generally assumed to be heterosexual and am treated as such, at least up until the point where the disclosure of my gender calls this into question. At the same time, in many queer spaces, there is no lack of celebration of (white) trans men; their bodies fill the spaces of photography projects, popular online sites, and even queer porn. However, these images are rarely consumed outside of the queer community, leaving trans men on the margins of mainstream discussions of transgender identity and making black trans men, for the most part, culturally invisible.

Shifting Liberation

These examples of black trans male privilege and the consequences of black masculinity are important to the larger LGBT community. They demonstrate the ways in which men of all genders benefit from the complicit oppression of black women, while revealing the similarities of gender discrimination experienced by black trans men and black trans and cis women. This intersectional awareness serves as a point of entry in which to insert black trans men into the dominant conversations of LGBT equality from which we are largely absent. Additionally, they help us to more fully understand the ways in which some black trans men resist racist expectations of black manhood as a process of survival. Such stories ultimately afford all black men a type of social humanity that is often denied as the result of a culture saturated with stereotypes and mischaracterizations of our identity.

Most importantly, exploring the ways in which black trans men navigate the privileges and disprivileges of masculinity, both inside and outside the LGBT community, only extends the possibilities of what transgender means. Surely, it is our diverse lived experiences that matter in this moment in which trans people across the globe are breaking ground in multiple fields.

19

gay and jewish

The "Advantages" of Intersectionality

Seth Goren*

> Do I contradict myself?
> Very well then I contradict myself,
> (I am large, I contain multitudes.)
> —WALT WHITMAN, "SONG OF MYSELF"

Nearly three decades ago, Peggy McIntosh's classic 1988 essay on White privilege captured the imagination of progressives worldwide and has served as a foundational piece for diversity and inclusion education ever since. Among the essay's most captivating portions is an inventory of how White privilege is manifested, providing specific examples of the ways in which White individuals reap racial privilege's benefits, ways they are often unaware of.[†]

Following McIntosh's example, other lists have sprouted up surrounding a particular identity and the privilege it brings with it. By drawing attention to the privileges surrounding ability, wealth, sexual orientation, class, gender, gender identity, and religion, these enumerations have proven efficient

---

[†] Among McIntosh's examples are one's race being an asset in social and professional situations, having positive educational curricula and media coverage of one's race, and not being taken as a representative of one's race.

and effective ways to educate readers with specific examples of how privilege operates.

At the same time that these privilege lists have proliferated, scholars have elaborated on privilege and pursued the ongoing development of privilege and related studies. Among these developments have been explorations of intersectionality, a term coined by Kimberlé Crenshaw referring to the ways in which a person's various identities interact and their combined impact on lived experiences (1989). Much of the literature in this area has focused on the compounding negative impact of marginalized identities, with the experiences of Black women providing one such example (Crenshaw, 1991).

While the privilege inventories mentioned above provide excellent examples of privilege along a variety of single axes, few address intersectionality or more than one identity at a time.* This could be because much of the literature on intersectionality focuses on two or more marginalized identities and how those identities interact to magnify oppression, or because of the inherent difficulty of disentangling two specific threads of identity from the elaborate, complicated tapestry that makes up a human being. Regardless, as more privilege conversations include intersectionality as a vehicle for understanding and educating (Ferber), the classic McIntosh-style list format has the potential to be a helpful tool for individuals exploring a variety of intersecting identities.

While I carry a number of privileged identities (*e.g.*, White, male, cisgender), I also have (at least) two non-privileged identities: I identify religiously and visibly as Jewish, and I am openly gay. Individually, each of these independently marks me for exclusion in society as a whole, as numerous researchers have pointed out, and on a regular basis, I run into the ill effects of either straight privilege, religious privilege, or both.

My experiences as an openly gay Jew generally affirm the negative synergies often associated with the intersectionality of two marginalized identities. Religious privilege flows through the queer community, just as it does the rest of society, presenting expected challenges in being Jewish rather than Christian (at least culturally Christian) in queer contexts. Similarly, Jewish settings are not free from heteronormativity and sexual orientation

---

* The one example of an intersectional list I was able to find is "The Black Male Privileges Checklist" (available at http://jewelwoods.com/node/9), which focuses on the privileges enjoyed by Black men, and the acute marginalization of Black women.

privilege, and it is easier to be a straight Jew than a gay one. Several studies have highlighted the collision of these two identities and the difficulties faced by gay and lesbian Jews in integrating these two aspects of who they are (Abes, 2011; Schnoor, 2006), as well as the lower rates of practice and engagement for lesbian, gay, and bisexual Jews when compared to the Jewish community as a whole (Cohen, 2009).

That said, the intersectional effect of being both gay and Jewish is, oddly enough, not entirely disadvantaging, when compared to the experience of those who are gay and not Jewish. Having had repeated conversations with gay non-Jews, I am struck by the way in which I enjoy certain unearned benefits that they do not, based on my being Jewish. It is almost as if my Jewish identity, and the resources that flow from it, grant me entrance to a queer-friendly (or at least a queer-friendlier) sanctuary from some of the heteronormativity and homophobia in the world at large.

For those more visually inclined among us, the following figure may be useful:*

| CHRISTIAN | LGBT | JEWISH |

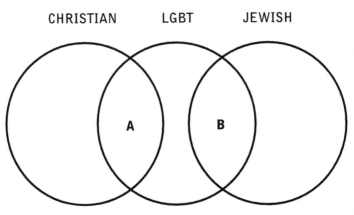

In essence, my experience as a resident of Area B is, in some ways, more advantaged than that of Area A dwellers. Because those in Area A carry religious privilege that I do not, this seems counterintuitive. Nevertheless, examples of my Jewish identity giving me support unavailable to LGBT Christians are surprisingly numerous.

---

* This figure makes Jewish and Christian religious identities mutually exclusive. While there may be some overlap in Christian religious identities with Jewish ethnic identities, Jewish and Christian religious identities are typically thought of in the mainstream Jewish community as incompatible.

Increasingly mindful of these benefits and inspired like so many others by Peggy McIntosh, I have put together a list of specific things that I, as a gay Jew, take for granted and that gay non-Jews are less likely to have. Some are particular to my being gay and Jewish, while others apply more generally to LGBT or queer Jews. The items listed are not exclusively or universally Jewish; there are others who reap similar benefits, such as gay Unitarian-Universalists or LGBT individuals who affiliate with the Metropolitan Community Church or United Church of Christ,* and the advantages I have included are uneven in their spread through the Jewish world, particularly pronounced in certain settings and nearly absent in others.† Even so, what strikes me as unusual is their widespread, visible, mainstream and at times even dominant nature in the Jewish community as a whole, in a way I have not seen in Christianity writ large or almost any other overarching religion.

This list is not without caveats. Although I have done my best to isolate these two identities and how they interrelate, I am certain that other aspects of who I am have seeped in. Moreover, to be clear, this is not a "privilege list" along the lines of those enumerated elsewhere, and does not obviate the need to confront systemic oppression; it is difficult to see how a gay Jew could be "privileged" based on those identities in the way that men, straight people, White people or other holders of dominant identities are. This is, rather, an exploration of my own intersectionality, the gay-Jewish perks I often forget are not universal and the unexpected ways in which two salient, marginalized aspects of who I am interact.

With that introduction, the following is a list of benefits that I enjoy as a gay Jewish man and that are largely unavailable to gay non-Jews:

---

* There certainly are LGBT-welcoming Christian denominations, and LGBT persons in those denominations would "score" relatively highly on this inventory. That said, even in this time of substantial flux on queer issues in the North American religious world, most Christian movements and organizations at best continue to struggle with LGBT issues, limiting opportunities for inclusion and contributing to a perception of Christianity, on the whole, as unwelcoming.

† Many of these benefits accrue in a most pronounced manner in larger metropolitan areas and in pluralistic Jewish or non-Orthodox Jewish organizations and places of worship. That said, I have often been surprised at the way in which these benefits accumulate even in less densely populated areas and in the Orthodox Jewish world (e.g., Rapoport, 2004).

1. Should I marry someone of the same gender, there is religious liturgy readily available for me to use, either verbatim or as a starting point for designing my own liturgy, and there are abundant clergy of my religion willing to officiate at same-gender wedding ceremonies.

2. Numerous institutions, agencies, places of worship and community organizations affiliated with my religion have workplace protections based on sexual orientation and gender expression or identity.

3. Multiple denominations or movements within my religion have taken progressive stances on issues related to sexual orientation and gender identity, and historically have demonstrated support for marriage equality and legal protections for LGBT individuals.

4. My religion has numerous queer-inclusive rituals, including rituals for coming out, transitioning, assisted reproduction and same-gender divorce, available for use and widely disseminated, and has been using them for a significant stretch of time.

5. Mainstream organizations and conferences for my religious group offer programs and sessions that present and have professionals who speak to LGBT issues in a positive way.

6. Those who identify with my religion often experience marginalization and oppression or are exposed to the history of past oppressions, providing ready narratives for non-LGBT coreligionists to connect and empathize with my experience as an LGBT individual.

7. There are numerous lesbian, gay, bisexual, transgender and allied clergy I can turn to for pastoral counseling, spiritual guidance and other forms of religious and spiritual support.

8. If I choose to become a clergyperson or lay leader in my religious community, I would have several options to select from in pursuing my goals, and being lesbian, gay, bisexual or transgender would not be an inherent obstacle to pursuing any of them.

9. Among the sacred texts of my religion are stories, narratives and directives that easily lend themselves to supporting queer perspectives and inclusive stances.

10. In public surveys, my religious community demonstrates comparatively strong support for issues of importance to the queer community.

11. In filling out forms to join most religious organizations, it is unlikely that I will have to modify the membership form to make it fit me and my family.

12. There are numerous organizations and gatherings that focus on my religion specifically and its intersections with LGBT identities.

13. When celebrating anniversaries and other relationship milestones, I can find a religious community that will honor them.

14. Dating websites that cater to people of my religion are likely to have searches for same-sex partners as an option.

15. There are numerous books, websites, studies and other resources that respond to the intersectionality of my religion and LGBT identity in a positive way.

16. My experience with religious privilege, marginalization and oppression prepared me and gave me skills to respond to heteronormativity and straight privilege.

17. In looking nationally and internationally, I can see LGBT role models who share my religious identity in public life, including politics, academics and the arts with little effort.

18. In seeking out a mentor my religious community, I am able to find someone with a sexual orientation or gender identity identical to my own.

19. People's general unfamiliarity with my religion makes it less likely that they will sense or point out any perceived conflict between me being religious and me being openly queer.

20. If my partner of the same gender passed away, a significant portion of adherents and leaders would accord me the appropriate respect due a mourner in my position.

All told, this presents what could be read as a contradiction: when taken together, two marginalized and oppressed aspects of who I am create benefits that holders of only one of those identities are less likely to carry. It is almost as if these two "negative" identities (insofar as they are both marginal) produce something of a positive result, an outcome that holds in mathematics, but a phenomenon that feels somewhat contradictory in speaking of privilege.

The effects of intersectionality, especially as they reflect privilege and marginalization, are nuanced and subtle, and the fast-changing pace of LGBT acceptance in religious settings requires us to be especially attentive of how these combinations play out. As we become increasingly aware of the benefits of an intersectionality-based approach to identity, power, and privilege education, it would not surprise me if the *contradictions* multiply because surely, to paraphrase Walt Whitman, each of us carries contradictions and contains multitudes.

references

Abes, E. S. (2011). Exploring the Relationship between Sexual Orientation and Religious Identities for Jewish Lesbian College Students. *Journal of Lesbian Studies*, 15(2), 205–225.

Cohen, S. M., Aviv, C., & Kelman, A. Y. (2009). Gay, Jewish, or both: Sexual orientation and Jewish engagement. *Journal of Jewish Communal Service*, 84(1/2), 154–166.

Crenshaw, K. (1989). Demarginalizing the intersection of race and sex: A Black feminist critique of antidiscrimination doctrine, feminist theory and antiracist politics. *University of Chicago Legal Forum*, 139.

Crenshaw, K. (1991). Mapping the margins: Intersectionality, identity politics, and violence against women of color. *Stanford Law Review*, 1241–1299.

Coyle, A., & Rafalin, D. (2001). Jewish gay men's accounts of negotiating cultural, religious, and sexual identity: A qualitative study. *Journal of Psychology & Human Sexuality*, 12(4), 21–48.

Ferber, A. and O'Reilly Herrera, A. "Privilege as Key in the Pedagogy of Intersectionality." Unpublished.

McIntosh, P. (1988). White privilege: Unpacking the invisible knapsack. *Race, Class, and Gender in the United States: An Integrated Study*, 4, 165–169.

Rapoport, C. (2004). *Judaism and homosexuality: An authentic Orthodox view*. Mitchell Vallentine & Company.

Schnoor, R. F. (2006). Being gay and Jewish: Negotiating intersecting identities. *Sociology of Religion*, 67(1), 43–60.

20

the middle easterner as the other

The Slippery Slope from Friendly Foreigner
to Enemy Alien, Enemy Alien to Enemy Race

John Tehranian*

Inextricably intertwined with the rising tide of discrimination facing persons of Middle Eastern descent is the mythology surrounding racial construction and related religious and sociocultural perceptions. For prior generations, Middle Eastern Americans came closer to matching our constructed notions of whiteness. They were largely Christian; they came from an exotic but friendly, romantic, and halcyon foreign land imagined to contain magic lanterns, genies, flying carpets, and belly dancers; and they served as a chief vessel of the philosophical and cultural heritage of the West. Thus, in previous generations, people of (what we now call) Middle Eastern descent were, more often than not, blended into the white category. When the Levant was perceived as a desert hinterland, irrelevant to Western interests, its people were not collectivized into a Middle Eastern taxonomy. But once the region took on geopolitical and economic significance, the Middle East leaped into existence as a concept imbued with social meaning. As James C. Scott has argued, the naming process is intricately related to exercise of power. Specifically, the creation of synoptic categories represents an essential step in a state's nation-building process in that it advances the government's ability to track and control both its

* Tehranian, John. "The Middle Easterner as the Other." *Whitewashed: America's Invisible Middle Eastern Minority,* pp. 68–75. © 2009 by John Tehranian. All rights reserved. Reprinted by permission of NYU Press.

subjects and those who might pose a threat from without. Race comes into existence only when a group grows sufficiently large, in terms of both numbers and power, as to become a threat.

In an era when we view the most immediate threat to our national security as emanating from the Middle East, it is not surprising that monolithic images of the Middle East and the Middle Easterner have leaped into existence. Middle Easterners have been irretrievably associated with Islam; they appear to hail from a decidedly unfriendly foreign land imagined to contain nothing but terrorists, obstreperous mobs chanting "Death to America," unabashed misogynistic polygamists, and religious fundamentalists; and they seem to represent a wholly different civilization from our own—one with which the inevitable and apocalyptic clash of civilizations is unfolding. Thus, they are the quintessential Other, and the Middle Easterner category, imposed on them by society at large, has become their appellation.

In popular perception, in which the notion of assimilability constitutes the sine qua non of the majority's acceptance of an immigrant group, it is not surprising that Middle Easterners have fared poorly. As Karen Engle has noted, the past century has witnessed a radical transformation in majority perceptions of Middle Eastern individuals: they are, in short, no longer thought capable of assimilation. The changing religious composition of Middle Eastern immigrants to the United States has played a key role in this transformation. As the naturalization cases make clear, perceptions of race are frequently conflated with perceptions of religion. In 1924, about two hundred thousand Arabs resided in the United States. Of these, 80 percent were from Syria and Lebanon, of which group a startling 90 percent were Christian. Many of these immigrants had fled oppression and persecution under the Ottoman Empire. Indeed, an early study of the emerging Syrian and Lebanese community at the turn of the century in New York City found that only 2 of 2,482 residents were Muslim. As the author of the study noted, "The Moslems, Druses and Metàwely are not found in sufficient numbers to warrant more than passing mention."

Given the tendency to conflate race with religious affiliation, and Christianity with assimilability, it is not surprising that, at the beginning of the twentieth century, courts declared Armenians and even some Arabs white by law, thereby entitling them to the privileges of whiteness, including naturalization. However, the composition of the Middle Eastern American population has undergone a dramatic change in recent years, especially in the public imagination. Contrary to popular perceptions, only 25 percent of present-day Arab Americans are Muslim. However, about 60 percent of Arab immigrants arriving in the United States since 1965 identify themselves as Muslim. As it has grown less Christian, the Middle Eastern population in the United States is thought of as less assimilable and, consequently, less white.

As faith in their assimilatory capacity has diminished, Middle Easterners have come to represent enemy aliens, and even an enemy race, in the popular imagination. In the past, the paradigmatic noncitizen was the "Mexican illegal alien, or the inscrutable, clannish Asian." Today, it is the Arab terrorist, and this vision has firmly taken hold of our immigration policies. As Victor Romero argues, "post-9/11, the age-old stereotype of the foreign, Arab terrorist has been rekindled, and placing our immigration functions under the auspices of an executive department charged with 'homeland security' reinforces the idea that immigrants are terrorists." The recent wave of registration and deportation policies aimed at individuals of Middle Eastern descent also highlights this trend. Take, for example, the National Security Entry-Exit Registration System (NSEERS), which was formally announced by the attorney general on June 6, 2002, and then supplemented with a special "call-in" registration in November 2002. The NSEERS singles out a limited class of noncitizens—male, nonimmigrant visa holders over the age of sixteen who are from one of twenty-five Muslim and Middle Eastern countries—for special registration requirements.

The changing perceptions of the Middle East are exemplified with a perusal through one of the earliest reflections on the Middle Eastern population in the United States. At the turn of the twentieth century, Lucius Hopkins Miller, a professor of biblical studies at Princeton University, published a study on the Arab community in New York City. His analysis—which sheds a generally positive light on these new immigrants, embraces their assimilability, and endorses their admission to the Republic—reflects certain stereotypes, both positive and negative, about Middle Easterners that seem quite ill-fitting with contemporary perceptions. For example, Miller's strongest critique of Arabs is their allegedly well-known mendacity. Wholeheartedly acknowledging the duplicitous and perfidious ways of persons descending from the Middle East, Miller notes,

> A main charge brought against the Syrian character is that of sharpness and deceit—a prevalent Oriental strain. Its existence is admitted in the Arabic proverb 'A lie is the salt of man' and in the Arabic story of Satan's journey

through the earth. With twelve packs of lies on his back, while crossing Mount Lebanon, he tripped and fell, spilling the contents of ten bags upon the land of Syria.

To temper the implications of this charge, Miller then argues that Middle Eastern chicanery is not inherent or congenital but a symptom of circumstance:

> When it is remembered that in his own land the only alternative has often been 'lie or die,' it will be seen that Syrian deceitfulness has been largely nurtured by an adverse environment. In this he has shared with every downtrodden race in history. American residence should work improvement in this respect. . . . Nevertheless, the cold fact remains that the inability to tell the truth is the chief blot upon the Syrian immigrant's character.

Interestingly enough, Miller also heaps a number of "positive" stereotypes—unusual by today's popular standards—on the Syrians, particularly emphasizing their law-abiding character. In remarkable language, Miller explains,

> In his love of law and order the Syrian cannot be excelled. Personal inquiry at police stations and among patrolmen, as well as careful search in the reports of the Commissioners of Charities and Correction, failed to bring out the slightest flaw. The Syrians do not become public charges and they mind their own business. The universal testimony of the police authorities is that there is no more peaceful or law abiding race in New York city. The humane spirit is very strong among the Syrians.

Ironically, at the turn of the next century, Middle Easterners would be perceived as the greatest threat to American national security.

Perceptions of the humane spirit described by Miller resonated at least through the eve of the oil embargoes and the Middle Eastern tumult of the 1970s. In an episode of the children's cartoon *Scooby Doo, Where Are You?* that aired in the late 1960s, for example, the gang takes pains to highlight the Persians' renowned kindness, generosity, and hospitality—a message scarcely conveyed by the mass media today. The Persian custom of *larof*—an elaborate system of ceremonial politeness—was doubtless the inspiration for such a generalization.

Events in the region have led to a dramatic change in media portrayals during recent years. The image of the Levant as an exotic and charming land has given way to a nightmarish vision of the Middle East as a dangerous, anarchic world teeming with perfidious oil sheiks, Islamic fundamentalists and maniacal terrorists. But before we document and assess the impact of these changing perceptions, we must consider the particular processes that have fueled this transformation.

The Negotiation of Middle Eastern Identity: Selective Racialization and Covering

The negotiation of the Middle Eastern identity is mediated by a twofold process that moves both from the top down and from the bottom up. From the top down, society at large engages in a practice that can best be described as *selective racialization*. From the bottom up, Middle Easterners, both privileged and damned by their proximity to the white dividing line, engage in persistent (and frequently effective) covering of their ethnic background. These two social forces combine to create a pernicious stereotyping feedback loop that enervates the political strength of the Middle Eastern community, heightens its invisibility, and leaves little effective resistance to the growing assaults against its civil rights.

A Theory of Selective Racialization

In a landmark article published two decades ago, civil rights scholar Charles Lawrence advanced a powerful critique of existing equal protection jurisprudence and its problematic immunization of unconscious racism from judicial scrutiny. Under existing Supreme Court precedent, plaintiffs cannot raise a cognizable equal protection claim unless they establish that a challenged action purposefully sought to discriminate against a protected group, such as a racial minority. This intent requirement, argues Lawrence, has rendered our civil rights laws wholly inadequate to fight the pernicious systemic racism that pervades our society. As Lawrence explains, "Americans share a common historical and cultural heritage in which racism has played and still plays a dominant role. . . . [This] culture—including, for example, the media, an individual's parents, peers, and authority figures—transmits certain beliefs and preferences . . . [that] seem part of the individual's rational ordering of her perceptions of the world." Lawrence therefore warns us that, by limiting the remedial powers of courts to only those government policies that stem from overt animus, we ignore our broader culture of unconscious racism, its role in shaping our institutions, and its profound impact on our social, political, and economic lives.

The immediate thrust of Lawrence's argument deals with the equal protection doctrine, which attaches solely to state action—governmental regulations and policies. But Lawrence's core insight also has wider implications: to truly eradicate discrimination from our society, we must remedy both intentional and unconscious racism. To accomplish this task, we must scrutinize all forms of unintentional racism, including the social processes by which stereotypes are formed, transmitted, and perpetuated. With respect to individuals of Middle Eastern descent, the act of identification and racialization is laden with tacit associations that fuel negative stereotypes. Drawing on Lawrence's insights on the power of unconscious racism, this section examines the social mechanisms that have exacerbated the rising ride of discrimination against Middle Eastern Americans, fueled their relative invisibility in the body politic and civil society, and frustrated any semblance of a civil rights movement for them.

Specifically, in society at large, Middle Easterners are consistently subjected to a process of *selective racialization*. This largely undocumented and predominantly subconscious mechanism has profound ramifications. Systematically, *famous* individuals of Middle Eastern descent are usually perceived as white. Meanwhile, *infamous* individuals of Middle Eastern descent are usually categorized as Middle Eastern. When Middle Eastern actors conform to social norms and advance positive values and conduct, their racial identity as the Other recedes to the background as they merge into the great white abyss. By contrast, when Middle Eastern actors engage in transgressive behavior, their racial identity as the Other immediately becomes a central, defining characteristic of who they are. The result is an endless feedback loop that calcifies popular prejudices. Wholesome and socially redeeming activities, which might otherwise subvert public misperceptions of the community, do not get associated with Middle Eastern identity. By contrast, the image of transgression is continually correlated with the Middle Eastern racial category, serving only to reinforce negative connotations with the community.

Our country is filled with individuals of Middle Eastern descent who have contributed constructively to American society. Yet surprisingly few of these Americans are actually perceived as Middle Easterners. Instead, their ethnicity is frequently whitewashed. On one hand, this fact highlights the assimilability of Middle Eastern immigrants in the United States. On the other hand, it creates a problematic signposting of Middle Eastern identity when it becomes associated with transgressive activities.

The long list of Middle Eastern Americans includes individuals from virtually every aspect of American life, including athletes such as tennis player Andre Agassi (Persian/Armenian), Indy 500 champion Bobby Rahal (Lebanese), and NFL quarterbacks Doug Flutie and Jeff George (both Lebanese).

Some observers might point to the whitewashing of Americans of Middle Eastern descent as evidence of our evolving colorblindness. But such an argument is belied by the systematic racialization of transgressive individuals. When individuals lie at the cusp of the white/nonwhite divide, we unconsciously categorize them as the Other when they engage in wrongdoing but blend them into the white when they behave within social norms. Andre Agassi is a (white) tennis player, and Ralph Nader is a (white) politician. But Osama bin Laden is labeled an Arab terrorist and the Ayatollah Khomeini was a Middle Eastern Islamic fundamentalist. The act of selective racialization is by no means limited to geopolitical struggles. It occurs on a far more pedestrian, but nevertheless important, level. Take the case of Dodi Al-Fayed, the wealthy businessman who was dating Princess Diana following her divorce from Prince Charles. The escapades of the two, rumored to be engaged at the time of their deaths, were the subject of extensive media coverage. Throughout their relationship, Al-Fayed was repeatedly portrayed as an *Arab* businessman and *Middle Eastern* playboy—not merely an Englishman or a businessman without reference to his race. In other words, he was racialized. And the reason is clear: he was engaging in transgressive behavior, stealing away with the People's princess.

Other examples abound. The process of selective racialization occurs with regularity in the mass media, serving to bolster and legitimize existing stereotypes. Although all the characters in the Middle Eastern–themed Disney film *Aladdin* share Arab descent, they are only selectively racialized. The chief wrongdoers—the greedy bazaar merchants, the thief Kazim, and the main antagonist, Jafar—all possess exaggerated stereotypical features. Both Kazim and Jafar sport thick Arab accents, facial hair, and prominent hooked noses. By contrast, the movie's sympathetic protagonists—Aladdin, Princess Jasmine, and the Sultan—possess few of the features traditionally associated with Arabs. Instead, their physiognomy is quintessentially European, and they speak with no trace of a Middle Eastern accent. In other words, the transgressive characters are Arabized and the wholesome characters Anglicized, thereby heightening negative stereotypes linked to Middle Easterners while concurrently reinforcing positive associations with whiteness.

discussion questions and activities

Discussion or Journal Questions

1. What were some of the most powerful or memorable insights for you in this section?
2. Each chapter in this section examines the intersections of multiple social identities. For each chapter, identify some of the ways in which our knowledge of one specific social identity would be limited by examining it in isolation. For example, in Kimmel and Coston's chapter, how would our understanding of masculinity be limited by ignoring ability and sexual identity? What would some of the consequences be?
3. Considering Part Three as a whole, why is intersectionality so important to our understanding of social identities, privilege, and oppression?
4. Can you think of any research topic where an intersectional approach would not be possible, or beneficial?

Personal Connections

The following questions and activities are designed to be completed either on your own or in class, and then discussed as a group with others. As you share your insights with others, think about the patterns and similarities that emerge, as well as the differences among your answers.

A. Dissecting Privilege and Intersectionality in Your Own Life
- Identify one of the most significant social identities in your life. When you begin to examine that prominent identity in the context of your privileged identities, does it change anything? Reveal anything? Make you think about yourself or others differently in any way? For

example, if you have always seen being a woman as the most significant identity in your life, does considering your race, class, sexual identity, ability, religion, or nationality lead to a different understanding of your experience as a woman?

B. Bringing Privilege and Intersectionality into Your Studies

- Select one book or article you have read for another class or project that focuses specifically on only one social identity. Identify and discuss the ways that knowledge of the issue would be advanced by bringing an intersectional perspective into the research.

- Select one of the topics you would be most interested in researching. Approaching the topic from an intersectional perspective, which social identities do you think would be most important for you to examine, and why?

part four

making new connections, moving forward

Finally, we ask, what can we do? After all, every one of us has some privilege, and every one of us is marginalized in some way. Can we develop a language to talk through our differences instead of talking past each other?

All the essays in this section suggest that we need to think in new ways. For example, Carol Mukhopadhyay advises that we get rid of the word *Caucasian*, since it is inaccurate and creates a false origin of "whiteness." M. E. Lee suggests we rethink notions of mobility when it comes to class, since it is the only status that we think of as a continuum rather than a fixed status. Perhaps we can use the emerging understanding of a gender continuum to understand class positioning and changes.

Abby Ferber cautions against false solutions such as color-blindness or "postfeminism" that suggest one could simply transcend or surpass the influence of gender or race on social life as an act of individual will.

And finally, Patricia Hill Collins, Mark Warren, and Caitlin Deen Fair describe the politics that might emerge from an understanding of the intersections of privilege and marginality, subordination and superordination. Such awareness of these intersections need not place us in ever-shrinking silos of marginality, in which we end up feeling despairing, hopeless, and isolated. Rather, seeing these intersections creates new possibilities for new political coalitions across all these divides. That, it seems to us, is the promise of a genuine intersectional politics of multiculturalism.

21

getting rid of the word "caucasian"

Carol C. Mukhopadhyay*

Racial labels and categories, like all terms and concepts, are human-made classifying devices that we learn, internalize, and then use to interpret the everyday world in which we live. But conventional American racial categories are rooted in colonialism, slavery, and an elaborate ideology developed to justify a system of racial inequality. Given racial categories' sociohistorical rather than biological roots, the notion that "races" describe human biological variation has been officially rejected by the American Anthropological Association. As we critique outmoded systems of racial classification, we must also question the labels we use for "races."

The Civil Rights Movement dismantled the most explicit forms of racism, including many biological-sounding racial labels. Terms like "Negroid," the "Red Man" and the "Yellow Race" were replaced—often by group members themselves—with words like "Black" or "African American," "Native American," and "Asian," which indicate that these groups are political, not biological, realities. Today, terms like "Oriental" would immediately mark the user as seriously out of touch with current understandings. Yet there is one striking exception in our modern racial vocabulary: the term "Caucasian." Despite being a remnant of a discredited theory of racial classification, the term has persisted into the twenty-first century, within as well as outside of the educational community.

* Mukhopadhyay, Carol C. "Getting Rid of the Word 'Caucasian.'" Excerpt from *Everyday Antiracism: Getting Real about Race in School* © 2008 by Mica Pollock. Reprinted by permission of the New Press. www.thenewpress.com.

It is high time we got rid of the word Caucasian. Some might protest that it is "only a label." But language is one of the most systematic, subtle, and significant vehicles for transmitting racial ideology. Terms that describe imagined groups, such as Caucasian, encapsulate those beliefs. Every time we use them and uncritically expose students to them, we are reinforcing rather than dismantling the old racialized worldview. Using the word Caucasian invokes scientific racism, the false idea that races are naturally occurring, biologically ranked subdivisions of the human species and that Caucasians are the superior race. Beyond this, the label Caucasian can even convey messages about which groups have culture and are entitled to recognition as Americans.

The term Caucasian originated in the eighteenth century as part of the developing European science of racial classification. After visiting the region of the Caucasus Mountains, between the Caspian and Black seas, German anatomist Johann Blumenbach declared its inhabitants the most beautiful in the world, the ideal type of humans created in "God's image," and deemed this area the likely site where humans originated. (Humans actually originated in Africa.) He decided that all light-skinned peoples from this region, along with Europeans, belonged to the same race, which he labeled Caucasian.

Blumenbach named four other races that he considered physically and morally "degenerate" forms of "God's original creation." He classified Africans (excepting lighter-skinned North Africans) as "Ethiopians" or "black." He split non-Caucasian Asians into two separate races: the "Mongolian" or "yellow" race of China and Japan, and the "Malayan" or "brown" race, including Aboriginal Australians and Pacific Islanders. Native Americans were the "red" race.

Blumenbach's system of racial classification was adopted in the United States. American scientists tried to prove that Caucasians had larger brains and were smarter than people of other races. Racial science dovetailed with nineteenth-century evolutionary theories, which ranked races from more "primitive" "savages" to more "advanced" or "civilized," with Caucasians on top. Racial hierarchies were used to justify slavery and other forms of racial discrimination.

The U.S. legal system drew on Blumenbach's definitions to decide who was eligible to become a naturalized citizen, a privilege the 1790 Naturalization Act restricted to "whites." This schema created dilemmas. Blumenbach's Caucasians included such groups as Armenians, Persians (Iranians),

North Indians, Arabs, and some North Africans. In 1923, however, the U.S. Supreme Court rejected the naturalization petition of an immigrant from North India, saying he was Caucasian but not white and citing, among other things, his skin color.

The constant tweaking of categories like "Caucasian" to include or exclude newcomers provides evidence of these categories' social rather than biological basis. By the 1920s, eugenicists (who were concerned with the improvement of the species through the reproduction of the "superior" race) had divided Caucasians into four ranked sub-races: Nordic, Alpine, Mediterranean, and Jew (Semitic), and designated Nordics intellectually and morally superior. These subdivisions were used to justify discriminatory immigration laws that preserved the ethnic dominance of northern and western Europeans. Not until after World War II, when theories of "Aryan" racial superiority were thoroughly discredited by their association with the Nazis, did these distinctions begin to dissolve and European Americans become fully homogenized into the category "white." The status of groups like Armenians, Iranians, and South Asians remained ambiguous, demonstrating that "white," like "Caucasian," was a category that could easily be bent to exclude those deemed unworthy.

The North American system of racial classification continues to shift in response to historical, economic, and political events. Yet the basic conceptual framework imagining biologically distinct racial categories remains surprisingly stable. The word Caucasian is still used in many forms of data collection, medical circles, and popular discourse. Most other labels have changed. New terms more accurately reflect geographic locations or ancestral origins, broadly defined. In contrast, the more biological-sounding word Caucasian stubbornly persists. I suggest that each time we, as educators, use or subject our students uncritically to the term Caucasian, we are subtly re-inscribing key elements of the racist worldview.

Caucasian has more explicitly biological connotations than other contemporary racial terms. To most of us, the Caucasus does not signify a geographical area. Virtually none of our students and probably very few of us could locate the Caucasus on a map or specify what countries or regional groups it includes today (answer: Georgia, Armenia, Azerbaijan, parts of north Iran, and central southern Russia). So what does it mean to designate someone Caucasian? It does not, at least in the twenty-first century United States, suggest anything cultural—that is, a shared set of behaviors and beliefs. U.S. Caucasians do not speak Caucasian. Since it does not connote location or language, it implies something more "natural" than cultural—a profoundly dangerous assumption.

Of course, categories such as Asian, African, and Native American are human-made classifications, too. These labels also falsely imply that clear dividing lines exist between geographically defined "races." For example, the category Asian is internally diverse and has shifting boundaries. It includes Chinese, Japanese, Korean, and Vietnamese people, but what about the peoples of the Indian subcontinent, the Indonesian archipelago, or the Pacific islands? Still, students can identify specific languages and countries in Asia or Africa. Unlike Caucasian, labels like African, Asian, and Native American, while oversimplified, connote culture-bearing historical and political entities.

Anthropologists have long struggled to convince the public that races are not discrete, bounded, biologically based categories but artificial inventions, arbitrary divisions in a continuum of human diversity. Using the label Caucasian masks the equally arbitrary and invented character of this racial category. It renders invisible the diverse ethnic, linguistic, religious, and political groups that make up Europe, which constituted the significant identities of most European Americans until the past half century. The term Caucasian implies that people of European descent form a coherent, stable, homogeneous, biological entity, reinforcing obsolete biological notions of "race."

Using the word Caucasian also tends to imply that whites (the two terms are often used interchangeably) differ from other major racial groupings in the United States in being just plain Americans whose immigrant origins remain unmarked. Yet European Americans originally arrived as immigrants and refugees and were often unwanted by those who had preceded them. Today, they are no more authentically American than any other group. Compared to Native Americans, all European Americans are recent immigrants. Most African Americans' ancestors were brought to these shores before the ancestors of most European Americans arrived. Yet the term Caucasian, because it now lacks any geographic connotation, masks this group's foreign ancestry while other labels, such as Asian American or African American, highlight those groups' foreign roots.

The word Caucasian also reinforces the tendency to equate "American" with people of European descent because, as a one-word designation, Caucasian reinforces the "hyphenated" status of other American groups.

Linguistically, adding a modifier to a generic term—for example, adding Asian or African to American—generally signifies that the modified form is less "normal." The more fundamental, typical, "normal" form is left unmarked. (For example, we add the gender modifier "male" to mark the unusual, abnormal category of "male" nurses. "Nurse" refers to the typical, taken-for-granted, "normal" nurse, who is female.) Most standard U.S. racial labels today other than Caucasian add a specific modifier to American. These modifiers, unless used for all racial-ethnic groups, subtly marginalize the "marked" groups, implying they are not fully American. Some groups remain framed eternally as immigrants, regardless of how many generations they have been in the United States.

Finally, for those designated Caucasian, the term subtly erases their ethnicity, their own ancestry, cultural traditions, and experiences. Ironically, we are starting to talk as if ethnicity and culture are attributes of only some groups, especially marginalized groups. My university has an umbrella organization for the diverse cultural groups on campus, but it does not include any European American ethnocultural groups. But of course, what is Caucasian culture? The category is empty.

Being more specific about origins allows European American students the opportunity to explore their ethnic identities and ancestries. Linking histories or cultural practices to specific cultural or linguistic regions by calling them English, German, Italian, Polish, and so forth, situates them as one among many cultural traditions brought to the United States by immigrants.

European American is a more precise substitute for Caucasian than white—at least as long as we feel the need to classify U.S. residents into a few large groupings. If we wish to describe lived experiences of privilege and the distribution of opportunities based upon ancestry, both "European American" and "white" can be useful. The label European American (or "Euro") may sound bulky or strange at first, but so did African American!

We can also challenge the notion of "pure races" by substituting a more accurate term, "multiracial," for "of mixed race." The terminology of mixture draws upon the old notion of distinct races. In fact, the history of our species is one of constant interaction and mating between populations; that is why humans have remained one species. Moreover, in the process of "mixing," one element gets "diluted." The term "multiracial" connotes the possibility of multiple cultural traditions, multiple identities, and a richer, rather than diluted, cultural legacy.

What can we do beyond using language that reinforces the ideas we want to convey? We can encourage our students to think about everyday, popular language, its roots, and the subtle meanings it conveys. We can invite them to alter their own everyday talk.

references

Carol C. Mukhopadhyay, Rosemary Henze, and Yolanda T. Moses. 2007. *How Real Is Race? A Sourcebook on Race, Culture, and Biology.* Lanham, MD: Rowman & Littlefield.

22

"maybe I'm not class mobile; maybe I'm class queer"

Poor Kids in College, and Survival Under Hierarchy

M. E. Lee*

As a kid from a lower-class home who was privileged enough to attend university, I spent two years in women's studies classrooms watching the same token superficial analyses of racism and classism get regurgitated over and over again. Few academics that I encountered were comfortable or even conscious enough to deal with the ways that university works as a mechanism to perpetuate class hierarchy. I was not an ideal candidate to broach the subject either—as a poor kid, I was in that classroom precisely to get myself out of the lower-class social group that I had been a part of my whole life. If I spoke up against the classist aspects of the academic industry and the values that permeate it, I knew that I would be attacking everyone in the classroom, including myself. I didn't know if my thoughts were rational or if they were simply the product of misplaced resentment,

* Lee, M. E. "'Maybe I'm Not Class Mobile, Maybe I'm Class Queer': Poor Kids in College, and Survival Under Hierarchy." From *Feminism for Real: Reconstructing the Academic Industrial Complex of Feminism*, Jessica Yee, Ed., pp. 85–92. © 2011 by Canadian Center for Policy Alternatives. This work is protected by copyright and the making of this copy was with the permission of Access Copyright. Any alteration of its content or further copying in any form whatsoever is strictly prohibited unless otherwise permitted by law. Reprinted with permission.

and I didn't know if I could even speak for a group that I was in the process of trying to escape. I laid low for a long time.

Getting educated didn't just entail a change in my C.V. and prospective earnings; the institution and the student body were permeated by a value-set and worldview that pressured me to alter my language, my appearance, the elements of my personal background that I learned to conceal, the values that I was expected to hold, my relationships, my alliances, my family ties, and my identity as a person. My women's studies classes were supposed to be a respite and a support, a place where I could voice my uneasiness with the institution and where I could sort out these conflicted ideas. Instead, I was met with sleight-of-hand, apologist pandering, and dismissal. Wherever I tried to raise the issue, it was acknowledged briefly but the discussion quickly shifted before anything meaningful was said. Academic institutions reinforced class privilege, but academic feminism, for all its espoused anti-oppressive commitments, did not want to get into the details.

For a while, I kept my personal life a complete secret. The fact that my immediate family was on social assistance was something that was not to be talked about if I was to accomplish the transformation from poor to not-poor. To mark myself as different was to raise the issue that class privilege is not merely a social starting-point established at birth, but perpetuated and reconstructed at every moment of our lives. Being in university made us complicit in the reconstruction and perpetuation of class hierarchy. The issue was not one of blame—who could blame someone for not wanting to live in poverty? But it still tasted bitter. Nobody wanted to talk about it.

At home, though, it was impossible to ignore the fact that I was going to school while my family members were on social assistance or working low-paying manual labour jobs—my education tested and transformed my relationships with my family. We talked often about what it meant for me to "move up" in terms of class, to "leave this life behind." My mother had always pushed me to achieve as much as I could, so that I would not have to suffer the degradations that she had, living in poverty; however, as I began to put down roots in the middle-class professional world, it became clear that there was a lot of unresolved, even unacknowledged tension and anger with regard to those with class privilege. We had not constructed this "us and them" world, but we had lived in it all of our lives, and suddenly, I was becoming a "them."

My mother is sometimes afraid that I will become privileged and that I will internalize the classist values that paint her as a failure, a loser, a welfare bum, and a "bad mother." She sometimes feels pain and jealousy because I have so many opportunities that she never had. She sometimes feels abandonment, because I am inhabiting realms of experience that she has always been situated on the outside of. She used to go through cycles of resentment because she feared that I would become like the many privileged young professionals in public interest fields who claim to understand the experience of being oppressed by virtue of their education and rely on the authority of their education to silence and ignore the actual experiences of oppressed people. In contrast, there were times when she wanted to cut off all contact with me because she was afraid that my ties to my family would "drag me down" and prevent me from living an easier life. Every fierce, complex, and conflicted emotion that she has felt towards me, I have also felt towards myself. We are still in the process of sorting it all out.

The personal/political exercise of self-examination and communication that my family and I are engaged in is the main site on which my feminism is practiced. I re-read Andrea Smith's piece on white supremacy, which (among other things) talks about rethinking the concept of family as something that unites diverse members with complicated relationships to one another. This idea resonated with me at a profound level, since my relationship with my family has been the main force guiding my feminism. Growing up, my single mom struggled to keep my brother and me fed, clothed, and safe from an abusive father, and to give us the kind of foothold in the world that she herself had never had. She fought her whole life to survive, and that spirit of tooth-and-nail survivalism permeated my childhood and is the bedrock of my feminist convictions. I was raised with the understanding that in this upward battle, it is not only our bodies but our minds and identities that must endure and remain whole.

In my family, we are diverse individuals who occupy distinct social locations, but we are deeply invested in the survival of the whole. We are a family of hapas; our roots are Chinese, Black, Western-European and Native. I have always been able to pass as white, and my white privilege has significantly affected the academic, social and professional circles that I have been a part of. Unlike the rest of my family, I have the safety and luxury of being racially invisible when I choose to be. I am privileged by the same racist systems that oppress my mother and my brother; at the same time, my brother is privileged by heteronormative patriarchal systems that subordinate me as a lesbian. Ignoring these dangerous dynamics is not an option—not for my family, and not for any human being who wishes to participate in the creation of an anti-oppressive movement. We need to understand these mechanisms of oppression in order to understand and love one another.

My family has been engaged in a loving, open dialogue about difference for years, and at this moment, we have never been stronger—as individuals or as a unit. But it took a lot of work and energy on all sides to keep this dialogue going and to keep our family strong. It took a lot of openness that was, more often than not, painful for everyone involved. We were lucky that our relationship was strong enough at the outset, that our ties to one another were able to survive the crush of poverty, sexual abuse, assault, drugs, mental illness, and repeated brutalizing hospitalization. We were lucky that our efforts to listen and self-examine were able to produce such positive growth. There were many, many times when I thought that our family would not survive, when I was forced to leave my home because of conflict, when I wanted to drop out of school completely, and when I felt like my identity and what I thought was my family and my home had been shattered into a million irreparable pieces.

From talking to the few-and-far-between university students from poor backgrounds that I've encountered, don't think that my experience is idiosyncratic. Poverty is not simply having no money—it is isolation, vulnerability, humiliation and mistrust. It is not being able to differentiate between employers and exploiters and abusers. It is contempt for the simplistic illusion of meritocracy—the idea that what we get is what we work for. It is knowing that your mother, with her arthritic joints and her maddening insomnia and her post-traumatic stress disordered heart, goes to work until two in the morning waiting tables for less than minimum wage, or pushes a janitor's cart and cleans the shit-filled toilets of polished professionals. It is entering a room full of people and seeing not only individual people, but violent systems and stark divisions. It is the violence of untreated mental illness exacerbated by the fact that reality, from some vantage points, really does resemble a psychotic nightmare. It is the violence of abuse and assault, which is ignored or minimized by police officers, social services, and courts of law. Poverty is conflict. And for poor kids lucky enough to have the chance to "move up," it is the conflict between remaining oppressed or collaborating with the oppressor.

I live in a province where university tuition is extremely subsidized (I pay about $3,000 a year for my law degree) and where need-based financial aid is mostly available. Yet I can count on one hand the number of poor kids that I have met in university. Financial barriers to education are a serious issue, and I do not wish to minimize the importance of fighting for accessible education—however, it is not enough on its own. The fight for accessible education has to be a panoramic fight against poverty—against dehumanization, ghettos, exploitation, and fear. It needs to be the fight for anti-racist collectives and radical immigration reform, and it needs to be the fight against the non-profit industrial complex wherein some organizations, under the guise of anti-oppressive activism, re-enforce the status of the privileged (for they are the educated professionals) and remain invested in the oppression of the poor and racialized (for they are the "clients" who legitimize the non-profit organization). The fight for accessible education has to seek to change universities from institutions that reinforce oppressive hierarchies to institutions that break oppressive hierarchies down.

From my own experience, I feel that separatism in a world of oppression is not sufficient to create justice—at least, with regards to class-oppression. In fact, systems of privilege benefit from separatism because they allow the privileged to persist in their justificatory narrative without being troubled by the rage of those whose backs their privilege is built upon. The current model of "class-mobility" reinforces separatism and class-hierarchy because it posits that in order to escape oppression, one must become an oppressor—and universities do not merely mediate the boundary between professional and labourer, they teach the body of knowledge, the worldview, the values that mark a person as professional, as "belonging" to the middle- or upper-class.

Universities teach us to renounce our sense of identification with the poor; they teach this by mainly ignoring the existence of poor people, and by treating us as "other" when we do become the subject of discussion. Universities teach us not to care too much, because it will undermine our professional role. Universities teach us that we are separate from where we came from, that we are "qualified" (which suggests that our families and peers are not), that we are justified in having power over people, in speaking for the subjects of our study. Universities teach us that we are "too good" to wait tables and clean houses, with the implication that those who do those jobs are "not good enough" to deserve better.

Poor people tend to see university as a way out for their kids, but university is also a way in to the class of people whose success is premised on the oppression of the poor. In the course of my upbringing, I was exposed to a lot of conflicted ideas surrounding university and class mobility. "Moving up" was seen as both highly desirable and worthy of derision and scorn. It was the subject of envy, resentment and outright hatred. Some of the black kids on my block got called "white" for reading books; it made sense, since the educated professionals whose houses were cleaned and whose children were reared by lower-class people of colour were mostly white. Education had a strong class and race connotation to it, and contrary to what most privileged people tend to think, going to college was not something that evoked uncomplicated positive feelings in most of the poor people I knew, myself included. For a kid to become educated meant that he or she would live an easier life that was premised on the oppression and invisibility of the very communities s/he came from. This left a foul taste in many mouths.

I have had that foul taste in my mouth for years, and I have come to the provisional conclusion that it is the taste of injustice—of being forced to choose between the indignity of remaining poor and the ethically repellant strategy of privilege-seeking. To a poor kid who has the chance to go to college or university, participating in an institution that she identifies as oppressive (either before attending or in the course of her education) might seem like the best choice with regards to her survival, but it is a conflicted survival.

University is a classist institution—not only in the sense that financial barriers render it inaccessible to most poor people but in the sense that the culture of university imposes a homogeneous set of classist values, including dangerous delusions of meritocracy. My experience of women's studies in particular has been deeply alienating since the program claims "fighting oppression" as one of its objectives. Ideas about justice and empowerment that had been my tools of survival were present in our course materials, but they were rendered so abstract, and they were so dissociated from their real-world application that they were barely recognizable. Issues of racism and classism were identified as "problematic" and left at that. I found myself in a classroom sitting next to a blonde girl who raised her hand to complain that she didn't know how to talk to black people because she was uncomfortable with the idea that "they" might be hostile towards her. There were a couple of black women in the room, and I wish to god that I could transcribe their facial expressions because their faces said it all. Even when the oppressed person is sitting right there, the university setting permits everyone to talk about us in the third person.

Sometime during my fourth semester, I started ranting in seminars, arguing with professors after-hours, and disclosing my background to my peers. A few responded with respect and interest, but most responded with discomfort, disinterest, defensiveness, and anger. Of the former, most came from similar class backgrounds or had similar feelings of ambivalence and alienation within the university setting due to their race or cultural roots.

To talk with other people who are engaged in the same difficult task of working out the conflicts in their own narrative, I have started to imagine a new kind of interstitial identity: citizenship within no man's land. When we work together, we can go beyond the question of what university is doing to us, and we can start thinking about what we can do to the university. Academic institutions have the power to construct one group of people as "professional" or "qualified" and thus relegate everyone else to the status of "unqualified"—moreover, they are not about to lose this power anytime soon. But we can get ahold of some of that power, and we can control how it is used. We can change the internal composition of the institution by staying in school and getting more of our own people in. We can participate in the institution on our own terms rather than on theirs, and we can redefine what an educated professional looks and sounds like. We can challenge what knowledge is seen as legitimate and what is seen as illegitimate. And most of all, we can identify the role of the university itself, and the way that it sustains class divisions, the way that it functionally excludes people based on their economic status, and the way that it alienates the few who make it through the cracks. Academic feminism belongs too much to the oppressive white educated-class culture that infuses academia as a whole, but it is the most logical place to begin asserting our presence. We need to speak up in order to make room—psychologically and intellectually—for the ones who come after us. We need to carry our roots with us, and not forget or whitewash where we come from.

note

I've spent four years in university—first women's studies, now law school. There are still a good number of mornings that I wake up feeling like a compradora and I hate myself inside and out. (Because I am seen as a valuable enough prospect, my university and government collaborate to give me free psychiatric counseling, which helps—although I'd feel better if my family also had access to comparable care. But I digress.) I know that I am where I am largely due to my privilege. I did grow up far below the poverty line, I am a lesbian and a survivor of sexual abuse, and I suffer from mental illness. But I am also a Canadian citizen and a Quebec resident, meaning that I can access extremely cheap post-secondary education and extremely cheap health care, among other things. I look more-or-less white and I am cisgendered. I am highly privileged. While I believe I'm in a decent position from which to examine the relationship between class and education, I know that my ideas and my efforts to understand the systems we live are greatly enriched by other perspectives, and I invite dialogue.

23

we aren't just color-blind, we are oppression-blind!

Abby L. Ferber*

The ideology of color-blind racism, the contemporary framework for understanding and defending white privilege, is part of a broader, overarching ideology I refer to as "oppression-blindness." It is not only race-based
privilege that we actively render invisible today, but many other systems
of oppression and privilege as well, including class, gender, sexuality, nationality, ability, age, and religion. We have already examined most of these
systems throughout this book, and read about many examples where these
systems interact and intersect in shaping our lives. We have read important
arguments by leading scholars compelling us to consider these social identities not as discrete, stand-alone properties, but as specific axes of power
that imbue the social structures we shape and are shaped by day in and day
out. In this chapter I will take these arguments further by examining the
multifaceted ways in which the ideological justifications for each of these
various systems of inequality work to reinforce one another. Each one is
made stronger by its placement in the broader context of a hierarchically
organized society with ever-evolving narratives that work to rationalize
and justify inequality as natural and inevitable. Situating these specific systems of oppression and privilege within this broader narrative framework

* This chapter is a slightly revised version of the article that appeared as "The Culture
of Privilege: Color-blindness, Post-feminism, and Christonormativity," by Abby L. Ferber.
Article first published online: 19 MAR 2012. *Journal of Social Issues* 68, no. 1, March 2012,
pp. 63–77. DOI: 10.1111/j.1540–4560.2011.01736.x. © 2012 by The Society for the Psychological Study of Social Issues. Reprinted by permission of John Wiley and Sons.

can help us to understand why each one remains so elusive and difficult to abolish despite the work of active social justice movements over the past three hundred years.

Intersectionality

Kimberlé Crenshaw coined the term "intersectionality" to direct attention to the interaction of multiple social identities in shaping the reality of oppression and privilege (African American Policy Forum, 2009). She argues that we must embrace an intersectional approach to analyze social problems and develop more effective social movement responses. An intersectional framework can be employed at every level of analysis. Traditionally, analysts of racial inequality and racism have identified three levels for analysis: the individual level, the cultural level, and the structural level (Blumenfeld, 2006; Hardiman and Jackson, 1997).

Intersectional analyses focus most often on those who are multiply disadvantaged by numerous systems of inequality. There is less research, however, examining systems of privilege intersectionally (Coston and Kimmel, 2012). In this chapter, I examine privilege from an intersectional perspective and focus specifically on the level of culture. Culture gives meaning to our experiences and shapes the ways we make sense of the world. Race itself is a cultural construct, and it is through culture that we learn to "see" and "read" race (Ferber, 1998; Hartigan, 2010). Culture is key in socializing people into a system of racial inequality, and cultural constructions of race shape our own individual identities, as well as our participation in institutions and systems that reproduce inequality (Blumenfeld, 2006; Hardiman and Jackson, 1997).

Researchers from many disciplines identify racial ideology as one of the most important factors in ongoing racial inequality (Blumenfeld, 2006; Bonilla-Silva, 2010; Feagin, 2001; Ferber, 1998; Hartigan, 2010). Ideology is a central feature of culture that "consists of broad mental and moral frameworks, or 'grids,' that social groups use to make sense of the world, to decide what is right and wrong, true or false, important or unimportant" (Bonilla-Silva, 2010, p. 62). Racial ideology mediates individuals and institutions, providing rationalization for the nature of current race relations. It provides a system of assumptions and rules that inform individuals' decisions, behaviors, and interactions. Racial ideology is an interpretive repertoire that provides story lines, narratives, and common frames for making sense of race relations.

The Defense of White Privilege: Color-Blind Ideology

Sociologists, psychologists, social workers, and economists continue to research the ways in which racial oppression remains entrenched in the United States (Feagin, 2001; Plaut, 2010). Centuries of what Feagin (2001) calls "undeserved impoverishment and undeserved enrichment" (p. 21) provide some people a huge head start and plenty of help along the way.

Yet many white people believe that discrimination against people of color is a thing of the past (Plaut, 2010). For example, despite all evidence to the contrary, white people generally believe that whites are actually more likely to face job discrimination than people of color (Pincus, 2003). As Collins (2004) argues,

> Recognizing that racism even exists remains a challenge for most White Americans, and increasingly for African-Americans as well. They believe that the passage of civil rights legislation eliminated racially discriminatory practices and that any problems that Blacks may experience now are of their own doing. (p. 5)

To understand this gap between reality and the stories we tell, we need to examine the cultural framework informing our stories. Plaut (2010) argues that we must

> [examine] the cultural ideas and beliefs that are prevalent in people's social worlds. These socially, culturally, and historically constituted ideas and beliefs, or cultural models, get inscribed in institutions and practices (e.g., language, law, organizational policies), and daily experiences (e.g., reading the newspaper, watching television, taking a test) such that they organize and coordinate individual understandings and psychological processes (e.g., categorization, attitudes, anxiety, motivation) and behavior. (p. 82)

Over time our hegemonic stories and narratives about race change, connected to the changing social and economic organization of race relations. Just when the blatantly discriminatory policies and practices of Jim Crow racism were finally crumbling under attack, the early foundations of a "new racism" were taking form (Irons, 2010). This new racism is much less overt, its predominant operating narrative characterized as an ideology of color-blind racism that avoids the use of blatantly racist terminology (Bonilla-Silva, 2010; Irons, 2010; Plaut, 2010).

A color-blind perspective assumes that discrimination is a thing of the past and denies the reality of race and racial inequality today. This approach argues that we should treat people as simply human beings, rather than as racialized beings (Plaut, 2010).

According to Bonilla-Silva (2010), color-blind ideology consists of four key frames that organize our understandings of racial inequality:

1. *Abstract liberalism*: relies upon the language of political liberalism, referring to abstract concepts of equal opportunity, rationality, free choice, individualism, etc. (i.e., discrimination is no longer a problem, and any individual who works hard can succeed).
2. *Naturalization*: reframes ongoing inequality as the result of natural processes, rather than social relations (i.e., segregation today is the result of the natural inclination of people to live near others of the same race).
3. *Cultural racism*: reframes ongoing inequality as the result of inherent cultural differences between racialized groups.
4. *Minimization of racism*: assumes that we now have a fairly level playing field, everyone has equal opportunities to succeed, and racism is no longer a real problem.

Color-blind racism assumes racial discrimination has ended, people are being treated in a color-blind fashion, and any differences we see in the success of racial groups is therefore due to inherent differences in the groups themselves. Color-blind ideology leads to the conclusion that we've done all we can. For many whites, the election of Barack Obama as president has been evoked to confirm their assumptions of a color-blind nation (Bonilla-Silva, 2010; Cunnigen and Bruce, 2010). While many people naively embrace this view as nonracist, it reinforces and reproduces contemporary systemic racial inequality by denying its reality.

These scripts are so ubiquitous that they are drawn upon to explain other forms of inequality as well. Color-blind racism needs to be examined from an intersectional perspective, making visible the ways it is connected and mutually constitutive of other ideologies of privilege. In the remainder of this chapter, I will examine discourses of oppression and privilege that rationalize male and Christian privilege, and argue that we must examine how these ideologies mirror color-blind racism and reinforce one another. Postfeminism has emerged to justify and rationalize gender inequality, just as Christonormativity works to naturalize and protect Christian privilege. As Plaut argues, these cultural ideologies work together; therefore, each one must be dismantled to advance the cause of social justice.

From New Racism to Postfeminism

Intersectional analyses of both the civil rights and women's movements of the 1960s have revealed how their failures to address the concerns, needs, and demands of women of color limited their success. Exclusion of women from leadership in the civil rights movement, and the women's movement's failure to fully engage issues of race and sexuality (both the first and second waves), led to divisions in both movements.

There are also striking similarities among the predominant narratives of backlash to both of these movements, yet efforts to respond and attack these narratives still proceed from separate silos, with little collaboration. I argue that the same four frames of color-blindness identified by Bonilla-Silva operate to defend and normalize gender inequality (Ferber, 2007). It is common today for journalists and conservative commentators to argue that we have moved beyond the need for feminism, and have entered a *postfeminist* phase. Like the civil rights movement, the women's movement did much to advance formal, legal equality for women. Nevertheless, gender inequality remains widespread, and feminist scholars have observed the rise of a new discourse around gender, remarkably similar to new racism's color-blind framework.

The ideology of postfeminism assumes that the law and society are now "gender-blind" in their treatment of men and women, reflecting the use of a "minimization of racism/discrimination" frame. Mainstream media promote the assumption that the women's movement has accomplished its goals and barriers facing women have been removed. According to the advocates of postfeminism, men and women now have equal opportunities: women now have the right to vote, legal protection from discrimination, and the same legal rights as men (Douglas, 2010; McRobbie, 2004).

Some commentators argue that the push for equality has gone too far, saying that men are now victims of feminist frenzy. Just as the advocates of color-blind racism believe that racial inequality is a thing of the past and that further attempts to remedy inequality lead to "reverse discrimination" against whites, we see similar arguments about gender. This rearticulation of the minimization of discrimination frame leads to reifying the values of *abstract liberalism*, where feminism is attacked for violating the values of individualism and equal opportunity. After all, if everyone is already equal, then interventions aimed at women violate the principle of equal opportunity and hurt men. Faludi (1991) examines the "steady stream of indictments" of feminism that began in the 1980s in the mainstream media. Problems women face are often framed as the result of feminism, and women's push for equality, rather than the product of inequality itself. In this way, feminism is discredited and claims of ongoing inequality dismissed. McRobbie (2004) writes that postfeminist culture is undermining the gains of the women's movement and feminism, arguing that "equality is achieved, in order to install a whole repertoire of new meanings which emphasize that it is no longer needed" (p. 255).

Consistent with the abstract liberalism frame, women's status today is depicted as a product of their own individual choices. According to the logic of the postfeminist story line, women legally have the same opportunities and rights as men; therefore, if women are more likely to be found in low-paying, part-time jobs, it must be because of their own choosing, since "women are now free to choose for themselves" (McRobbie, 2004, p. 259). Job segregation and the persistent wage gap are often dismissed with the "prevailing ideological constructions of women as carers," which are also used to explain why women are more likely to be found in the home, responsible for child care, elder care, and housework. Further, as an extension of women's caregiving "natures," they are assumed to be more likely than men to choose careers in nursing, teaching, day care, or social work, knowing that these jobs pay significantly less compared to male careers requiring similar skills and education levels (Glenn, 2010). Here we have moved into the frames of *naturalization* and *cultural racism/sexism*. Both natural, biological differences between men and women, as well as gender-based cultural differences, are invoked to rationalize gender inequality (Cole, Avery, Dodson, and Goodman, 2012). In *Forced to Care*, Glenn (2010) examines the ways this gender ideology of caring, in conjunction with ideologies of race, relegate women of color to the lowest-paying, least valued caregiving jobs, such as working in nursing homes. She strikingly reveals the coercion at the heart of this enterprise, examining the state's role in enforcing women's obligation to provide "care," including the training of Native American women in boarding schools and the formal "American-ization" programs for immigrant women. A tremendous amount of effort and force has been extended to make women acquiesce with the ideology of women as natural caregivers.

Yet postfeminism makes this history and enforcement invisible; "there is little trace . . . of the enduring inequities which still mark out the relations between men and women" (McRobbie, 2004, p. 260). Any inequality be-tween men and women, therefore, is seen as a result of men's and women's different natures, and the choices men and women make. Both color-blind racism and postfeminism ignore the vast body of literature that examines the ways the social institutions of education, work, health care, criminal justice, and the family shape and constrain all of our choices and oppor-tunities (Crittenden, 2001; Faludi, 1991; Feagin, 2001; Glenn, 2010; Lewis, 2003; Van Ausdale and Feagin, 2001).

Given the ideological similarities of color-blind racism and postfem-inism, we need to examine both discourses within a broader framework of political backlash against the social movements of the 1960s and '70s. According to Coppock, Haydon, and Richter (1995), "The proclamation of 'post-feminism' has occurred at precisely the same moment as acclaimed feminist studies demonstrate that not only have women's real advance-ments been limited, but also that there has been a backlash against fem-inism of international significance" (p. 3). The concept of postfeminism itself is part of this backlash, an "attempt to retract the handful of small and hard-won victories that the feminist movement did manage to win for women" (Faludi, 1991, p. 12).

Similarly, Bonilla-Silva (2003) argues that color-blind racism "has be-come a formidable political tool for the maintenance of the racial order [serving] as the ideological armor for a covert and institutionalized system [of racial oppression] in the post–Civil Rights era" (p. 3). Both postfeminism and color-blind racism are part of an ideology of "oppression-blindness" that operates to defend the culture of privilege against perceived attacks (Ferber, 2003, 2007; Ferber and Samuels, 2010; Pratto and Stewart, 2012).

This discourse results in blaming the victim for his or her own oppres-sion. William Ryan first described the contours of blaming the victim in 1971. Ryan emphasizes that blaming the victim is essentially a defense of privilege: "those who buy this solution with a sigh of relief are inevitably blinding themselves to the basic causes of the problems being addressed.

They are, most crucially, rejecting the possibility of blaming, not the victims, but themselves" (p. 583). In this way, blaming the victim allows privilege to remain intact and unexamined, not simply rationalizing, but reproducing, privilege.

Christonormativity

I now turn to a third category, Christian privilege. Christonormativity refers to the normalization and privileging of Christianity as the dominant religious and spiritual culture in the United States (Steinberg and Kincheloe, 2009). Todd (2010) argues that Christianity "not only dominates other religious and atheistic traditions in this country, but is implicated in virtually every other category of oppression: racism, sexism, heterosexism, ableism, classism . . . every one of these categories has been undergirded by Christian theological justifications" (p. 142). Indeed, Christianity played a central role historically in constructing racial categories, and continues to affect decisions over who counts as "white." Tehranian's (2009) work on Middle-Eastern Americans demonstrates that when the majority of Arab immigrants to the United States were Christian, they were more likely to be defined legally as white, yet as the percentage of Arab immigrants who are Muslim has grown, that is changing. "As it has grown less Christian, the Middle Eastern population in the United States is thought of as less assimilable and, consequently, less white" (p. 70).

A few years back, I published a blog examining the pervasive atmosphere of Christian privilege I was observing (Ferber, 2009). In the blog, I argue that Christonormativity is a system of privilege that marginalizes and excludes those who are not Christian, especially during the winter holiday season. In the blog, I described a typical December day:

I woke up and turned on my favorite morning show. I learned new recipes for the favorite holiday drink—egg nog; tips on how to decorate for the holidays on a budget by trimming the mantel and staircase with wreaths, green swags, and small lights; followed by the best toys to buy for kids this holiday season. I then read my local newspaper, which featured a big story about how the Colorado governor's mansion has been decorated for the holidays, accompanied by a large photo of the Christmas tree. . . . I entered my office building, where a large Christmas tree sat in the lobby. Due to concerns raised a few years back about the heavy focus on Christmas, the tree has now been renamed "The Giving Tree." It is decorated by ornaments made by children at the campus day care center, with requests for donations as a part of our annual Holiday Service Project. I wonder how Jewish, Muslim, and other non-Christian students feel each time they enter the building.

On my way home, I stop off on a few errands. In the grocery store, I am greeted by another large Christmas tree. As I wander the aisles I hum along to "Jingle Bells," "All I Want for Christmas," "Blue Christmas," "Feliz Navidad," and "Here Comes Santa Claus." . . . So you see, while it may not seem like a big deal that someone wishes me a "Merry Christmas," and I genuinely appreciate the good will and cheer being offered, for non-Christians like myself, this time of year can be anything but merry (24% of the U.S. population of about 304 million do not define themselves as Christian). . . . Not only is it all-pervasive, all day long, when I do the math, I discover that it adds up to about ten years of my life that I live in this exclusionary Christian culture. (If I live to be eighty, one and a half months per year of that time adds up to ten years over a lifetime!). . . . The question is *not* how do we stop the celebrations, but instead, how do we create a more inclusive culture, a climate where everybody feels included? (full text of blog can be found at www.huffington post.com/abby-ferber/please-dont-wish-me-a-mer_b_389824.html)

My arguments here are threefold. First, I introduce the concept of Christonormativity, documenting the manner in which Christian culture has become the normative, dominant culture in the United States at this time of year. Like other forms of privilege, it is often invisible and unexamined. Second, I highlight the way attempts to make Christian privilege visible are rearticulated as an attack on Christianity. This is another example of blaming the victim. Finally, I ask that we think about what it means to be inclusive.

Defending Christian Privilege

I received a flood of negative responses to this blog. The blog appeared on the *Huffington Post*, a news/blog site generally characterized as liberal. I have a regular blog there, and in previous blogs I have received a maximum of twenty-one comments, while this post received seventy-nine comments. I often focus on issues of race and gender. I wrote an entry titled "I Am Racist" and have often written about white privilege, yet received very few negative responses. I was therefore shocked by the number of negative responses to this post. Of the seventy-nine, forty were explicitly negative or sarcastic and contained elements of an oppression-blind ideology. The remaining responses consisted of short replies to other posts, were neutral, or were positive. In examining the responses, there is a clear pattern that can be discerned. Like the discourses of color-blind racism and postfeminism, these oppression-blind ideologies minimize Christian privilege and reframe the issue in the abstract liberal terms of free choice and individualism.

One of the most common themes I found was the *minimization of discrimination* and the concomitant attempt to preserve the culture of privilege:

- "The only thing Christian about Christmas is the name 'Christ'mas . . . about 95% of all Christmas traditions are non-Christian . . . growing up I never really noticed the Christ in Christmas. . . . To me it's like Thanksgiving."
- "Christ was born in September, the holiday that you are so offended by is a secular holiday, there are no real Christian holidays. . . . The American Christmas is a family celebration of giving and love . . . everyone can join in, it's really not Christian in any real sense."
- "May I suggest you go to 'Blintzes and Bling' and get a Star of David necklace the size of a hub cap so that I know you are Jewish. Then I promise to wish you a Happy Hanukkah. . . . People of all faiths are dying across the globe for their religious beliefs. December is a month of hope and light and joy for most faiths—and also for those of no particular faith—who can enjoy the secular spirit of giving and cheer."

These quotes and many others argue that there is no evidence of privilege or exclusion. Christmas is reframed in universal terms, depicted as good fun that everyone can be a part of. These responses also provide evidence of the *naturalization* of Christianity. Christian values are naturalized as simply human values inherent in all people. As one respondent put it, "These are universal beliefs, that for this time of year, just happen to be wrapped in green and red bows."

Not only do the respondents minimize and trivialize Christian discrimination and privilege, they draw upon the abstract liberalism frame by emphasizing the abstract principles of individualism, rationality, and free choice:

- "What an awful whiner. . . . The vast majority of this country is Christian, and even many secular people celebrate Christmas; is it any wonder that the average person is assumed to celebrate it? Anybody who is 'offended' or 'uncomfortable' really needs to find something new to complain about."
- "You have two choices. You can either be terribly offended and act pissy when someone smiles and wishes you a Merry Christmas or you can embrace the friendly, positive sentiment as it was intended and smile back. How you react says much about who you are."
- "We can choose to continue to live in a world where we seek out an offense where none is intended and continue down this dangerous path of perpetuating the 'us vs. them' mentality that serves to divide us more than we are already. Or we can decide to be participants in a world where we look beyond our differences."
- "As an atheist, I am constantly bombarded with God from the government, from friends and strangers alike. However, I am not offended by anyone wishing me Merry Christmas, Happy Hanukkah, Happy Kwanzaa etc. . . . I would be in a constant state of irritation if I let these things bother me."
- "I am not a Christian. I could choose to feel excluded and marginalized because a lot of people are celebrating a holiday important to their religion, or I can choose my own interpretation of a winter holiday with rituals and traditions that I select and enjoy the lights and colors and giving and general goodwill. It's of no relevance to me what the holiday means to anyone else, and mine is of no matter to them. If I choose to forgo Christmas completely (and I've done that in previous years), I certainly don't resent others continuing to celebrate nor do I take offense that they assume that I share in their celebration."

These arguments are the very same arguments used to justify color-blind racism and postfeminism. They erase from view Christian privilege, reinscribing Christianity as normative. They blame the victim for choosing to focus on differences. Like advocates of affirmative action or those "frenzied feminists," anyone who argues that race, gender, and religious differences still matter in shaping people's daily lives is attacked. The reality of institutional inequality is ignored, and the issue is reduced to simply one of individual choice.

Our failure to examine the interconnections among these three narratives carries consequences and undermines our efforts to advance social justice. When we only interrogate this cultural story line of privilege and oppression in terms of its implications for racial inequality, we leave the broader story line in place. While the goals of most research on white privilege are to contribute to antiracist activism, approaches that focus only on race have limited potential. For example, the belief that legal obstacles to equality have been removed and everyone has equal opportunities to succeed is used to justify not only race, but gender and religious inequality, which is rearticulated as the product of the poor choices of individuals, rather than a systemic issue. When we hear the very same arguments offered to explain each of these systems of inequality, it gives them more legitimacy. The more familiar the arguments, the more they feel intuitively right to people. The frames are more likely to resonate and to feel like "common sense." Wherever we are situated, we will have greater potential for success if we attack the entire ideology of oppression-blindness and victim blaming in all of its forms, rather than only one of its manifestations.

Focusing on only one social classification, such as race, is like trying to pull one strand out of a tapestry. Even if we are successful, the tapestry itself remains intact, and thus that strand can always be picked up and woven back in; perhaps in new ways, so that the overall pattern and design shift over time. Nevertheless, the ever-present tapestry remains in place and ready to reincorporate new threads.

It is the entire tapestry we must unravel. We need to analyze all of our "-isms" as strands in a broader, comprehensive ideological tapestry explaining away inequality and trying to naturalize and justify oppression and privilege.

references

African American Policy Forum. 2009. A primer on intersectionality. http://aapf.org/wp-content/uploads/2009/03/aapf_intersectionality_primer.pdf.

Blumenfeld, W. 2006. "Christian Privilege and the Promotion of 'Secular' and not-so 'Secular' Mainline Christianity in Public Schooling and in the Larger Society." *Equity and Excellence in Education* 39: 195–210. doi: 10:1080/10665680600788024

Blumenfeld, W. J., and K. Jaekel. "Exploring Levels of Christian Privilege Awareness Among Preservice Teachers." *Journal of Social Issues* 68: 128–144.

Blumenfeld, W. J., K. Y. Joshi, and E. E. Fairchild. 2009. *Investigating Christian Privilege and Religious Oppression in the United States*. Rotterdam, Denmark: Sense Publishers.

Bonilla-Silva, E. 2010. *Racism Without Racists: Color-blind Racism and the Persistence of Racial Inequality in the United States,* 3rd ed. Lanham, MD: Rowman & Littlefield.

———. 2003. "'New Racism,' Color-blind Racism, and the Future of Whiteness in America." In A. W. Doane and E. Bonilla-Silva, eds., *White Out: The Continuing Significance of Race.* New York: Routledge.

Brown, C., and T. Augusta-Scott. 2007. *Narrative Therapy: Making Meaning, Making Lives.* Thousand Oaks, CA: Sage.

Case, K. 2012. "Discovering the Privilege of Whiteness: White Women's Reflections on Antiracist Identity and Ally Behavior." *Journal of Social Issues* 68, no. 1: 78–96.

Cole, E. R., L. R. Avery, C. Dodson, and K. D. Goodman. 2012. "Against Nature: How Arguments About the Naturalness of Marriage Privilege Heterosexuality." *Journal of Social Issues* 68, no. 1: 42–62.

Collins, P. H. 2000. *Black Feminist Thought: Knowledge, Consciousness, and the Politics of Empowerment,* 2nd ed. New York: Routledge.

———. 2004. *Black Sexual Politics: African Americans, Gender, and the New Racism.* New York: Routledge.

Coppock, V., D. Haydon, and I. Richter, 1995. *The Illusions of "Post-feminism."* London: Taylor and Francis.

Coston, B. M., and M. S. Kimmel, 2012. "Seeing Privilege Where It Isn't: Marginalized Masculinities and the Intersectionality of Privilege." *Journal of Social Issues* 68: 97–111.

Crittenden, A. 2001. *The Price of Motherhood: Why the Most Important Job in the World Is Still the Least Valued.* New York: Henry Holt.

Cunnigen, D., and M. Bruce. 2010. *Race in the Age of Obama.* Bingley, UK: Emerald Group Publishing.

Doane, A. W. 2003. "Rethinking Whiteness Studies." In A. W. Doane and E. Bonilla-Silva, eds., *White Out: The Continuing Significance of Race* (pp. 3–18). New York: Routledge.

Doane, A. W., and E. Bonilla-Silva, eds. 2003. *White Out: The Continuing Significance of Race.* New York: Routledge.

Douglas, S. 2010. *Enlightened Sexism: The Seductive Message That Feminism's Work Is Done.* New York: Times Books.

Fairchild, E. E. 2009. "'I Believe' in Education." In W. J. Blumenfeld, K. Y. Joshi, and E. E. Fairchild, eds., *Investigating Christian Privilege and Religious Oppression in the United States* (pp. 151–157). Rotterdam, Denmark: Sense Publishers.

Faludi, S. 1991. *Backlash: The Undeclared War Against American Women.* New York: Doubleday.

Feagin, J. R. 2001. *Racist America: Roots, Current Realities, and Future Reparations.* New York: Routledge.

Ferber, A. L. 1998. *White Man Falling: Race, Gender, and White Supremacy.* Lanham, MD: Rowman & Littlefield.

———. 2003. "Defending the Culture of Privilege." In M. S. Kimmel and A. L. Ferber, eds., *Privilege: A Reader* (pp. 319–329). Boulder, CO: Westview Press.

———. 2007. "Whiteness Studies and the Erasure of Gender." *Sociology Compass* 1: 265–282, doi 10.1111/j.1751–9020.2007.00014.x

———. 2009. "Please Don't Wish Me a Merry Christmas." *Huffington Post,* www.huffingtonpost.com/abby-ferber/please-dont-wish-me-a-mer_b_389824.html.

Ferber, A. L., C. Jimenez, A. H. O'Reilly, and D. Samuels, eds. 2008. *The Matrix Reader: Examining the Dynamics of Privilege and Oppression.* New York: McGraw-Hill.

Ferber, A. L., and D. Samuels. 2010. "Oppression Without Bigots." Factsheet. *Network News.* Sociologists for Women in Society, Winter.

Glenn, E. N. 2010. *Forced to Care: Coercion and Caregiving in America.* Cambridge, MA: Harvard University Press.

Hardiman, R., and B. Jackson. 1997. "Conceptual Foundations for Social Justice Courses." In M. Adams, L. A. Bell, and P. Griffin, eds., *Teaching for Diversity and Social Justice Courses* (pp. 16–29). New York: Routledge.

Hartigan, J. Jr. 2010. *Race in the 21st Century: Ethnographic Approaches.* New York: Oxford University Press.

Irons, J. 2010. "Reconstituting Whiteness: The Mississippi State Sovereignty Commission." Nashville, TN: Vanderbilt University Press.

Kendall, F. E. 2006. *Understanding White Privilege: Creating Pathways to Authentic Relationships Across Race.* New York: Routledge.

Kimmel, M. S., and A. L. Ferber, eds. 2009. *Privilege: A Reader,* 2nd ed. Boulder, CO: Westview Press.

Kincheloe, J. L. 2009. "Selling a New and Improved Jesus: Christotainment and the Power of Political Fundamentalism." In S. Steinberg and J. L. Kincheloe, eds., *Christotainment: Selling Jesus Through Popular Culture* (pp. 1–22). Boulder, CO: Westview Press.

Lewis, A. 2003. *Race in the Schoolyard: Negotiating the Color Line in Classrooms and Communities.* New Brunswick, NJ: Rutgers University Press.

McRobbie, A. 2004. "Post-feminism and Popular Culture." *Feminist Media Studies* 4: 255–264. doi 10.1080/1468077042000309937

Nelson, J. 2009. "Christian Teachers and Christian Privilege." In W. J. Blumenfeld, K. Y. Joshi, and E. E. Fairchild, eds., *Investigating Christian Privilege and Religious Oppression in the United States* (pp. 135–149). Rotterdam, Denmark: Sense Publishers.

Pincus, F. L. 2003. *Reverse Discrimination: Dismantling the Myth.* Boulder, CO: Lynne Rienner.

Plaut, V. C. 2010. "Diversity Science: Why and How Difference Makes a Difference." *Psychological Inquiry* 21: 77–99. doi: 10.1080/10478401003676501

Pratto, F., and A. L. Stewart. 2012. "Group Dominance and the Half-blindness of Privilege." *Journal of Social Issues* 68, no. 1: 28–45.

Ryan, W. 1971. *Blaming the Victim.* New York: Pantheon Books.

Steinberg, S. 1995. *Turning Back: The Retreat from Racial Justice in American Thought and Policy.* Boston: Beacon Press.

Steinberg, S. R., and J. L. Kincheloe. 2009. *Christotainment: Selling Jesus Through Popular Culture.* Boulder, CO: Westview Press.

Stewart, T. L., I. M. Latu, and H. T. Denney. 2012. "White Privilege Awareness and Efficacy to Reduce Racial Inequality Improve White Americans' Attitudes Toward African Americans." *Journal of Social Issues* 68, no. 1: 11–27.

Sutton, B. 2010. *Bodies in Crisis: Culture, Violence, and Women's Resistance in Neoliberal Argentina.* New Brunswick, NJ: Rutgers University Press.

Tehranian, J. 2009. *Whitewashed: America's Invisible Middle Eastern Minority.* New York: New York University Press.

Todd, J. 2010. "Confessions of a Christian Supremacist." *Reflections: Narratives of Professional Helping* 16: 140–146.

Van Ausdale, D., and J. R. Feagin. 2001. *The First R: How Children Learn Race and Racism.* Lanham, MD: Rowman & Littlefield.

24

toward a new vision

Race, Class, and Gender as Categories
of Analysis and Connection

Patricia Hill Collins*

*The true focus of revolutionary change is never merely the
oppressive situations which we seek to escape, but that piece of
the oppressor which is planted deep within each of us.*
  —AUDRE LORDE, *SISTER OUTSIDER*

Audre Lorde's statement raises a troublesome issue for scholars and activists working for social change. While many of us have little difficulty
assessing our own victimization within some major system of oppression,
whether it be by race, social class, religion, sexual orientation, ethnicity,
age, or gender, we typically fail to see how our thoughts and actions uphold someone else's subordination. Thus, White feminists routinely point
with confidence to their oppression as women but resist seeing how much
their white skin privileges them. African-Americans who possess eloquent
analyses of racism often persist in viewing poor White women as symbols
of white power. The radical left fares little better. "If only people of color
and women could see their true class interests," they argue, "class solidarity
would eliminate racism and sexism." In essence, each group identifies the

---

 * Collins, Patricia Hill. "Toward a New Vision: Race, Class, and Gender as Categories of
Analysis and Connection." Adapted from an article originally published in *Race, Sex, and
Class* 1, no. 1, Fall 1993. Reprinted by permission of Jean Ait Belkhir, Founder and Editor of
the *Race, Gender & Class* journal.

type of oppression with which it feels most comfortable as being fundamental and classifies all other types as being of lesser importance.

Oppression is full of such contradictions. Errors in political judgment that we make concerning how we teach our courses, what we tell our children, and which organizations are worthy of our time, talents, and financial support flow smoothly from errors in theoretical analysis about the nature of oppression and activism. Once we realize that there are few pure victims or oppressors, and that each one of us derives varying amounts of penalty and privilege from the multiple systems of oppression that frame our lives, then we will be in a position to see the need for new ways of thought and action.

To get at that "piece of the oppressor which is planted deep within each of us," we need at least two things. First, we need new visions of what oppression is, new categories of analysis that are inclusive of race, class, and gender as distinctive yet interlocking structures of oppression. Adhering to a stance of comparing and ranking oppressions—the proverbial "I'm more oppressed than you"—locks us all into a dangerous dance of competing for attention, resources, and theoretical supremacy. Instead, I suggest that we examine our different experiences within the more fundamental relationship of domination and subordination. To focus on the particular arrangements that race, class, and gender take in our time and place without seeing these structures as sometimes parallel and sometimes interlocking dimensions of the more fundamental relationship of domination and subordination may temporarily ease our consciences. But while such thinking may lead to short-term social reforms, it is simply inadequate for the task of bringing about long-term social transformation.

While race, class, and gender as categories of analysis are essential in helping us understand the structural bases of domination and subordination, new ways of thinking that are not accompanied by new ways of acting offer incomplete prospects for change. To get at that "piece of the oppressor which is planted deep within each of us," we also need to change our daily behavior. Currently, we are all enmeshed in a complex web of problematic relationships that grant our mirror images full human subjectivity while stereotyping and objectifying those most different from us. We often assume that the people we work with, teach, send our children to school with, and sit next to . . . will act and feel in prescribed ways because they belong to given race, social class, or gender categories. These judgments by category must be replaced with fully human relationships that transcend the legitimate differences created by race, class, and gender as categories of analysis. We require new categories of connection, new visions of what our relationships with one another can be. . . .

[This discussion] addresses this need for new patterns of thought and action. I focus on two basic questions. First, how can we reconceptualize race, class, and gender as categories of analysis? Second, how can we transcend the barriers created by our experiences with race, class, and gender oppression in order to build the types of coalitions essential for social exchange? To address these questions I contend that we must acquire both new theories of how race, class, and gender have shaped the experiences not just of women of color, but of all groups. Moreover, we must see the connections between the categories of analysis and the personal issues in our everyday lives, particularly our scholarship, our teaching, and our relationships with our colleagues and students. As Audre Lorde points out, change starts with self, and relationships that we have with those around us must always be the primary site for social change.

How Can We Reconceptualize Race, Class, and Gender as Categories of Analysis?

To me, we must shift our discourse away from additive analyses of oppression (Spelman, 1982; Collins, 1989). Such approaches are typically based on two key premises. First, they depend on either/or, dichotomous thinking. Persons, things, and ideas are conceptualized in terms of their opposites. For example, Black/White, man/woman, thought/feeling, and fact/opinion are defined in oppositional terms. Thought and feeling are not seen as two different and interconnected ways of approaching truth that can coexist in scholarship and teaching. Instead, feeling is defined as antithetical to reason, as its opposite. In spite of the fact that we all have "both/and" identities (I am both a college professor and a mother—I don't stop being a mother when I drop my child off at school, or forget everything I learned while scrubbing the toilet), we persist in trying to classify each other in either/or categories. I live each day as an African-American woman—a race/gender–specific experience. And I am not alone. Everyone has a race/gender/class–specific identity. Either/or, dichotomous thinking is especially troublesome when applied to theories of oppression because every individual must be classified as being either oppressed or not oppressed. The both/and position of simultaneously being oppressed and oppressor becomes conceptually impossible.

A second premise of additive analyses of oppression is that these dichotomous differences must be ranked. One side of the dichotomy is typically labeled dominant and the other subordinate. Thus, Whites rule Blacks, men are deemed superior to women, and reason is seen as being preferable to emotion. Applying this premise to discussions of oppression leads to the assumption that oppression can be quantified, and that some groups are oppressed more than others. I am frequently asked, "Which has been most oppressive to you, your status as a Black person or your status as a woman?" What I am really being asked to do is divide myself into little boxes and rank my various statuses. If I experience oppression as a both/and phenomenon, why should I analyze it any differently?

Additive analyses of oppression rest squarely on the twin pillars of either/or thinking and the necessity to quantify and rank all relationships in order to know where one stands. Such approaches typically see African-American women as being more oppressed than everyone else because the majority of Black women experience the negative effects of race, class, and gender oppression simultaneously. In essence, if you add together separate oppressions, you are left with a grand oppression greater than the sum of its parts.

I am not denying that specific groups experience oppression more harshly than others—lynching is certainly objectively worse than being held up as a sex object. But we must be careful not to confuse this issue of the saliency of one type of oppression in people's lives with a theoretical stance positing the interlocking nature of oppression. Race, class, and gender may all structure a situation but may not be equally visible and/or important in people's self-definitions. In certain contexts, such as the antebellum American South and contemporary South America, racial oppression is more visibly salient, while in other contexts, such as Haiti, El Salvador, and Nicaragua, social class oppression may be more apparent. For middle-class White women, gender may assume experiential primacy unavailable to poor Hispanic women struggling with the ongoing issues of low-paying jobs and the frustrations of the welfare bureaucracy. This recognition that one category may have salience over another for a given time and place does not minimize the theoretical importance of assuming that race, class, and gender as categories of analysis structure all relationships.

In order to move toward new visions of what oppression is, I think that we need to ask new questions. How are relationships of domination and subordination structured and maintained in the American political economy? How do race, class, and gender function as parallel and interlocking systems that shape this basic relationship of domination and subordination? Questions such as these promise to move us away from futile theoretical struggles concerned with ranking oppressions and toward analyses that assume race, class, and gender are all present in any given setting, even if one appears more visible and salient than the others. Our task becomes redefined as one of reconceptualizing oppression by uncovering the connections among race, class, and gender as categories of analysis.

1. Institutional Dimension of Oppression

Sandra Harding's contention that gender oppression is structured along three main dimensions—the institutional, the symbolic, and the individual —offers a useful model for a more comprehensive analysis encompassing race, class, and gender oppression (Harding, 1989). Systemic relationships of domination and subordination structured through social institutions such as schools, businesses, hospitals, the workplace, and government agencies represent the institutional dimension of oppression. Racism, sexism, and elitism all have concrete institutional locations. Even though the workings of the institutional dimension of oppression are often obscured with ideologies claiming equality of opportunity, in actuality, race, class, and gender place Asian-American women, Native American men, White men, African-American women, and other groups in distinct institutional niches with varying degrees of penalty and privilege.

Even though I realize that many . . . would not share this assumption, let us assume that the institutions of American society discriminate, whether by design or by accident. While many of us are familiar with how race, gender, and class operate separately to structure inequality, I want to focus on how these three systems interlock in structuring the institutional dimension of oppression. To get at the interlocking nature of race, class, and gender, I want you to think about the antebellum plantation as a guiding metaphor for a variety of American social institutions. Even though slavery is typically analyzed as a racist institution, and occasionally as a class institution, I suggest that slavery was a race-, class-, and gender-specific institution. Removing any one piece from our analysis diminishes our understanding of the true nature of relations of domination and subordination under slavery.

Slavery was a profoundly patriarchal institution. It rested on the dual tenets of White male authority and White male property, a joining of the political and the economic within the institution of family. Heterosexism was assumed and all Whites were expected to marry. Control over affluent White women's sexuality remained key to slavery's survival because property was to be passed on to the legitimate heirs of the slave owner. Ensuring affluent White women's virginity and chastity was deeply intertwined with maintenance of property relations.

Under slavery, we see varying levels of institutional protection given to affluent White women, working-class and poor White women, and enslaved African women. Poor White women enjoyed few of the protections held out to their upper-class sisters. Moreover, the devalued status of Black women was key in keeping all White women in their assigned places. Controlling Black women's fertility was also key to the continuation of slavery, for children born to slave mothers themselves were slaves.

African-American women shared the devalued status of chattel with their husbands, fathers, and sons. Racism stripped Blacks as a group of legal rights, education, and control over their own persons. African-Americans could be whipped, branded, sold, or killed, not because they were poor, or because they were women, but because they were Black. Racism ensured that Blacks would continue to serve Whites and suffer economic exploitation at the hands of all Whites.

So we have a very interesting chain of command on the plantation—the affluent White master as the reigning patriarch; his White wife helpmate to serve him, help him manage his property, and bring up his heirs; his faithful servants, whose production and reproduction were tied to the requirements of the capitalist political economy; and largely propertyless, working-class White men and women watching from afar. In essence, the foundations for the contemporary roles of elite White women, poor Black women, working-class White men, and a series of other groups can be seen in stark relief in this fundamental American social institution. While Blacks experienced the most harsh treatment under slavery, and thus made slavery clearly visible as a racist institution, race, class, and gender interlocked in structuring slavery's systemic organization of domination and subordination.

Even today, the plantation remains a compelling metaphor for institutional oppression. Certainly the actual conditions of oppression are not as severe now as they were then. To argue, as some do, that things have not changed all that much denigrates the achievements of those who struggled for social change before us. But the basic relationships among Black men, Black women, elite White women, elite White men, working-class White men, and working-class White women as groups remain essentially intact.

A brief analysis of key American social institutions most controlled by elite White men should convince us of the interlocking nature of race, class, and gender in structuring the institutional dimension of oppression. For example, if you are from an American college or university, is your campus a modern plantation? Who controls your university's political economy? Are elite White men overrepresented among the upper administrators and trustees controlling your university's finances and policies? Are elite White men being joined by growing numbers of elite White women helpmates? What kinds of people are in your classrooms grooming the next generation who will occupy these and other decision-making positions? Who are the support staff that produce the mass mailings, order the supplies, fix the leaky pipes? Do African-Americans, Hispanics, or other people of color form the majority of the invisible workers who feed you, wash your dishes, and clean up your offices and libraries after everyone else has gone home?

If your college is anything like mine, you know the answers to these questions. You may be affiliated with an institution that has Hispanic women as vice presidents for finance, or substantial numbers of Black men among the faculty. If so, you are fortunate. Much more typical are colleges where a modified version of the plantation as a metaphor for the institutional dimension of oppression survives.

2. The Symbolic Dimension of Oppression

Widespread, societally sanctioned ideologies used to justify relations of domination and subordination comprise the symbolic dimension of oppression. Central to this process is the use of stereotypical or controlling images of diverse race, class, and gender groups. In order to assess the power of this dimension of oppression, I want you to make a list, either on paper or in your head, of "masculine" and "feminine" characteristics.

If your list is anything like that compiled by most people, it reflects some variation of the following:

Masculine	Feminine
aggressive	passive
leader	follower
rational	emotional
strong	weak
intellectual	physical

Not only does this list reflect either/or dichotomous thinking and the need to rank both sides of the dichotomy, but ask yourself exactly which men and women you had in mind when compiling these characteristics. This list applies almost exclusively to middle-class White men and women. The allegedly "masculine" qualities that you probably listed are only acceptable when exhibited by elite White men, or when used by Black and Hispanic men against each other or against women of color. Aggressive Black and Hispanic men are seen as dangerous, not powerful, and are often penalized when they exhibit any of the allegedly "masculine" characteristics. Working-class and poor White men fare slightly better and are also denied the allegedly "masculine" symbols of leadership, intellectual competence, and human rationality. Women of color and working-class and poor White women are also not represented on this list, for they have never had the luxury of being "ladies." What appear to be universal categories representing all men and women instead are unmasked as being applicable to only a small group.

It is important to see how the symbolic images applied to different race, class, and gender groups interact in maintaining systems of domination and subordination. If I were to ask you to repeat the same assignment, only this time, by making separate lists for Black men, Black women, Hispanic women, and Hispanic men, I suspect that your gender symbolism would be quite different. In comparing all of the lists, you might begin to see the interdependence of symbols applied to all groups. For example, the elevated images of White womanhood need devalued images of Black womanhood in order to maintain credibility.

While the above exercise reveals the interlocking nature of race, class, and gender in structuring the symbolic dimension of oppression, part of its importance lies in demonstrating how race, class, and gender pervade a wide range of what appears to be universal language. Attending to diversity in our scholarship, in our teaching, and in our daily lives provides a new angle of vision on interpretations of reality thought to be natural, normal, and "true." Moreover, viewing images of masculinity and femininity as universal gender symbolism, rather than as symbolic images that are race, class, and gender specific, renders the experiences of people of color and of non-privileged White women and men invisible. One way to dehumanize an individual or a group is to deny the reality of their experiences. So when we refuse to deal with race or class because they do not appear to be directly relevant to gender, we are actually becoming part of someone else's problem.

Assuming that everyone is affected differently by the same interlocking set of symbolic images allows us to move forward toward new analyses. Women of color and White women have different relationships to White male authority, and this difference explains the distinct gender symbolism applied to both groups. Black women encounter controlling images such as the mammy, the matriarch, the mule, and the whore, that encourage others to reject us as fully human people. Ironically, the negative nature of these images simultaneously encourages us to reject them. In contrast, White women are offered seductive images, those that promise to reward them for supporting the status quo. And yet seductive images can be equally controlling. Consider, for example, the views of Nancy White, a 73-year-old Black woman, concerning images of rejection and seduction:

> My mother used to say that the black woman is the white man's mule and the white woman is his dog. Now, she said that to say this: we do the heavy work and get beat whether we do it well or not. But the white woman is closer to the master and he pats them on the head and lets them sleep in the house, but he ain't gon' treat neither one like he was dealing with a person. (Gwaltney, 1980, p. 148)

Both sets of images stimulate particular political stances. By broadening the analysis beyond the confines of race, we can see the varying levels of rejection and seduction available to each of us due to our race, class, and gender identity. Each of us lives with an allotted portion of institutional privilege and penalty, and with varying levels of rejection and seduction inherent in the symbolic images applied to us. This is the context in which we make our choices. Taken together, the institutional and symbolic dimensions of oppression create a structural backdrop against which all of us live our lives.

3. The Individual Dimension of Oppression

Whether we benefit or not, we all live within institutions that reproduce race, class, and gender oppression. Even if we never have any contact with members of other race, class, and gender groups, we all encounter images of these groups and are exposed to the symbolic meanings attached to those images. On this dimension of oppression, our individual biographies vary tremendously. As a result of our institutional and symbolic statuses, all of our choices become political acts.

Each of us must come to terms with the multiple ways in which race, class, and gender as categories of analysis frame our individual biographies. I have lived my entire life as an African-American woman from a working-class family, and this basic fact has had a profound impact on my personal biography. Imagine how different your life might be if you had been born Black, or White, or poor, or of a different race/class/gender group than the one with which you are most familiar. The institutional treatment you would have received and the symbolic meanings attached to your very existence might differ dramatically from what you now consider to be natural, normal, and part of everyday life. You might be the same, but your personal biography might have been quite different.

I believe that each of us carries around the cumulative effect of our lives within multiple structures of oppression. If you want to see how much you have been affected by this whole thing, I ask you one simple question—who are your close friends? Who are the people with whom you can share your hopes, dreams, vulnerabilities, fears, and victories? Do they look like you? If they are all the same, circumstance may be the cause. For the first seven years of my life I saw only low-income Black people. My friends from those years reflected the composition of my community. But now that I am an adult, can the defense of circumstance explain the patterns of people that I trust as my friends and colleagues? When given other alternatives, if my friends and colleagues reflect the homogeneity of one race, class, and gender group, then these categories of analysis have indeed become barriers to connection.

I am not suggesting that people are doomed to follow the paths laid out for them by race, class, and gender as categories of analysis. While these three structures certainly frame my opportunity structure, I as an individual always have the choice of accepting things as they are, or trying to change them. As Nikki Giovanni points out, "We've got to live in the real world. If we don't like the world we're living in, change it. And if we can't change it, we change ourselves. We can do something" (Tate, 1983, p. 68). While a piece of the oppressor may be planted deep within each of us, we each have the choice of accepting that piece or challenging it as part of the "true focus of revolutionary change."

How Can We Transcend the Barriers Created by Our Experiences with Race, Class, and Gender Oppression in Order to Build the Types of Coalitions Essential for Social Change?

Reconceptualizing oppression and seeing the barriers created by race, class, and gender as interlocking categories of analysis is a vital first step. But we must transcend these barriers by moving toward race, class, and gender as categories of connection, by building relationships and coalitions that will bring about social change. What are some of the issues involved in doing this?

1. Differences in Power and Privilege

First, we must recognize that our differing experiences with oppression create problems in the relationships among us. Each of us lives within a system that vests us with varying levels of power and privilege. These differences in power, whether structured along axes of race, class, gender, age, or sexual orientation, frame our relationships. African-American writer June Jordan describes her discomfort on a Caribbean vacation with Olive, the Black woman who cleaned her room:

> Even though both "Olive" and "I" live inside a conflict neither one of us created, and even though both of us therefore hurt inside that conflict, I may be one of the monsters she needs to eliminate from her universe and, in a sense, she may be one of the monsters in mine. (1985, p. 47)

Differences in power constrain our ability to connect with one another even when we think we are engaged in dialogue across differences. Let me give you an example. One year, the students in my course "Sociology of the

Black Community" got into a heated discussion about the reasons for the upsurge of racial incidents on college campuses. Black students complained vehemently about the apathy and resistance they felt most White students expressed about examining their own racism. Mark, a White male student, found their comments particularly unsettling. After claiming that all the Black people he had ever known had expressed no such beliefs to him, he questioned how representative the viewpoints of his fellow students actually were. When pushed further, Mark revealed that he had participated in conversations over the years with the Black domestic worker employed by his family. Since she had never expressed such strong feelings about White racism, Mark was genuinely shocked by class discussions. Ask yourselves whether that domestic worker was in a position to speak freely. Would it have been wise for her to do so in a situation where the power between the two parties was so unequal?

In extreme cases, members of privileged groups can erase the very presence of the less privileged. When I first moved to Cincinnati, my family and I went on a picnic at a local park. Picnicking next to us was a family of White Appalachians. When I went to push my daughter on the swings, several of the children came over. They had missing, yellowed, and broken teeth, they wore old clothing, and their poverty was evident. I was shocked. Growing up in a large eastern city, I had never seen such awful poverty among Whites. The segregated neighborhoods in which I grew up made White poverty all but invisible. More importantly, the privileges attached to my newly acquired social class position allowed me to ignore and minimize the poverty among Whites that I did encounter. My reactions to those children made me realize how confining phrases such as "well, at least they're not Black" had become for me. In learning to grant human subjectivity to the Black victims of poverty, I had simultaneously learned to demand White victims of poverty. By applying categories of race to the objective conditions confronting me, I was quantifying and ranking oppressions and missing the very real suffering that, in fact, is the real issue.

One common pattern of relationships across differences in power is one that I label "voyeurism." From the perspective of the privileged, the lives of people of color, of the poor, and of women are interesting for their entertainment value. The privileged become voyeurs, passive onlookers who do not relate to the less powerful, but who are interested in seeing how the "different" live. Over the years, I have heard numerous African-American students complain about professors who never call on them except when a so-called Black issue is being discussed. The students' interest in discussing race or qualifications for doing so appear unimportant to the professor's efforts to use Black students' experiences as stories to make the material come alive for the White student audience. Asking Black students to perform on cue and provide a Black experience for their White classmates can be seen as voyeurism at its worst.

Members of subordinate groups do not willingly participate in such exchanges but often do so because members of dominant groups control the institutional and symbolic apparatuses of oppression. Racial/ethnic groups, women, and the poor have never had the luxury of being voyeurs of the lives of the privileged. Our ability to survive in hostile settings has hinged on our ability to learn intricate details about the behavior and worldview of the powerful and adjust our behavior accordingly. I need only point to the difference in perception of those men and women in abusive relationships. Where men can view their girlfriends and wives as sex objects, helpmates, and a collection of stereotyped categories of voyeurism—women must be attuned to every nuance of their partners' behavior. Are women "naturally" better in relating to people with more power than themselves, or have circumstances mandated that men and women develop different skills? . . .

Coming from a tradition where most relationships across difference are squarely rooted in relations of domination and subordination, we have much less experience relating to people as different but equal. The classroom is potentially one powerful and safe space where dialogues among individuals of unequal power relationships can occur. The relationship between Mark, the student in my class, and the domestic worker is typical of a whole series of relationships that people have when they relate across differences in power and privilege. The relationship among Mark and his classmates represents the power of the classroom to minimize those differences so that people of different levels of power can use race, class, and gender as categories of analysis in order to generate meaningful dialogues. In this case, the classroom equalized racial difference so that Black students who normally felt silenced spoke out. White students like Mark, generally unaware of how they had been privileged by their whiteness, lost that privilege in the classroom and thus became open to genuine dialogue. . . .

2. Coalitions Around Common Causes

A second issue in building relationships and coalitions essential for social change concerns knowing the real reasons for coalition. Just what
brings people together? One powerful catalyst fostering group solidarity
is the presence of a common enemy. African-American, Hispanic, Asian-
American, and women's studies all share the common intellectual heritage
of challenging what passes for certified knowledge in the academy. But
politically expedient relationships and coalitions like these are fragile because, as June Jordan points out:

> It occurs to me that much organizational grief could be avoided if people
> understood that partnership in misery does not necessarily provide for part-
> nership for change. When we get the monsters off our backs all of us may
> want to run in very different directions. (1985, p. 47)

Sharing a common cause assists individuals and groups in maintaining relationships that transcend their differences. Building effective coalitions involves struggling to hear one another and developing empathy for
each other's points of view. The coalitions that I have been involved in that
lasted and that worked have been those where commitment to a specific
issue mandated collaboration as the best strategy for addressing the issue
at hand.

Several years ago, master's degree in hand, I chose to teach in an in-
ner-city parochial school in danger of closing. The money was awful, the
conditions were poor, but the need was great. In my job, I had to work with
a range of individuals who, on the surface, had very little in common. We
had White nuns, Black middle-class graduate students, Blacks from the
"community," some of whom had been incarcerated and/or were affiliated
with a range of federal anti-poverty programs. Parents formed another
part of this community, Harvard faculty another, and a few well-meaning
White liberals from Colorado were sprinkled in for good measure.

As you might imagine, tension was high. Initially, our differences
seemed insurmountable. But as time passed, we found a common bond
that we each brought to the school. In spite of profound differences in our
personal biographies, differences that in other settings would have ham-
pered our ability to relate to one another, we found that we were all deeply
committed to the education of Black children. By learning to value each
other's commitment and by recognizing that we each had different skills

that were essential to actualizing that commitment, we built an effective coalition around a common cause. Our school was successful, and the children we taught benefited from the diversity we offered them. . . .

None of us alone has a comprehensive vision of how race, class, and gender operate as categories of analysis or how they might be used as categories of connection. Our personal biographies offer us partial views. Few of us can manage to study race, class, and gender simultaneously. Instead, we each know more about some dimensions of this larger story and less about others. . . . Just as the members of the school had special skills to offer to the task of building the school, we have areas of specialization and expertise, whether scholarly, theoretical, pedagogical, or within areas of race, class, or gender. We do not all have to do the same thing in the same way. Instead, we must support each other's efforts, realizing that they are all part of the larger enterprise of bringing about social change.

3. Building Empathy

A third issue involved in building the types of relationships and coalitions essential for social change concerns the issue of individual accountability. Race, class, and gender oppression form the structural backdrop against which we frame our relationship—these are the forces that encourage us to substitute voyeurism . . . for fully human relationships. But while we may not have created this situation, we are each responsible for making individual, personal choices concerning which elements of race, class, and gender oppression we will accept and which we will work to change.

One essential component of this accountability involves developing empathy for the experiences of individuals and groups different from us. Empathy begins with taking an interest in the facts of other people's lives, both as individuals and as groups. If you care about me, you should want to know not only the details of my personal biography but a sense of how race, class, and gender as categories of analysis created the institutional and symbolic backdrop for my personal biography. How can you hope to assess my character without knowing the details of the circumstances I face?

Moreover, by taking a theoretical stance that we have all been affected by race, class, and gender as categories of analysis that have structured our treatment, we open up possibilities for using those same constructs as categories of connection in building empathy. For example, I have a good White woman friend with whom I share common interests and beliefs. But we know that our racial differences have provided us with different experiences. So we talk about them. We do not assume that because I am Black, race has only affected me and not her or that because I am a Black woman, race neutralizes the effect of gender in my life while accenting it in hers. We take those same categories of analysis that have created cleavages in our lives, in this case, categories of race and gender, and use them as categories of connection in building empathy for each other's experiences.

Finding common causes and building empathy is difficult, no matter which side of privilege we inhabit. Building empathy from the dominant side of privilege is difficult, simply because individuals from privileged backgrounds are not encouraged to do so. For example, in order for those of you who are White to develop empathy for the experiences of people of color, you must grapple with how your white skin has privileged you. This is difficult to do, because it not only entails the intellectual process of seeing how whiteness is elevated in institutions and symbols, but it also involves the often painful process of seeing how your whiteness has shaped your personal biography. Intellectual stances against the institutional and symbolic dimensions of racism are generally easier to maintain than sustained self-reflection about how racism has shaped all of our individual biographies. Were and are your fathers, uncles, and grandfathers really more capable than mine, or can their accomplishments be explained in part by the racism members of my family experienced? Did your mothers stand silently by and watch all this happen? More importantly, how have they passed on the benefits of their whiteness to you?

These are difficult questions, and I have tremendous respect for my colleagues and students who are trying to answer them. Since there is no compelling reason to examine the source and meaning of one's own privilege, I know that those who do so have freely chosen this stance. They are making conscious efforts to root out the piece of the oppressor planted within them. To me, they are entitled to the support of people of color in their efforts. Men who declare themselves feminists, members of the middle class who ally themselves with anti-poverty struggles, heterosexuals who support gays and lesbians, are all trying to grow, and their efforts place them far ahead of the majority who never think of engaging in such important struggles.

Building empathy from the subordinate side of privilege is also difficult, but for different reasons. Members of subordinate groups are understandably reluctant to abandon a basic mistrust of members of powerful groups because this basic mistrust has traditionally been central to their survival.

As a Black woman, it would be foolish for me to assume that White women, or Black men, or White men or any other group with a history of exploiting African-American women have my best interests at heart. These groups enjoy varying amounts of privilege over me and therefore I must carefully watch them and be prepared for a relation of domination and subordination.

Like the privileged, members of subordinate groups must also work toward replacing judgments by category with new ways of thinking and acting. Refusing to do so stifles prospects for effective coalition and social change. Let me use another example from my own experiences. When I was an undergraduate, I had little time or patience for the theorizing of the privileged. My initial years at a private, elite institution were difficult, not because the coursework was challenging (it was, but that wasn't what distracted me) or because I had to work while my classmates lived on family allowances (I was used to work). The adjustment was difficult because I was surrounded by so many people who took their privilege for granted. Most of them felt entitled to their wealth. That astounded me.

I remember one incident of watching a White woman down the hall in my dormitory try to pick out which sweater to wear. The sweaters were piled up on her bed in all the colors of the rainbow, sweater after sweater. She asked my advice in a way that let me know that choosing a sweater was one of the most important decisions she had to make on a daily basis. Standing knee-deep in her sweaters, I realized how different our lives were. She did not have to worry about maintaining a solid academic average so that she could receive financial aid. Because she was in the majority, she was not treated as a representative of her race. She did not have to consider how her classroom comments or basic existence on campus contributed to the treatment her group would receive. Her allowance protected her from having to work, so she was free to spend her time studying, partying, or in her case, worrying about which sweater to wear. The degree of inequality in our lives and her unquestioned sense of entitlement concerning that inequality offended me. For a while, I categorized all affluent White women as being superficial, arrogant, overly concerned with material possessions, and part of my problem. But had I continued to classify people in this way, I would have missed out on making some very good friends whose discomfort with their inherited or acquired social class privileges pushed them to examine their position.

Since I opened with the words of Audre Lorde, it seems appropriate to close with another of her ideas. . . .

Each of us is called upon to take a stand. So in these days ahead, as we examine ourselves and each other, our works, our fears, our differences, our sisterhood and survivals, I urge you to tackle what is most difficult for us all, self-scrutiny of our complacencies, the idea that since each of us believes she is on the side of right, she need not examine her position. (1985)

I urge you to examine your position.

references

Butler, Johnella. 1989. "Difficult Dialogues." *Women's Review of Books* 6, no. 5.

Collins, Patricia Hill. 1989. "The Social Construction of Black Feminist Thought." *Signs.* Summer.

Gwaltney, John Langston. 1980. *Drylongso: A Self-Portrait of Black America.* New York: Vintage.

Harding, Sandra. 1986. *The Science Question in Feminism.* Ithaca, New York: Cornell University Press.

Jordan, June. 1985. *On Call: Political Essays.* Boston: South End Press.

Lorde, Audre. 1984. *Sister Outsider.* Trumansburg, New York: Crossing Press.

———. 1985. "Sisterhood and Survival." Keynote address, conference on the Black Woman Writer and the Diaspora, Michigan State University.

Spelman, Elizabeth. 1982. "Theories of Race and Gender: The Erasure of Black Women." *Quest* 5: 36–32.

Tate, Claudia, ed. 1983. *Black Women Writers at Work.* New York: Continuum.

25

winning hearts and minds

Mark R. Warren*

John Brown worked not simply for black men—he worked with them; and he was a companion of their daily life, knew their faults and virtues, and felt, as few white Americans have felt, the bitter tragedy of their lot.

—W. E. B. DU BOIS

With these words, W. E. B. Du Bois opened his biography of John Brown, the white abolitionist who led an armed assault against slavery. Brown had a religiously inspired moral vision of an America freed of the sin of slavery. As Du Bois indicated, Brown identified closely with African Americans, saw their cause as a common one, and deeply believed that he was working in the best interests of both blacks and whites. Brown certainly had fire in his heart. In the words of Reverend Joseph Lowery, referenced in the subtitle of this book, Brown came to deeply embrace the cause of racial justice. So do many white activists who work for racial justice today. How did they come to do so? . . .

How can white Americans come to care enough about racism that they move from passivity to action for racial justice? I decided to look for clues to answer that question by examining the lives and self-understanding of

*Warren, Mark R. "Winning Hearts and Minds." From *Fire in the Heart: How White Activists Embrace Racial Justice* by Warren (2010) pp. 211–233. By permission of Oxford University Press, USA. Notes included in the original have been removed from this reprinted excerpt.

white people who have made that move and became committed activists for racial justice. . . .

Head, Heart, and Hand

Americans place great faith in education as a force for social change. If whites knew about racism, so this thinking goes, and understood that it continues to exist and oppress people of color, they would come to oppose it. I did find that awareness of racism proves important to the development of commitment on the part of the interviewees, but only partly so. Rather, I found that the activists in this study came to support racial justice through a combination of cognitive and emotional processes at the heart of which lay moral concerns.

Activists begin their journey to racial justice activism through a direct experience that leads to an awareness of racism, but the real action does not lie in the knowledge gained. What makes this experience a seminal one for them is that through it they recognize a contradiction between the values with which they have grown up and the reality of racial injustice. When they confront this value conflict, activists express anger at racial injustice. They care about racism at first because they believe deeply in the values that are being violated. They express what I call a moral impulse to act.

If we stop here, however, we are left with the do-gooder, the white person who helps people of color but remains at a distance. I find that relationships with people of color begin to undermine that separation. Whites learn more deeply about the reality of racism through these relationships. But more than the head is involved here, too. Personal relationships and stories tug at the heart; that is, they create emotional bonds of caring. Whites become concerned about racism because it affects real people they know. Rather than working *for* people of color, they begin to work *with* them, their commitment nurtured by an ethic of care and a growing sense of shared fate.

As whites take action for racial justice, they build more than individual relationships with people of color. Working collectively in activist groups, they prefigure the kind of human relationships they hope will characterize a future America. In other words, as they attempt to create respectful collaborative relationships, they construct a more concrete sense of the kind of society for which they are working, what I call a moral vision. They find purpose and meaning in a life that works for the kind of society they want for themselves, their children, and all people across racial lines. Some refer to this as a calling, but they all begin to express a direct interest for themselves in a life committed to racial justice activism. Activists come to see that racism harms whites, as well as people of color. It denies whites their full humanity and blocks progress toward a society that would benefit everyone, one that would be in the interest of whites, as well as people of color. Forging community in multiracial groups deepens a sense of shared fate and bonds of caring as it fosters hope for the possibilities of social change. If the moral impulse represents what activists are against, an emerging moral vision represents what they are for, a truly human or beloved community. It provides a foundation for shared identities as multiracial political activists.

Activists develop commitment and deepen their motivations over time, in part through their experiences taking action against racism. Activism provides whites an opportunity to build relationships with people of color, as well as other white activists, and to construct the kind of multiracial community in which they develop and implement a vision of a future society. This is not a linear process but rather a cycle or perhaps a spiral. Indeed, a model of motivation leading to action is too simplistic. Rather, I find that activists develop commitment over time and through activism. Indeed, there may be setbacks or a need for constant vigilance as the pressures of the dominant society constantly push whites back toward a white world and worldview.

For the sake of clarity, I have presented the processes in an ordered form, starting with a moral impulse and leading to a moral vision. To some extent, this order is represented in the activists' lives. However, some activists inherit a sense of a moral vision from their families or their religious traditions and so have elements of a vision at the beginning. For others, relationships come earlier rather than later. Meanwhile, activists continue to express moral outrage even after they deepen their commitment through relationships and construct a moral vision. Each of these processes has its own particular effects on developing commitment. Yet each represents a piece of the larger puzzle of commitment. I have illustrated [on p. 80] how they work together to forge a deep commitment to racial justice on the part of white activists (Figure 25.1).

It may be useful to summarize the relationship between these processes by visualizing them as a cycle. If we start with the heart, anger at the violation of deeply held values leads some white activists to take action for racial

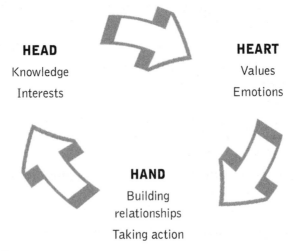

HEAD
Knowledge
Interests

HEART
Values
Emotions

HAND
Building
relationships
Taking action

Figure 25.1

justice and thereby build relationships with people of color. These connections create knowledge about the experiences of people of color and begin to shape a sense of common interests. By working in emergent multiracial communities, white activists develop caring and hope while generating a moral vision of a multiracial society with justice at its center. They continue to experiment with building respectful, collaborative associations in multiracial activist groups, all the while developing a sense of their personal interest in racial justice as they find that activism offers a meaningful life.

Within the context of the interactive approach just elaborated, I found moral concerns to play a key role in the development of commitment and action. This approach lies in stark contrast to most thinking on racial justice, which focuses on the cognitive domain. As noted earlier, we place great emphasis on educating white Americans about racism. Certainly, one must understand that racism is an important problem if one is to take action against it. In that sense I did find the processes of learning about the history and experiences of people of color and of developing a racial justice framework to be important to the activists in this study. Moreover, cognitive knowledge about racism, including research and analysis of how it works, is necessary to know what to do about it. However, by itself, knowledge does not motivate one to take action. It answers the "what" to do but not the "why" to do it.

Motivation comes primarily from a moral source even as its character develops from impulse to care and vision. White activists start with a
moral impulse that racism is wrong because certain values they care about
are being violated. Through relationships they deepen their commitment
as they develop an ethic of caring. The many children of color who drop
out of high school are no longer just numbers but rather real people to
whom they are connected. Eventually activists make the cause their own
through the construction of a moral vision of a just, multiracial, and human community.

The other way in which cognitive processes are typically emphasized is
through a focus on the rational calculation of self-interest. If whites can
come to see their common material interests with people of color (in better
health care, for example), then they are likely to find common cause with
people of color. Or if whites can see that it will cost them less to educate
children than to incarcerate them after they drop out of high school and
get into trouble, then they will likely support a more just educational system. These are important arguments. Yet I found almost no evidence that
rational, interest-based understandings like these motivated the activists
in my study.

I do not want to counterpose morality and interests. Rather, what I discovered is that activists find a way to get them to work together and to reinforce each other. In particular, as white activists construct a moral vision of
a future society based upon their values, they develop a way to understand
white interest in racial justice. As we have seen, these visions encompass
material concerns. Activists are working today to address poverty, rebuild
communities, and create better educational systems. The future society
they envision would offer more equitable social provision for people of
color and for most whites as well. Yet it would perhaps more fundamentally
be a community based upon what activists see as deeply human values,
where people treat each other with respect and caring across lines of race.
Out of these values, better material provision can emerge. While interests
and morality work together, in the end, activists embed an understanding
of white people's interests into their vision of human community, and that
is why I argue that moral sources are primary.

Pursuing a moral vision does not mean working altruistically *for* people of color. The activists in this study have developed a clear sense of their
own direct stake in racial justice. In order to understand how morality and

interests can work together at the individual level, we have to break from the notion that equates moral action with altruism—doing for someone else rather than for yourself. Nathan Teske, in his study of political activists, has criticized the duality of self-interested versus altruistic action. He shows instead that when activists uphold their most deeply held values by working for the common good, they are also benefiting themselves in ways that are quite rational. They construct an identity for themselves as moral persons, which allows them to gain a meaningful life and a place in history.

Teske reconciles morality and self-interest at the individual level, but I also found that activists resolve the dichotomy at the collective level, too, by embedding an understanding of the collective interests of white Americans in a moral vision. The two levels are in fact related. Activists derive meaning in their lives by pursuing that vision. As activist Roxane Auer captured it, "I'm contributing to the world I want to live in." In other words, activists develop a strong and direct interest in living their lives in the present in accordance with the principles on which that beloved community would be founded. Indeed, along with other activists they attempt to work out those principles by implementing them in the present.

It is also a mistake to counterpose cognitive understanding and emotions. Traditionally, we have understood emotionally based activity as nonrational and suspect in politics. Yet there is a large and growing literature in several fields that shows that emotions and cognition are closely connected. Political scientist George Marcus draws upon recent work in neuroscience to show the role of emotion in reasoning. He has argued that emotions are critical to democratic life, and so, in his view, "sentimental citizens" are the only ones capable of making reasoned political judgments and putting them into action. Political theorist Sharon Krause also shows that emotions can enhance, not detract from, democratic deliberation. She begins her critique of the distinction between passions and reason with words that echo the findings of this study: "Our minds are changed when our hearts are engaged."

Emotions play a particularly important role in cognitive processes regarding racial justice precisely because the minds of white Americans need to be changed. Whites need to break from the dominant color-blind ideology and adopt a racial justice framework. That seems to happen in crystallized moments when a direct experience of racism brings powerful emotions into play. These experiences shock whites out of a complacent belief in the fairness of American society and sear a new racial justice awareness into their consciousness.

In sum, many scholars of race relations and many policymakers have sought to make rational arguments that will convince whites that they have more to gain than lose by working together with people of color. Yet this study suggests that such an approach, however important, is ultimately too narrow. Rather, whites come to find common cause with people of color when their core values are engaged, when they build relationships that lead to caring and a sense of common identity, and when they can embed an understanding of their interests in a vision of a future, racially just society that would benefit all—that is, when the head, heart, and hand are all engaged. . . .

Moral, Visionary Leadership

I turn now to some of the broader lessons of this study for moving white Americans from passivity to action for racial justice. . . .

One of the key implications of this study is the need to bring values to the fore and assert moral leadership in the struggle for racial justice. There are two ways of thinking about morality in this regard, however, captured in my distinction between the moral impulse and a moral vision. Whites can be exhorted to do the right thing, or they can be offered a chance to join in an effort to pursue the moral project of a better society for all with justice at its core. To some extent, as we have seen, probably both appeals are necessary. Nevertheless, an appeal to conscience alone is insufficient. If whites feel only moral impulse, the result may be moralism rather than moral leadership. Perhaps that is the case for many well-meaning white people today. They believe racism is wrong, but they have not gone through the relationship-building and practice-based experiences that engage them in efforts to create and pursue values for a better society.

From this moralist point of view alone, the problem of racism is lodged in "bad" white people. Other whites are the problem, and moralists can easily denounce them. Even if they understand how racism functions in the institutional structure of American society, this still has nothing to do with them. Moralists have yet to discover two important and related lessons. First, as one activist in this study, Z. Holler, said, quoting Pogo, "The enemy is us." In other words, all white people have been affected by racial indoctrination. Rather than dichotomizing the world into good and bad and simply blaming others, all white Americans have to take a close look at their own beliefs and behaviors.

Second, the perpetuation of racism is a complex problem. Whites need a serious, sustained effort to create institutional change and to deal with difficult challenges as they arise. Denouncing racism can make some whites feel good. Laboring in the trenches of the educational and criminal justice systems for sustained racial justice change, for example, is not all feel-good work even if it results in a rewarding life. The IAF organizers in this study, Perry Perkins and Christine Stephens, balked at my labeling them as activists because, in IAF thinking, activism represents short-term, unfocused action. I do not think the label "activism" necessarily means inconsistency or lack of commitment, but I do think their concerns help us appreciate that making serious advances in racial justice requires long-term engagement in public work to build power and new kinds of relationships that lead to real and positive change.

Part of this serious work involves creating respectful, collaborative relationships with people of color. The moralists, the do-gooders working for people of color rather than with them, may continue to keep that separation. People of color are perhaps rightly suspicious of the white heroes who think they can solve problems for them. Rather, moral leadership involves building reciprocal relationships in common pursuit of justice goals. . . .

Moralism in relationship to other whites presents a constant challenge even for the most seasoned racial justice activists. They struggle with honest confrontation with the racial beliefs and behaviors of other whites in a way that does not create defensiveness. They foster a sense of responsibility on the part of whites for action against racism. Responsibility is one thing, however; shaming and guilt trips are another. We have not seen much evidence in this study that shaming individual whites motivates a great deal of action. Indeed, the moral impulse arises not from shaming an individual as a bad person but from engaging positive values that people believe in and care about. Moral leadership lies in offering a moral vision, something to work for, a chance to become part of the racial justice family, as activist Christine Clark put it.

This study lends little support to the idea that confronting whites with their racial privilege constitutes an effective strategy to move them to action. Racial privilege may be a complex reality that white people need to grasp. Indeed, much important work to move whites toward racial justice understanding and action occurs under this banner. However, stressing privilege as a strategy to engage whites seems to emphasize the wrong thing. It focuses on the narrow and short-term benefit whites receive from a racial hierarchy rather than their larger interest in a racially just future. Alone, it seems to engage shame and guilt rather than anger at injustice and hope for a better future. It is moralistic rather than visionary.

Moralism ignores interests in favor of altruism. By contrast, moral leadership takes interests seriously but reshapes white people's understanding of their interests and asks them to join a larger project that promises to create a better society for all. There is a material agenda here, one that offers better economic conditions and better social provision for people of color, as well as white families. However, this interest-based agenda is set and framed within a larger moral vision and political project.

There is evidence that suggests that this kind of moral leadership can be effective. Indeed, we are witnessing the rise of values-based activism in a variety of fields. For some, those values come from a religious faith that calls them to care for community and to act for social justice. Faith-based community organizing, for example, has emerged as a powerful force for engaging people in political action in their local communities. Indeed, several activists in this study are faith-based organizers and leaders. This kind of organizing engages value traditions while working for concrete, material improvements in the quality of people's lives in housing, jobs, and education.

These values can also have secular roots like those based in the American democratic traditions of fairness, freedom, and justice. They can also be newer creations. Many activists in the environmental movement, for example, work not just to prevent ecological devastation but also to establish a new kind of society based upon the principles of working in balance and harmony with the world and caring about all forms of life. Environmentalists today try to live those values out in their relationships to each other and to the environment. In practice, both old and new values can be blended, as can religious and secular ones. More and more we are realizing that people care deeply about their values and can be engaged around them in progressive politics and other activist endeavors.

In the end, moral leadership is about creating a vision that engages values to shape people's understanding of how their interests relate to racial justice. . . .

286 ■ making new connections, moving forward

Building Multiracial Community

Another clear lesson of this study is the need to increase multiracial contact and collaboration in the United States. The activists in this study came to understand and care about racism through the people of color they knew personally. Certainly whites can teach other whites about racism. Indeed, the white activists in this study take that responsibility seriously. However, hearing stories directly from people of color engages the heart, as well as the head, and proves powerful. Through such relationships whites begin to care—and not just to know—about racism, and they begin to develop a sense of common identity and shared fate. Relationships, it appears, create the microfoundation for the broader visionary project of racial justice.

Studies of social capital, that is, social connections and ties between people, highlight the importance of these findings. Scholars of social capital like Robert Putnam have suggested that creating "bridging" ties across lines like race can create trust and cooperation and strengthen a sense of the common good. Yet we have far more "bonding" social capital, that is, ties among people who are like each other, than ties that bridge our differences. Nevertheless, despite persistent segregation, young people increasingly express a desire to be in a diverse setting. College may in fact be a particularly important place for whites to begin to create bridging ties.

Recent research by Robert Putnam highlights the importance of building these cross-racial ties. In studying racial diversity in localities across the United States, Putnam finds that areas with higher levels of racial diversity are lower in social trust. In other words, people appear to trust each other less when diversity is high. Whites trust blacks less and vice versa. Perhaps more surprisingly, however, people also trust other members of their own racial group less when diversity is high. In other words, diversity absent cross-racial relationships works against a sense of shared fate in the entire community. In this context, Putnam calls for investing in places where meaningful interactions across racial and ethnic lines occur, where people work, learn, and live together.

As Putnam and others realize, however, contact across race in and of itself may not move whites toward racial justice. Years ago, Gordon Allport put forward the "contact thesis," which argued that contact with black people lessens prejudice in whites but does so only under certain conditions. Contact reduces prejudice in situations where whites and blacks hold relatively equal status, share common goals, and cooperate with each other in some way and where social norms support the contact.

The findings of this study echo these themes. However, even more, they help us understand the processes that occur within these relationships to enhance support for racial justice. In other words, they open up the black box of bridging social capital to reveal what happens inside, which helps us understand how certain kinds of contact change minds.

Still, our interest goes beyond mere contact and the lessening of prejudice. We are concerned with the role of relationships in developing an understanding of racism and a commitment to racial justice. I find that many pressures work against racial equality within multiracial settings. Indeed, whites build relationships with people of color "under the weight of history," that is, in a context laden with unequal power relationships. Whites can unconsciously bring some of the prejudices they have learned from the larger society into multiracial settings, which leads people of color to mistrust their motives or commitments. In this context, positive action needs to be taken to construct institutional arrangements and policies that will promote truly collaborative relationships. . . . For example, explicit efforts to address racialized thinking or behavior prove important to lessening prejudice and moving whites toward racial justice. Moreover, I find that the more power that people of color hold in the situation, the more compelling the change in whites can be. More broadly, white activists emphasize the need for conversation based upon respect and honesty within these multiracial venues, as well as a genuine effort on their part to learn about the experience of people of color. To the extent that people can share stories across lines of race, mutuality and a sense of common cause develops.

We are also interested in more than creating one-on-one relationships across lines of race. Although those individual connections serve as a foundation for building collectivities, it is through creating community that whites can form shared identities with people of color and other justice-oriented whites. These groups, networks, and communities become the crucible where white activists develop a vision for a future multiracial society and work to implement it today. In other words, we are interested in fostering deeply democratic practices within multiracial institutions and communities.

26

an open letter to white "allies" from a white friend

Caitlin Deen Fair*

To my dearest White friends and acquaintances that identify as allies,

Thank you. Thank you for having a heart for justice and equality. Thank you for showing up. Thank you for doing work; and thank you for being open-minded and unfettered by your defenses as you read this beseeching petition to reconsider your allyship.

As of late, I have been both encouraged and deeply, deeply troubled by the convergence of White "allyship" with the fight for Black liberation and an end to police brutality; encouraged, because it is galvanizing to see masses of White people feeling called to action around a cause that likely does not directly affect them, but troubled because their participation, in many cases, has resulted in a co-opting of the message and of the movement. Troubled, because often times I find that White people unintentionally hang their "allyship" over the heads of the oppressed, as if it is a privilege that must be earned through good behavior; or worse, they hang their participation on their ability to control the message.

This is an inherent part of the problem that we are fighting against.

One of the biggest examples of this is the insistence by many White "allies" to use the phrase "All Lives Matter" in lieu of the message "Black Lives

* Fair, Caitlin Deen. "An Open Letter to White 'Allies' from a White Friend." *Understanding and Dismantling Privilege* 5, no. 2 (December 2015). Reprinted by permission of the author.

Matter," and the arguing or inserting of this message over the voices of those whom the movement represents. Listen, I get it. Saying "Black Lives Matter" is uncomfortable for you. It feels unrelated to you. And that's because it is. And it's supposed to be. Let me explain to you why: Historically, White life has not been undervalued or dehumanized. Period. Currently, we live within a system that was created by White Supremacist principles. Yes, White supremacy. It doesn't have to mean white hoods, nooses, burning crosses, and the Aryan Nation. The systems in this country were created to support and sustain White people. For my White women folk, White supremacy is as fundamental to this country's systems as patriarchy. Hopefully, that provides some perspective for you. With this being said, no argument needs to be made that "all" (which really equates to "White too!") lives matter, because from a systemic perspective, the value of White life is not, and never has been, in question. It is a given that White life in this country is valuable. This is not the case with Black life. Black life in this country is often viewed as inherently less valuable, even sub- or non-human. This is evidenced by the way Darren Wilson talked about Michael Brown in his ill-advised interview, referring to Mike as a demon. So here's the long and short of it: The insistence that "All Lives Matter" over the message that "Black Lives Matter" is racist. You are derailing and decentering the important conversation about the devaluing of Black lives in America and thereby silencing the voices of the very people you are claiming to be allies of. You are participating in Black erasure, actively exercising (and ignoring) your White privilege, and thereby, being racist. Even though you mean well. Even though you are at the march. Even though you are holding signs, and chanting, and have Black friends.

Let me provide a parallel:

You wouldn't go to a Lupus benefit and demand that the speakers acknowledge heart disease. You wouldn't go to the Susan G. Komen Race for the Cure with a T-shirt that says "All Cancer Matters!" Not because all cancer doesn't matter, but because well, we aren't talking about all cancer right now. We are talking about breast cancer; and because that's not what you're there for. You are there to show your love and support to people who have suffered from breast cancer. Period. So for you to try and make the conversation about anything other than breast cancer would be insensitive and selfish. It's hard for us to conceptualize this at times in the context of the "Black Lives Matter" movement however, because the message that is being preached, despite its truth, is one that doesn't include us. It is uncomfortable to subscribe to because we don't understand where we fit into it. And that's because it's not meant to serve or represent us. For that reason, being involved in this movement is going to be unavoidably uncomfortable for you; and you have to be OK with that.

Please understand, it is OK (and frankly, important) for you to feel uncomfortable in your participation in this movement at times. You will squirm. You will not know what to say. You will not know what to do. I, myself, feel incredibly awkward when someone says to raise your fists in the air. I get scared that I am going to do or say something, with the best of intentions, that is offensive. There will be moments when you want to run the other way and head for the hills. That is absolutely normal, and it's OK. That is the nature of being a White person who is involved in this cause. But please, hang in there.

I am going to provide a few guidelines that are important to understand when identifying as a White "ally." Admittedly, in my frustration with White "allies," it has become increasingly difficult for me to be patient and graceful in communicating some of these points, but I understand that in order to be effective, one must also be compassionate. I also understand that as a White person in the work, a large part of my responsibility is to help coach other White people in this area. So being that I am a Christian, and because I want to be effective, I am going to do my best to be gentle about it, as that is what God instructs me to do. However, I am also going to be straightforward and honest with you. So here we go:

1. If your "allyship" is contingent upon how you are treated or how you feel, you are not an ally.

It is important to understand that some Black people are angry. And many of them are angry with White people. This is not a personal attack on you. You must decentralize yourself, and depersonalize people's reactions to you. You need to understand, and accept, that not everyone is going to receive you with open arms. And that is OK. They don't have to. This should not impact your commitment to social justice and equality.

For example, when I was told by a fellow member of a group that I belonged to that the first step in the liberation of Black folks was to kill all the White women because they were tools of re-colonization, my gut reaction was to argue him down to the ground. But as uncomfortable, and hurt, and offended as I was in the moment, and as much as I may have disagreed with his point of view, I knew I couldn't engage him on that; primarily because I don't know what his lived experience has been. He may very well have had legitimate experiences that tell him that this is the most reasonable and effective solution to the problems that we face. In fact, rather than arguing with him about it, as I may have been initially inclined to do, I removed myself from the group because I did not want to become a distraction from the work that needed to be done, or make anyone uncomfortable or upset in what was intended to be a space primarily for Black folks. It wasn't until all the members of the group, including him, asked me to come back, that I rejoined the group. Sometimes, often times in fact, we have to fight our inclinations to engage on certain topics and make the conscious decision to stand down. Sometimes that is going to be the absolute hardest thing to do, but that doesn't mean it isn't the right thing to do. We can't know what others have experienced in their lifetime that has contributed to their current ideological view. That being said, it is safe to say that it would be imprudent to challenge or engage in a "discussion" (read: argument) about it, particularly in movement spaces; and, moreover, it will rarely be effective in those moments.

2. Our job, as White people, is not to dictate to people how to get free while our proverbial foot is on their necks.

Our only job lies in listening, aiding as requested, and stepping aside when suggested. We should not be trying to insert ourselves into spaces and conversations that we are not invited to or welcomed in. Sometimes our input is just not desired, and frankly, not needed. Recognize that you are not an expert on anyone else's experience besides your own. We should not be trying to control bullhorns and megaphones. We should be making space for people whose voices are underrepresented and often unheard. We should be helping other "allies" learn how to become better allies. But we should never, under any circumstances, be trying to control or lead the narrative.

3. Your voice should never be louder than that of the people you are supporting, and should never stand in the place of those voices.

Think of it this way: You are a backup singer to the movement. Your voice should merely serve as a part of the chorus, supporting the leading roles in the play, if you will.

4. This is not a photo-op or your nightly news debut.

If you are only here for (or even mainly here for) the pictures to post on Instagram and Facebook, or are itching for a reporter to interview you so you can share your righteousness with the prime-time audience, go home. This is not what we're here for.

5. Save your "I totally understand 'cause once I got made fun of for being White" stories.

This is not empathy, it is racism. As a rule of thumb: If the conversation is about Black people, it is safe to assume it would be both inappropriate and racist to start talking about your experience as a White person or any other topic relating to White people.

6. Educate yourself.

This doesn't mean go around to all the Black folk you know and ask them to explain to you what oppression and privilege are—because, well, that's oppressive. There are a plethora of phenomenal authors, bloggers, and other personalities that have discussed these topics at length. Do your Googles. Trudy of GradientLair.com does a phenomenal job of discussing the unique experience of Black womanhood and oppression in the form of misogynoir, as well as the role that White people play in perpetuating this and other forms of oppression. Robin DiAngelo has also discussed the concept of White fragility at length, and does a wonderful job of breaking down what it means and how to work against it. If you take the time to look around a bit, you will find that people have been discussing these issues for years. Jane Elliot's brown eyes experiment and Peggy McIntosh's article

"White Privilege: Unpacking the Invisible Knapsack," although both over 18 years old, are great examples of the way White people often interact (or fail to interact) with issues of race. There is even a whole conference you can attend to learn more! Founded and directed by Dr. Eddie Moore, Jr., The White Privilege Conference is in its eighteenth year. This four-day conference features national and international professionals and experts who host workshops, panels, and discussions that address issues of diversity, privilege, and leadership.

7. One of the best ways you can help in this movement is by educating your fellow White people on how to be an effective "ally."

Aka: Teach other White folks how not to be so racist (both intentionally and completely unintentionally) so that Black people don't have to keep spending their time trying to teach their oppressors how to set them free. And if a Black person happens to be so gracious and patient as to take the time to explain to you . . .

8. SHUT THE HECK UP AND LISTEN.

No explanation needed. Just listen, reflect, and internalize.

Lastly, and in my opinion most importantly,

9. Stop being a *BLEEPING* ally!

If you have been wondering why I have been using quotation marks around the word "ally" throughout this article, it is because I do not believe in the concept of allyship. Allyship implies contingency. It implies condition and impermanence rather than a true belief in and commitment to the movement and the cause, despite the possibility (and probability) of discomfort, inconvenience, and the potential for being received less than pleasantly. Don't be an ally. Be a brother. Be a sister. Be a shoulder. Be a hand. Show the people you are standing with that you are standing firmly by their sides, that this is about them, not you, and that you are good with that.

Friends, thank you. Thank you for having a heart for justice and equality. Thank you for showing up. Thank you for doing work; and thank you for being open-minded and unfettered by your defenses as you read this beseeching petition to reconsider your allyship. I love you.

Now go throw out your "All Lives Matter" signs. Please.

Love Peace,
Your White non-ally friend

discussion questions and activities

Discussion or Journal Questions

1. Why do you suspect some scholars or areas of study may resist embracing an intersectional approach?
2. Identify some examples of the power and importance of language in these readings.
3. How can an intersectional approach advance social change and social justice work?
4. Warren examines numerous reasons that compel white people to become antiracist activists. Which of the reasons do you, personally, find most compelling?
5. Why is relationship-building so central to ally work?
6. Does Warren's research shift/add to your understanding about the work of social justice activism in any way?

Personal Connections

The following questions and activities are designed to be completed either on your own or in class, and then discussed as a group with others. As you share your insights with others, think about the patterns and similarities that emerge, as well as the differences among your answers.

A. Responding to Resistance

Think about one person you know (either personally, or someone in the media) that adamantly rejects the concept of privilege or does not see privilege in their own life. Write a letter to that person trying to persuade them to recognize privilege (you do not need to actually send this letter—that is up to you).

B. Be an Ally

What does it mean to be an ally? You will find many websites that discuss what it means for a person with privilege to be an ally. Peruse the plethora of sources, and create a definition of what it means to you to be an ally. Next, create a list of at least five ways in which you can and will strive to be an ally. Be realistic, and create a list that is doable for you. Consider the social change act you chose to take in Part Two. Is this one thing you will continue? Why or why not?

C. Working for Social Justice

Surfing the Internet, identify at least five organizations working for social change and social justice, and describe what they do and why. Select one organization that you would be most interested in engaging with further (whether following, joining, learning from, etc., depending upon the type of organization).

D. Social Action Continuum

Online, search for the words "social action continuum." You will find popular continuums for self-assessment. Select one continuum, and discuss where you see yourself. Is this where you would like to be? Why or why not?

E. Social Identity Development

Return to your examination of the stages of social identity development in Part One. Do you think your stages have shifted at all? Why or why not?

index

Eurocentrism
and capitalist economy, 58
as form of prejudice that distorts
theoretical understanding, 58
and global privilege, 56, 57–59, 61
and modernisation and
Westernisation, 61
and non-Eurocentric history, 59
and non-Western intellectuals,
influence on, 58–59
and social science disciplines, 58
and Western global dominance,
and white cultural influence, 58
European Americans, 126–127,
234–235

fault, 70–71
female privilege. *See* white female
privilege; women
"feminine" and "masculine"
characteristics, as symbolic
dimension of oppression,
265–267
feminism, 2
backlash against, 251
indictment of, and the media, 250
and postfeminist phase of,
249–252
and university/college/education,
238
See also postfeminism; women
Fields, Karen and Mamie, 34
Flutie, Doug, 225
foreign aid
and concept of "helping" non-
West as instrument of power, 63
effectiveness and fairness of, 62–63
and exploitation and intervention,
63

and global privilege, 62–63
and IMF and World Bank, 62, 63
and international trading system,
as alternative to, 63
requested vs. imposed, 63
foreign policy, and Christianity,
dominant western, 145–146
Frankenstein (Shelley), 88
Frankenstein's monster, relating to,
and transgender betweener,
90–93, 96
free choice, 248, 254–255
free choice, and abstract liberalism,
248, 254–255
Freud, Sigmund, 81

gay and lesbian coming out stories,
in sport, 82
gay Jews
and intersectionality, of privilege/
marginality/social identity,
212–218
and intersectionality, of privilege/
marginality/social identity,
benefits of, 214–215, 215n,
217–218
and intersectionality, of privilege/
marginality/social identity,
benefits of (list), 216–217
and religious privilege, 213–214
See also men
gay men
and gay whitening practices,
182–194
HIV-negative, 194–199
and hypermasculinity, 171–172, 173
and intersectionality, of privilege/
marginality/social identity,
161–162, 170–174, 176–177

guilt, 3, 5–6, 9–10, 25, 26, 148, 196, 199, 284, 285
Gunn, Sakia, 210

Haiti, 262
Hall, Robert David, 170
hapas, 239
hate violence, transsexuals as targets of trans-specific, 88n
head, heart, and hand, and racial justice activism, 278–283, 280 (fig.)
Hedwig and the Angry Inch (movie), 110
hegemonic masculinity, 82, 162
hegemony, Christian. *See* Christian hegemony
heterosexism, 3
heterosexual privilege, 69
constructing heterosexual/masculine identity in context of sport, 83–84
ordinary ways of experiencing, 38–39
ordinary ways of experiencing (list), 38
heterosexuality, compulsory, 81, 171
heterosexual/masculine identity in context of sport, 79–85. *See also* identity
Hill, Marjorie, 191
history, and biography, 84
HIV-negative gay men, 194–199. *See also* men
Hogsett, Scott, 167–169
homophobia, 1, 81, 89, 171
and working-class men, 176

homosexuality, pathologization of, 176–177
homosexuals, and neo-Nazi skinheads, 75
House Armed Services Committee, 190
human beings, men's development as, and unearned privilege, 29
humiliation and humility, and transgender betweener, 104–105
hypermasculinity
and disabled men, 168
and gay men, 171–172, 173
and working-class men, 176

identity
and upper class, and class consciousness, 132
See also American identity; dominant-group identity; heterosexual/masculine identity in context of sport; intersectionality, of privilege/marginality/social identity; Jewish ethnic and religious identities; Middle Eastern identity; mythological identity; social identity; transgender identity
IMF, and foreign aid, 62, 63
immigration, and deportation policies, and stereotypes, 221
immigration laws, discriminatory, and racial classification, 232–233
imperialism, and development programs, 61
income inequality, 27

CPSIA information can be obtained
at www.ICGtesting.com
Printed in the USA
BVOW06s0224010917

493744BV00017B/254/P